Dictionary

of

Italian Cuisine

DICTIONARY ~ *of* ~ ITALIAN CUISINE

Maureen B. Fant
&
Howard M. Isaacs

THE ECCO PRESS

THE ECCO PRESS
100 West Broad Street
Hopewell, New Jersey 08525

Published simultaneously in Canada by
Publishers Group West, Inc., Toronto, Ontario
Printed in the United States of America

Library of Congress Cataloging-in-Publication Data
Fant, Maureen B.
Dictionary of Italian cuisine/Maureen B. Fant and Howard M. Isaacs.—1st ed.
p. cm.
Includes bibliographical references (p.).
ISBN 0-88001-612-4
1. Food—Dictionaries—Italian. 2. Cookery, Italian—Dictionaries—Italian.
3. Italian language—Dictionaries—English.
I. Isaacs, Howard M. II. Title.
TX350.F36 1998
641.3'0945'03—dc21 98-20276
CIP

9 8 7 6 5 4 3 2 1

FIRST EDITION 1998

Patri benemerenti. To the memory of my father, Edward D. Brown.

—M.B.F.

To my *sposa carissima,* Nadia Rigoni

—H.M.I.

~

Contents

Acknowledgments

OF the many friends and sources to whom we owe thanks, the first to be named must be our friend Judith Harris, an American journalist in Rome, who introduced us to each other and continues to be an inexhaustible source of ideas, information, and encouragement. Faith Heller Willinger, whose generosity and team spirit are legendary in the world of Italian food, made the next happy match—with our publisher, Daniel Halpern. Also at The Ecco Press, we thank Judith Capodanno and Emily Dolbear. The food experts who have allowed themselves to be pumped for information include Oretta Zanini De Vita and Lorenza Manzi, both of whom made useful comments on the manuscript, and June Di Schino. Scores of Italian restaurateurs, waiters, and food sellers never hesitated to answer our questions—however eccentric they may have found them, or us. In the Testaccio market in Rome, Liliana Alfonsi and her daughter Paola provided hands-on instruction in distinguishing the mints and the broccolis. Francesco Retacchi, a Roman butcher in Torino, provided advice on cuts of meat. We are particularly indebted to chef and butcher Dominick Lolacono, of Dom's Meat Market in Manhattan, one of that disappearing breed of butchers who still carve their own meat, and Jack Ubaldi, author, teacher, and retired butcher, for their many hours of help in trying to fit the Italian cow into an American frame. We are also obliged, in Rome, to Daniela Filippi and Jon Eldan, and, in New York, to Joe Puglisi, Flora Papini, and Alice Merwin.

This is the cyber age, and this book could not have been completed in a timely fashion by two people living more than three thousand miles apart were it not for computers, modems, and e-mail. But the computer has played yet another role in the writing of this book: we owe a large debt of gratitude to the many members of the Italian Forum on CompuServe who responded to our queries and calls for help.

It is unimaginable that a work such as this dictionary could come into being without any omissions or errors of fact. We welcome correspondence that may aid in the preparation of future editions. The authors can be reached, by mail, care of The Ecco Press, 100 West Broad Street, Hopewell, NJ 08525. On the internet our e-mail addresses are: **italtrav@compuserve.com** (Howard M. Isaacs); **MBFant@compuserve.com** (Maureen B. Fant).

It goes without saying—but we leave nothing to chance—that without our Italian helpmeets and tablemates, Nadia Rigoni and Francesco Filippi, we would never have had the chutzpah to attempt this project, let alone spread reference books the length of our respective apartments.

Our thanks to all, and only to us any blame.

Introduction

We compiled this dictionary for the most practical of reasons: we needed it ourselves in our daily work, writing about the food and restaurants of Italy. Our overfilled shelves lacked a handy and concise reference vocabulary of Italian food terms, which is what this book aims to be.

The best books on Italian cooking in English tend, rightly, to focus on a single region or food category—offering depth rather than breadth—and are usually aimed at cooks. The many travelers' vocabularies that have been published ignore the kitchen and concentrate on the menu. The panorama of other culinary dictionaries has a few bright lights, but nothing wide-ranging enough for the needs of a translator faced with an unfamiliar crustacean, a cook working from recipes in Italian, a wine writer trying to unravel cellar terms, or a traveler faced with a regional menu. We have chosen to cast a wide net in collecting our terms and have provided a bibliography for readers who want details. Using this book as an aid, readers should be able to get the gist of entries in Italian-language guides and reference books, and to follow an Italian recipe.

In Italy, all cooking, like politics, is local. Oh, some recipes and foods have spread up and down the country, but it is good to remember that even those ubiquitous pizzerias scarcely existed outside Naples two generations ago. Unification came late to Italy, and gastronomic unification has come even more slowly. Not long ago we found ourselves in a Milan restaurant explaining an item on the menu to a fellow diner, a Milan native. It was *trofie*, a well-known pasta in Liguria. But Liguria, sixty miles from where we sat, might as well have been the moon. We have also told a young Neapolitan about the Roman *pajata*, and explained Roman *puntarelle* to our hostess near Matera, in Basilicata, as she prepared a salad of *cicoria catalogna*—same plant, different word.

The common wisdom is that standard Italian is the triumph of merely a single dialect, Dante's Tuscan, but in fact, it has only been since the triumph of television that the country has been unified by a single tongue. Many dialects are alive and well, thank you, and thriving on the menu. In any case, even if the language were unified, culinary and gastronomic practices certainly would not be. And even if they were, they would not be dominated by Tuscany—contrary to the image carried by tourists and armchair travelers throughout the world. No one region would dominate.

Does this book claim to contain everything? Of course not. We will be collecting Italian food terms for the rest of our lives. However, its six thousand entries contain all the basic, standard-Italian menu items, ingredients, cooking techniques, and utensils as well as a great many regional synonyms and regional dishes, and a number of important place names (including all regions and provinces). The terminology of wine description is pretty well covered; some wines and grape varieties are also included for convenience, but more comprehensive lists are already available in English. Some broad and complicated categories (meat, fish, vegetables, herbs) could have been expanded with variant regional names, additional species, and the like. However, our object was to meet the needs of food lovers and culinary professionals, not of scientists.

In Greek mythology, the sea god Proteus had the power to repeatedly change form unless held firmly down, at which point he would resume his true shape and answer questions about things unknown. As we tried to make sense of several years of note-taking, we wrestled with, more than any other difficulty, the protean nature of our subject. Just when we thought we had pinned down a soup or grain or fish or cut of meat, a loose tentacle would thump us from behind and point to another name for the same food in a different region. Or the same name for a different food somewhere else. Or almost the same food with one new ingredient and the same or a different name. Or three scientific names for the same Italian fish, or herb, or salad green. In fact, perhaps the most astounding aspect of the sources we consulted, in both English and Italian, is the breezy confidence with which their authors list ingredients and assign localities.

Meat is particularly difficult. To imagine the problem, visualize a map of the New York City area. Draw a triangle whose base is in Newark on the west and crosses the Hudson to lower Manhattan on the east, and whose apex is somewhere in Connecticut. Then, take the map to a cartographer and ask, "So, what do we call that?" Using Italian meat charts and pictures, we inflicted this kind of question on U.S. butchers; their ensuing bafflement should explain why some of our definitions read more like driving directions than synonyms. The Italians cut up their animals in ways quite unlike American butchers. And just to make the matter worse, there are something like a dozen different traditional systems in Italy itself. Still worse, some of the same names are used to mean different cuts in different cities. And worse still, industrial meat processing in Italy adds further variation to the scheme. Except where noted, we have used the names and cuts from what is called the "national" system.

Fish nomenclature is notoriously complicated. The same fish may have several Latin names, fifty Italian names, and no commonly used name at all in English. Another problem is that sometimes the same Italian (or English) name is used to identify several very different creatures. We have tried to include information on what other fish these untranslatable specimens resemble.

Herbs have outrageous numbers of synonyms in every language. Where possible, the botanical taxonomy has been included, but even that is vexed; reference books and seed catalogues that contain both modern and Latin names do not list all the regional and local synonyms and varieties, and often the same herb has more than one botanical name. Nevertheless, in the end we did manage to sort out most of the herbs any English-speaking cook is likely to encounter in an Italian recipe. The vegetables were easier, even though the Brassicas (broccoli, cabbages) are numerous and their names and synonyms are thrown around with some abandon. *Broccolo, broccoli,* and *broccoletti* are three completely different vegetables, yet often interchangeable in recipes. Some vegetable and legume varieties are highly local, and there is not much you can do with a bean whose name is simply that of the town near which it is grown.

Then there is food-naming by creative analogy, and heaven help the literal-minded. Anything squishy that can fit in your hand, such as a chunk of mozzarella stuffed into a piece of veal, can be called an "oyster." A "bean" can be the legume or a bean-shaped sweet. A "rag" can be what you use to clean up, but it can also be an irregularly cut slice of beef, or pasta, or any number of other raggedy things. Body parts, the sexier the better, often lend their names to foods by analogy: *bocca di dama* and *coscia di monaca*, but also *palle del nonno*, are names of sweets. Naturally, the same nomenclature is also used for the real thing: *ostriche* may also be oysters, and there may be nothing metaphorical about a plate of *granelli*, or veal testicles. "Worms" are likely to be innocent pastas—but watch out for *formaggio del caglio*! Foods can also take their names from wishes, hence the large number of pastas whose names express the cook's vicarious desire to throttle the next clergyman to lift a fork. We usually provide a food name's literal meaning so that the reader will be prepared to find the same word assigned to a completely different dish.

The information presented here comes from four types of sources: Italian-language reference books and cookbooks; menus from all over Italy; interviews (often extremely informal) with Italian food experts; and our own experience. Needless to say, the sources are often contradictory. Even in a field where respect for tradition is considered highly desirable, things do change. Innovations are introduced, old dishes are rediscovered. Nor is Italy immune to food fads, though it has been slow to accept foreign influences.

The standard dictionaries (Italian dictionaries, never mind Italian-English ones) do not contain many food terms, and there is no guarantee that those listed are correctly defined according to current usage in every locality. In any case, the trattoria owner chalking the day's menu on a blackboard is probably not consulting a dictionary as he writes. More likely, he is spelling phonetically, and his pronunciation is probably not that of the evening news. Foreign loan words can be spelled any number of ways (*sauté, souté, soutè*), and foreign visitors quickly learn not to be too rigid in their expectation of standard terminology.

The Italian food vocabulary that has evolved within the boundaries of the Italian Republic—that is, not counting imports—includes at least French, German, Slovenian, Albanian, plus Sardinian, Sicilian, and any number of dialects. Thus, be aware, for example, that the French listings are not French dishes but Piedmontese or Valdaostan; the German-language food names are from the bilingual region of Trentino-Alto Adige, on the Austrian border. A general work on the food of Italy would not be complete without them.

The most common topics of conversation in Italy are food and politics, and if you think it's hard to follow the politics, well, at least, thanks to television, its practitioners are all obliged to speak a comprehensible form of standard Italian. But unlike politicians, cooks are expected to get palatable results to the table while they're hot, without rhetoric. In fact, one reason why Italians talk so much about food is partly that so many dishes need to be explained—so great is the room for variation in meaning of the language of food, as well as the many languages and dialects used. Those explanations are part of the fun, and this book aims to make them intelligible.

Maureen B. Fant and Howard M. Isaacs
Rome and New York
March 1998

words can be [illegible] anywhere [illegible] or way [illegible] names [illegible] of their [illegible] synonyms.

The [illegible] has [illegible] the [illegible] of the Italian Republic — [illegible] — [illegible] Although [illegible] French [illegible] food names [illegible] would not be [illegible]

For [illegible] conversation [illegible] all [illegible]

[illegible]

Instructions for Use

We don't read manuals either, but if you don't know much Italian and can't make sense of the listings, the following should help.

Compound entries (such as *pesce persico*, perch) are listed under the part we think people are most likely to look under (*persico;* under *pesce,* you'll just find that it's the word for fish), so if you don't find what you're looking for, try another part. Compounds that are intelligible from their separately listed component parts are probably not included.

The arrangement of the entries and definitions is meant to be as intuitive as possible. The main entries, those accompanied by definitions (not just a variant or synonym), are to be considered standard Italian or at least the principal names by which the foods, items, or activities are known. Where an entry is followed by "=" and a word in small capitals, the entry is to be considered a variant of the word in small caps. Many words cannot, of course, be translated, and these are defined, described, or whatever else is appropriate.

Nouns are given in the singular and plural, except where one or the other is practically never used. The gender of nouns is not given except where it is ambiguous. Unless noted, all nouns ending in "a" are feminine, and those ending in "o" are masculine. To make a regular plural, the masculine "o" becomes "i," the feminine "a" becomes "e," and any singular that ends in "e" becomes "i," no matter what the gender.

If a word in the left-hand column is a plural, the term in small capitals will be a plural as well. So when you see a reference to

FAGIOLI, you'll find the definition under the singular, *fagiolo.* When in doubt, scan the immediate alphabetical area.

Verbs are given in the infinitive and past participle. Note that the endings of past participles change like those of adjectives.

Adjectives are given in the masculine singular and are marked "*(adj.)*." Adjectives agree with the nouns they modify in number and gender, so their endings change accordingly:

Masc. sing.	*Fem. sing.*	*Masc. pl.*	*Fem. pl.*
romano	romana	romani	romane
milanese	milanese	milanesi	milanesi

Pronunciation of Italian is quite regular.

Stress is on the penult (next to last syllable) unless specified otherwise (usually over the final vowel) or unless it's an exception. Most exceptions have to be learned. In this book, accents over letters are to be considered part of the standard spelling of the word. Where no accent is normally written, the vowel or vowel cluster (vowels to be pronounced together) to be accented is underlined. Thus *cinghiale* is pronounced cheen–GYA–le, three syllables, not four.

The vowels are pronounced approximately as follows:

a	*as in* part
e	*as in* hey
i	*as in* ski
o	*as in* oh
u	*as in* noose

Very roughly speaking, consonants are pronounced as in English, but bear in mind the following:

W, when it occurs, is pronounced like *v*, *j* like *y*.

The explosive *p* and dental *t* of English speakers is much ridiculed by Italians, and some effort to tone them down is worth the trouble. (Watch any Laurel and Hardy movie dubbed into Italian to hear the English accent as Italians do.)

C and *g* are always hard unless followed by *i* or *e*. That *i* or *e* usually serves merely to soften the consonant, not to add another syllable. The name Giorgio has two syllables (Jor-jo), not three or four. *Gg* followed by an *i* has a strong *j* sound; hence, *formaggio* is pronounced for-mahdge-o (not "for-mazh-o" and certainly not "-ee-o.")

Gn in combination with *l* and *n* adds a *y* sound. Hence, *gnocchi* are NYOK-i; *tagliolini* are tal-yo-lee-nee.

S may be hard or soft, but *ss* is always hard. *Z* and *zz* may be pronounced as *tz* or *dz*. While these distinctions are important to correct speech, they are not essential to the use we expect readers to make of this book and are not given.

Double consonants are pronounced doubly, which can be very difficult for foreigners to hear and imitate, but some effort should be made. The words *alla* and *ala* are not pronounced the same.

The many dialect words listed should, taken all together, give the reader a feel for the sorts of linguistic changes that take place and the sorts of alternative spellings they should look for if the first word sought is not listed. Try replacing Sicilian, and other southern, *dd* with *ll* or *tt*, or *u* with *o*. Try doubling or undoubling consonants in general, especially *c, g, l, m, n, s,* and *t*; *ai* or *aj* sometimes replaces *agl*—as in *zabaione* for *zagaglione, ajo* for *aglio,* or *pajata* for *pagliata*. *B* changes to *v* or *p* and vice-versa. Or simply scan up and down a little in the list.

The geographical attributions given in parentheses should not be considered restrictive in any way. The same word or food, or a variation of it, may be found elsewhere.

Note

All Italian gastronomic terms (including German and French terms from bilingual regions of Italy) are in bold the first time they appear, then in italics. Non-gastronomic Italian and other foreign words are in italics. Cross-references are in small caps. The equal sign (=) is used to send the reader from a variant to the main or standard form of the word. It is not used in the case of two parallel terms with the same meaning. Both the singular and plural of most nouns are given as well as the past participle of most verbs, except where the forms are practically never used. Rules of pronunciation are given in "Instructions for Use." The accented vowel is underlined in entries where stress does not fall on the penult; two vowels underlined together should be pronounced as a diphthong.

A

aàlunga = ALALUNGA (Liguria)

Abate a brown-flecked yellow pear

abbacchio properly speaking, a milk-fed lamb less than two months old, but the term is now also used for lamb in general. It is originally and still principally a Latian term and applies largely to Roman lamb. Note that *abbacchio* is always well done. See also AGNELLO, the normal Italian term for lamb.

abbadia, abbazia abbey

abbastanza enough; unfortunately, Italian recipes presume the cook knows when enough is enough and hate to specify; cf. Q.B. (QUANTO BASTA)

abbespata a Calabrian salted and smoked ricotta

abbinare, *p.p.* **abbinato** to match or to pair, as a tie with a shirt or a wine with a food; **abbinamento** *(n.)*, matching

abboccare, *p.p.* **abboccato** to top up (a cask of wine)

abboccato *(adj.)* of wine, mellow, somewhere between semisweet (AMABILE) and medium dry (6–20 g/l of residual sugars). Customer: "Is this wine sweet or dry?" Wine seller: "It's not sweet. It's just slightly *abboccato.*"

abbruscare = ABBRUSTOLIRE

abbrustolire, *p.p.* **abbrustolito** to toast

abledda barley-flour rolls (Puglia)

abrì = LATTERINO (Liguria)

abruzzese *(adj.)* of Abruzzo; **all'abruzzese**, usually spicy

Abruzzo the Abruzzo region of central Italy, extending from the Apennines to the Adriatic. "The Abruzzi" is an archaic term that should not be used to mean the present-day region. Abruzzo and Molise used to be a single region (hence the traditional plural), but they are now separate.

acacia acacia. The flowers are edible.

acagiù, acajou, acajù = ANACARDIO

acceglio a fresh cheese made in summer from skimmed cow milk (Piemonte)

accendere, *p.p.* **acceso** to light (e.g., the gas)

accendigas a gas lighter with a flint that makes a spark

accia celery (Calabria)

acciaio steel; **acciaio inossidabile** is stainless steel

acciarino sharpening steel

acciuga, *pl.* **acciughe** anchovy (*Engraulis encrasicholus*)

accomodare, *p.p.* **accomodato** literally "accommodate," and in the reflexive, "sit down"; in recipes, however, it just means "put," as when you accommodate fish in a frying pan. In Italian recipes, many verbs enjoin the cook to treat the food with tenderness.

accorciare, *p.p.* **accorciato** to shorten

accosciare, *p.p.* **accosciato** to truss (a bird)

accostamento = ABBINAMENTO

acerbo *(adj.)* for fruit: sour, unripe, green; for wine: sour, harsh

acero maple tree (*Acer*); maple syrup is SCIROPPO **d'acero**

acetaia place where vinegar is produced

acetini pickles

aceto vinegar

aceto balsamico balsamic vinegar, a highly prized, highly concentrated sweet, dark vinegar (more properly called a condiment) made by long aging in wooden casks of the must of special Trebbiano grapes. The genuine article is called **Aceto Balsamico Tradizionale di Modena**; its production is centered in Modena and is watched over by a producers' consortium. **Aceto Balsamico di Modena** is the legal designation of the better imitations.

acetosa garden sorrel (*Rumex acetosa*)

acetosella sometimes used to mean ACETOSA, but actually a different, medicinal plant; wood sorrel (*Oxalis acetosella*)

acetosità sourness, acidity; vinegary taste

acetoso *(adj.)* sour, tart, vinegary

ache = AGUGLIA COMUNE (Puglia)

achillea yarrow, milfoil, a pungent herb (*Achillea*)

acidità acidity

acido *(adj.)* sour, acid, sharp-tasting; acidic (of wine); **panna acida** is sour cream; **zuppa acida** in Bolzano is tripe soup with vinegar and laurel

acido *(n.)* sour (one of the four basic tastes); acid

acidulare, *p.p.* **acidulato** to acidulate

acidulo *(adj.)* acidulous; slightly ACIDO

acino, *pl.* **acini** grape, berry (generic); small pasta shape for soup; **acini di pepe** are peppercorns

acitu = ACETO

aco = AGUGLIA COMUNE (Veneto, Venezia Giulia)

acora = AGUGLIA COMUNE (Puglia)

acqua (1) water; **acqua minerale** is mineral water. The choice is usually simplified to LISCIA (or NATURALE) or GASSATA, but spring water may have a trace of effervescence, depending on the brand (i.e., source) of the water. If the water is to be used for medicinal purposes, the choice becomes more complicated, but people with kidney trouble choose an *acqua* OLIGOMINERALE. (2) The word for water is also used in the names of sauces and soups: **acqua pazza** is a light tomato sauce for whole fish, originally a fish stock poured over pieces of bread and fish; **acqua bruciata** is soup based on a browned béchamel diluted with milk (Friuli-Venezia Giulia).

acquacotta a vegetable soup, usually spiced with peppers and thickened with bread, and sometimes containing egg and cheese; typical of coastal Toscana and upper Lazio (the Maremma), but varies widely from locality to locality

acquaio sink; also used to describe someone with a large and undiscriminating appetite, a bottomless pit

acquaiolo ambulatory water vendor, a typical figure of the South Italian past

acquarzente archaic word meaning ACQUAVITE

acquavite *(n.sing.)* *eau de vie*, brandy
acquicoltura aquaculture, fish farming
acquolina saliva: *mi fa venire l'acquolina in bocca* means "it makes my mouth water"
acquoso *(adj.)* watery
actinidia = KIWI
acu di mari = AGUGLIA COMUNE (Sardegna)
acugella = AGUGLIA COMUNE (Lazio)
acugghiu = AGUGLIA COMUNE (Sardegna)
acura = AGUGLIA COMUNE (Puglia)
adacciata melted prosciutto fat flavored with garlic and herbs (Abruzzo)
addensare, *p.p.* **addensato** to thicken
additivo additive
addolcire, *p.p.* **addolcito** to sweeten
adduzzu = ARGENTINA (Sicilia)
adotto = CERNIA (Sicilia)
adragante, gomma gum of Tragacanth; an emulsifier used in pastry making; also called *gomma di Tragacantha*
adulterazione adulteration
aduzzu di sciummi = LUCCIO DI ACQUA DOLCE (Sicilia)
affetta– slicer, used as a prefix: **affettapane**, bread slicer; **affettatartufi**, truffle slicer; **affettauova**, egg slicer; **affettaverdure**, vegetable slicer
affettare, *p.p.* **affettato** to slice
affettato *(n.)* something sliced; in the plural, **affettati**, cold–cuts, sliced meats
affettatrice slicer, slicing machine
affilare, *p.p.* **affilato** to sharpen
affilatrice knife sharpener
affinamento maturation (of wine)
affinare, *p.p.* **affinato** to sharpen
affinocchiato *(adj.)* with fennel flavoring (fresh or dry)
affiorato *(adj.)* flowered; when used of olive oil, it refers to the oil from the very first pressing
affogare, *p.p.* **affogato** literally, "to drown"; in gastronomy,

usually used figuratively in the past tense to mean poached or smothered. However, the favorite food of Pope Martin IV (immortalized by Dante for his gluttony) was eels kept in a tank of Vernaccia wine, in which they quite literally drowned before being cooked. **Affogato al (caffè)** describes ice cream over which (hot coffee) has been poured. The potential is endless.

affuca parrinu hard dry Sicilian cookies; literally, "strangle priests." The vocabulary of Italian gastronomy is riddled with such anticlerical sentiments.

affumicare, *p.p.* **affumicato** to smoke (food); to smoke a cigarette is FUMARE. **Affumicatore** is a smoker (container for smoking food); **affumicatura** is the smoking of food.

africano literally, "African"; a chocolate-covered sweet

afrodisiaco aphrodisiac

afrore nasty odor, as from a fermenting grape

afseplasti barley rolls (Puglia)

ag. abbreviation of AGOSTO

agarico agaric mushroom; a mushroom of the family Agaricaceae, which is to say mushrooms with gills

agghiata = AGLIATA (Calabria)

agghiotta = GHIOTTA (Sicilia)

aggiada = AGLIATA (Liguria)

aggio = AGLIO

aggiou = LATTERINO (Liguria)

aggiungere, *p.p.* **aggiunto** to add

aggiunta addition; labels may thus signal the addition of some substance

aggiustare, *p.p.* **aggiustato** to adjust (the salt), to repair (the washing machine)

aggiuva = ACCIUGA (Sardegna)

agglassatu, aggrassatu kid, or lamb, pot roast used as pasta sauce

aggrumarsi to lump or form lumps; see GRUMI

agio = AGLIO (Veneto)

agitatore = SHAKER

agliaceo *(adj.)* garlicky; used to describe defective wine that has undergone a chemical reaction between the ethyl alcohol and sulfur dioxide

Aglianico del Vulture robust red DOC wine and grape from Basilicata that is worth aging, considered among the best in the South

agliata a garlic sauce, sometimes containing crushed walnut meats, that comes in a number of regional variations, notably of Piemonte, Abruzzo, and Liguria

agliato a garlic-flavored cheese (Umbria)

aglietto (1) the young garlic plant, used whole; other wild, garlic-like herbs; (2) any of several wild plants that smell of garlic

aglio garlic (*Allium*); **aglio d'Oriente** (*Allium ampeloprasum*), wild leek; **aglio delle vigne**, syn. of **aglio pippolino**; **aglio orsino** (*Allium ursinum*), ramson, broad-leafed garlic; **aglio pippolino** (*Allium vineale*), crow (or field) garlic, wild garlic; **aglio romano, d'India, di Spagna**, = ROCAMBOLA; **aglio scalogno** (*Allium ascalonicum*), shallot; see also SCALOGNO

aglio dolce garlic that has been chopped and soaked in milk to make it "sweet" (Piemonte)

aglio e olio literally, "garlic and (olive) oil." It is a much-loved quick condiment for spaghetti consisting of olive oil in which garlic has been sautéed. It can also have PEPERONCINO and/or parsley.

aglio giallo = AGLIETTO

aglione spicy garlic sauce

agneddu = AGNELLO (Sicilia)

agnellino diminutive of AGNELLO

agnello pasquale (1) Pascal lamb; (2) Easter cake in the shape of a lamb

agnello, *pl.* **agnelli** lamb. Legally, lamb is distinguished from mutton by weight (22 lb) and diet (milk). Commercially, a further distinction is made. The milk-fed animal is called **agnello da latte** and is butchered at 3–4 weeks and with a weight under 22 lb, while *agnello* is applied to animals up to 8–10 weeks and under 31 lb which have known the taste of grass.

agnellotti = AGNOLOTTI

agnillini Sicilian AGNOLOTTI, filled with pork and ricotta and with a sausage and pork-rind RAGÙ

agnoli, sorbir d' a historical dish from Mantova (Lombardia) of a sort of CAPPELLETTI, stuffed with boiled capon, bone marrow, cinnamon, cloves, cheese, eggs, and spices, served in capon broth. Today, it is often found with the same stuffing used in AGNOLINI—a different pasta shaped almost like TORTELLINI—comprised of a beef stew cooked to a paste, eggs, cheese, and sausage, which is served either in broth or with RAGÙ, or butter and Parmesan.

agnolini a pasta like AGNOLOTTI (Lombardia)

agnolotti variously shaped and filled ravioli-like pasta, usually filled with meat

agnulot = AGNOLOTTI (Piemonte)

ago (1) needle; **da assaggio**, tasting needle, meaning the bone needle inserted into a PROSCIUTTO and then smelled to test the quality; **per cucire**, sewing needle; **per lardare**, larding needle; (2) = AGUGLIA COMUNE (Veneto, Venezia Giulia)

agonada = LATTERINO (Veneto, Venezia Giulia)

agone shad (*Alosa fallax lacustris*); cf. CHEPPIA; = LATTERINO (Marche)

agora = AGUGLIA COMUNE or COSTARDELLA, a related species (Marche)

agosta = ARAGOSTA (Veneto, Venezia Giulia)

agosto August, traditionally vacation month

agrario *(adj.)* agrarian

agreste *or* **agresto** *(adj.)* (1) pertaining to the field; (2) = AGRO

agresto *(n.)* unripe berry, verjuice; **salsa all'agresto** is an amalgam of bread crumbs, nuts, immature grapes, parsley, garlic, and sugar

agretti *(pl.)* (1) in northern Italy, = CRESCIONE INGLESE; (2) elsewhere *Lepidium sativum*, a green vegetable that looks like grass or chives, usually boiled and served with lemon and olive oil

agretto *(adj.)* sourish

Agrigento the name of a province and its capital city in the Sicilia region, best known for its Greek temples

agriturismo agrarian tourism; programs of farm stays and farm restaurants
agro *(n. and adj.)* sour, acid, bitter, tart, sharp; = ASPRO; **all'agro**, with oil and lemon; treatment for cold boiled or steamed vegetables
agrodolce sweet and sour
agrume, *pl.* **agrumi** citrus fruit
aguadella = LATTERINO (Marche, Lazio)
agucchia = AGUGLIA COMUNE (Toscana)
agugghia d'alice = AGUGLIA COMUNE (Sicilia)
aguglia comune garfish, greenbone, billfish (*Belone belone*)
aguin = AGUGLIA COMUNE (Liguria)
aguja = AGUGLIA COMUNE (Sicilia)
agusigola = AGUGLIA COMUNE (Venezia Giulia)
aia threshing floor
aidos = MALLOREDDUS
aio, ajo = AGLIO
ajada garlic, walnut, and bread-crumb sauce
al, all', alla, ai, agli in the manner of
ala, *pl.* **ale** wing
alaccia golden or gilt sardine (*Sardinella aurita*)
alalunga a species of tuna (*Thunnus alalunga*) generally considered more delicate than TONNO COMUNE
alambicco alembic, an archaic still
alampica = LAMPREDA (Sicilia)
alare *(n.)* andiron
Alba city in Piemonte, center of the principal white truffle zone; see TARTUFO
Albana di Romagna acidic white DOCG wine made from grapes from the hills of Emilia-Romagna; see also AMABILE and PASSITO
albarello (1) jar; apothecary jar with nipped-in waist; (2) Tuscan name for the gray PORCINELLO mushroom
Albarola white grape of Liguria
albatra fruit of the CORBEZZOLO
albatrello = ALBARELLO
alberino = PIOPPARELLO
albese *(adj.)* (1) of ALBA; usually indicates preparation with truffles;

(2) as noun, a kind of bottle. **Carne all'albese** is veal served raw, thinly sliced or ground, with olive oil or lemon juice and truffle or Parmesan.

Albese, l' the area around ALBA; practically = *le* LANGHE

albicocca, *pl.* **albicocche** apricot(s); **albicocco** is an apricot tree

alborella bleak (*Alburnus alburnus*), a lake and river fish of northern and central Italy

alboreto = PAGELLO (Veneto, Friuli)

albume, *pl.* **albumi** egg white

Alcamo white DOC wine from Sicily

alce elk

alchechengi alkekengi, winter cherry, Chinese lantern plant (*Physalis alkekengi*); a bitter dry cherry-like fruit used decoratively

alchermes from Arabic via Spanish, meaning "red," a sweet, deep-red liqueur from spices and roses, mainly used in pastry. It derives its strong coloring from cochineal (an oak- or cactus-dwelling insect). Once a traditional flavoring and colorant in ZUPPA INGLESE, now it is often replaced by combinations of other liqueurs. The Antica Farmacia S. Maria Novella in Florence still makes and stocks the classic version.

alchimilla lady's mantle (*Alchemilla vulgaris*)

alcol *or* **alcool** alcohol

alcolico *(adj.)* alcoholic; as a noun, **alcolico**, *pl.* **alcolici**, alcoholic beverage(s)

Aleatico sweet red wines from the blue-black grapes of the same name; **Aleatico di Puglia** DOC; **Aleatico di Gradoli**, from Lazio

alece = ACCIUGA (Puglia, Sicilia)

alenoto a sort of southern Italian haggis of lamb or goat innards (with regional variations)

Alessandria the name of a province and its capital city in the Piemonte region, abbreviated AL

aletta, *pl.* **alette** wing(s) of something small; **alette** are poultry wings with the skin still attached

Alezio DOC rosé wine from Salentina Peninsula in Puglia, the heel of the boot

alga, *pl.* **alghe** (1) algae; seaweed; (2) = TAGLIATELLE (Veneto)

ali cut of poultry from just below the neck to immediately below where the wings are attached; also called *pipistrello*, for its bat-like appearance

alice, *pl.* **alici** anchovy (*Engraulis encrasicholus*)

alice grande = RICCIOLA (Marche, Abruzzo)

aliciastra, *pl.* **aliciastre** = ACCIUGA (Calabria)

aligusta = ARAGOSTA (Abruzzo, Lazio)

alimentare *(adj.)* pertaining to food; **prodotti alimentari** are groceries

alimentare, *p.p.* **alimentato** to feed (transitive and reflexive). Note that, as in English, the word is used in many situations not related to food. You feed your car with gasoline and your bank account, when all goes well, with money.

alimentazione nourishment, feeding, diet, nutrition. "Il Giorno mondiale dell'alimentazione" is World Food Day, October 16.

alimento nourishment, food. In the plural, *alimenti* means alimony.

aliotide sea ear, abalone (*Haliotis lamellosa*); it is a large, single-shell mollusk that looks something like an ear

alisanzas Sardinian LASAGNE

Alkermes see ALCHERMES

allappante *(adj.)* of wine: rough, unpleasant, drying to the mouth

alleggerire, *(p.p.)* **alleggerito** to lighten

allodola, *pl.* **allodole** lark

alloro bay (*Laurus nobilis*); **foglia di alloro**, bay leaf

alluminio aluminum, aluminum foil

allungare, *p.p.* **allungato** to dilute; literally, "to lengthen"; *allungare il brodo*, to water the soup, is used figuratively for any sort of lengthening, including padding a piece of writing

allusta = ARAGOSTA (Marche, Abruzzo, Lazio)

alosa = CHEPPIA (Piemonte)

alpacca nickel silver, which is an alloy of copper, nickel, and zinc used in silversmithing

alterazione deterioration of food (food is said to be **alterato** if it is spoiled)

Alto Adige DOC wine designation in the region of TRENTINO–ALTO ADIGE

altoatesino *(adj.)* of Alto Adige
aluzzetiello = CICERELLO (Campania)
aluzzoteddi = CICERELLO (Sicilia)
aluzzu = LUCCIO MARINO (Campania, Puglia, Sicilia)
alzagola = ALZAVOLA
alzare, *p.p.* **alzato** to raise, lift
alzata tiered fruit or cake stand
alzavola teal (*Anas crecca*), a species of duck
amabile semi-sweet (of wine); sweeter than ABBOCCATO
amalgamare, *p.p.* **amalgamato** to mix well, amalgamate
amandola = MANDORLA
amandovolo = MANDOVO
amanita *Amanita,* genus of mushroom that includes the prized OVOLO
amarasca = MARASCA; a sour cherry, a type of AMARENA
amarella black cherry liqueur
amarena (1) morello cherry or sour cherry, *Prunus cerasus* var. *acida;* the tree is **amareno**. (2) A drink prepared with SCIROPPO *di amarena.*
amaretto, *pl.* **amaretti** (1) a cookie made with almonds, apricot kernels, sugar, and egg whites; (2) a liqueur of the same flavor
amarettus Sardinian almond cookies
amarezza bitterness
amaro *(adj.)* bitter, unsweetened. Coffee and tea are served either ZUCCHERATO or *amaro.*
amaro *(n.)* (1) any of numerous after-dinner liqueurs, ranging from the mildly bitter to near-poisons, like FERNET-BRANCA. Italians sip these after meals in the belief that they aid the digestion. (2) Bitter, bitterness, one of the four basic tastes.
amarognolo *(adj.)* somewhat bitter, pleasantly bitter
Amarone the full name of this deservedly admired full-bodied red wine from the Veneto is Recioto della Valpolicella Amarone DOC, or Amarone della Valpolicella. It is the dry (AMARO) version of the PASSITO Recioto.
amarou = ACCIUGA (Liguria)

amarula = ARTEMISIA

amatriciana, all' (pasta) with tomato, PECORINO, and GUANCIALE. We won't enter the debate about other ingredients (hot pepper and onion) or what kind of pasta should be served *all'amatriciana*, but anything other than SPAGHETTI, BUCATINI, OR RIGATONI is to be considered unusual. The name comes from that of the town of Amatrice in northern Lazio, so the homophonic variant "alla matriciana," though common, is technically wrong.

ambibba = ANGUILLA (Sardegna)

ambientare, *p.p.* **ambientato** to acclimate; *chambrer* (for wine)

ambrina = OMBRINA (Sicilia)

ambulau a Sardinian barley soup

amburnìja = ALBARELLO (Piemonte)

amendola = MENOLA (Liguria)

American bar a bar primarily for the service of alcohol instead of coffee

americana, all' a lobster sauce; its name is a misnomer for *all'amoricana*, which is the French *amoricaine*, which has the same problem

americano (1) in trendier Milanese cafés an *americano* is supposed to be something like American coffee, but is really more like a CAFFÈ LUNGO; (2) a cocktail of vermouth and Campari

amido starch; **amido di mais**, cornstarch

aminoacido amino acid. The granular quality of Parmesan and other GRANA-type cheeses is due to the presence of amino acids, visible as white specks.

ammantare, *p.p.* **ammantato** to cloak, to wrap

ammazzare, *p.p.* **ammazzato** to kill, to slaughter; **ammazzacaffè** literally means "coffee killer," in other words a GRAPPA or similar served after coffee

ammezzare, *p.p.* **ammezzato** to divide in half; the past participle means half done, half full, or half empty

ammiscato *(adj.)* mixed; mixed pasta shapes, usually added to bean soup

ammogghiu trapanisi spaghetti with fresh tomato, basil, garlic, oil, and sharp cheese

ammollare, *p.p.* **ammollato** to soak; cf. MOLLO

ammollicare, *p.p.* **ammollicato** to sprinkle with dry bread crumbs; see MOLLICA

ammollire, *p.p.* **ammollito** to soften, make tender

ammoniaca ammonia (the cleaning product)

ammonio ammonium bicarbonate (for baking), powdered baking ammonia, carbonate of ammonia, hartshorn

ammorbidire, *p.p.* **ammorbidito** to soften

ammostare, *p.p.* **ammostato** to crush grapes or other fruit to obtain the must

ammuddicare = AMMOLLICARE (South)

ammuffire, *p.p.* **ammuffito** to get moldy; *p.p.*, moldy

amolo plum

amorosi *(pl.)* elongated, tubular, twisted pasta

ampelografia ampelography, or the taxonomy of vines

amplona = ACCIUGA (Liguria)

ampolla cruet, small bottle, ampoule

ampolliera cruet holder, a fixture of the Italian table

amurena = MURENA (Puglia)

anacardio *or* **anacardo**, *pl.* **anacardi** cashew—not particularly common in Italy

anace = ANICE; **anaci** are anise seeds

anacio = ANICE

anadot duck (Milano)

analcolico *(n. and adj.)* nonalcoholic, soft drink; this includes the category of bitter nonalcoholic APERITIVI

ananas pineapple

anara Venetian variation of ANATRA; **anara col pien**, Venetian stuffed duck

anatra duck; **anatra di Barberia**, Barbary duck

anatroccolo duckling; also spelled *anitroccolo*. The ugly duckling of the fairy tale is "il brutto anatroccolo."

anca haunch, hip, leg; **coscia con anca** is a poultry leg and thigh

Ancellotta grape variety and DOC sweet wine of Emilia-Romagna

anchellini fried ravioli

anchidda = ANGUILLA (Sicilia)

anciddi = ANGUILLA (Puglia)

anciò = ACCIUGA (Veneto)
ancioja = ACCIUGA (Sicilia)
anciova = ACCIUGA (Sicilia)
anciva = ACCIUGA (Sicilia)
Ancona capital of the Marche region and of one of its four provinces, an important Adriatic port
andare, *p.p.* **andato** (irreg.) to go; **andare a male**, to go bad
anellini, anelletti (1) ring-shaped pasta, usually served in broth or TIMBALLO; (2) other small ring-shaped foods, e.g., fried cuttlefish rings
anello, *pl.* **anelli** ring; a ring-shaped mold or anything ring-shaped
anesone anise-seed liqueur
aneto dill (*Anethum graveolens*)
anfora amphora
anfouson = CERNIA (Liguria)
angarone = ANGUILLA (Puglia)
angelica angelica (*Angelica archangelica*), an herb. Its leaves and seeds are used in cooking and its celery-like stems are candied.
angelo, pesce angel shark, angel fish, monkfish; syn. SQUADRO
Anghelu Ruju full-bodied sweet red PASSITO from Sardegna made from CANNONAU grapes. The name, which means "red angel" in Sardinian, comes from a prehistoric necropolis near the Sella & Mosca winery (near Alghero).
anghi = ANGUILLA (Liguria)
anghilla di màa = ANGUILLA (Liguria)
anghira = ANGUILLA (Sardegna)
angidda = ANGUILLA (Calabria)
angioda = ANGUILLA (Sicilia)
angiola = ACCIUGA (Sardegna)
angioletto = *pesce* CAPPONE (Marche)
angiolottus, anzolottos = CULURJONES
angiouvitta = ACCIUGA (Sardegna)
angiulottus = CULURJONES
angosigola = AGUGLIA COMUNE (Venezia Giulia)
anguatula = SOGLIOLA (Marche, Abruzzo)
angudelo = LATTERINO (Venezia Giulia)

anguela = LATTERINO (Veneto, Venezia Giulia)
anguella = ANGUILLA (Abruzzo)
anguidda = ANGUILLA (Sardegna)
anguilla eel (*Anguilla anguilla*)
angulis Sardinian doughnuts topped with Easter eggs
anguria watermelon, from the Greek; common variant of COCOMERO
angusier = AGUGLIA COMUNE (Veneto, Venezia Giulia)
anice anise (*Pimpinella anisum*); **anice stellato**, star anise
anicino, *pl.* **anicini** Sardinian anise-seed cookies
anicione = ANESONE
anima literally, "soul," hence: center, core, pit, or stone of certain fruit; the hard center of pasta cooked *al* DENTE
animale, *pl.* **animali** animal, but also used for insects
animella, *pl.* **animelle** sweetbreads, the thymus and pancreas of veal or lamb
anisetta anisette (liqueur)
anitra duck; variant spelling of ANATRA
annacquare, *p.p.* **annacquato** to water down; **annacquamento,** watering (as of wine)
annata vintage, vintage year; cf. MILLESIMI
annecchia in Naples, veal less than a year old
annegare, *p.p.* **annegato** literally, "to drown"; the participle means braised; cf. AFFOGARE
annegati slices of roast saddle of veal with white wine, held together by skewers
annianu = TACCHINO (Calabria)
anno year; cf. ANNATA
annu = AGNELLO (Calabria)
Annurca, mela a slightly tart apple
annutolo young water buffalo
anoi Piedmontese designation for part of a beef hindquarter, roughly coextensive with the FESA, SCAMONE, and GIRELLO
anolino, *pl.* **anolini** small stuffed pasta (Parma, Piacenza); = AGNOLOTTI
anona fruit similar to cherimoya (*Anona reticulata*)
anserino *(adj.)* pertaining to geese

Ansonica a Tuscan white grape variety and DOC wine
anteriore *(adj.)* anterior
antiaderente *(adj.)* non-stick
antibotritici antibotrytics
anticipo advance, advance notice, down payment; **in anticipo** means "early," as for a dinner date
antico *(adj.)* ancient, antique, old
antiossidante antioxidant
antipastiera platter with several compartments for serving ANTIPASTO
antipastino diminutive of ANTIPASTO
antipasto appetizer course; the world knows this is the Italian preview course (the pasta or soup being the official PRIMO PIATTO), but many think it means "before the pasta," while it actually means before the meal (PASTO). In posher dining establishments, the antipasto is preceded by a STUZZICHINO. **Antipasto magro**, meatless antipasto; **antipasto misto all'italiana**, less exciting than it sounds, contains prosciutto, salami, and a few pickled vegetables.
anvein pasta disks filled with cheese, topped with meat sauce or cream
anzile = ANGUILLA (Venezia Giulia)
anzoletto = *pesce* CAPPONE (Veneto, Venezia Giulia)
aola = ALBORELLA (Veneto)
Aosta capital of the VALLE D'AOSTA region and its only province, called Aoste in French, abbreviated AO
aostano *(adj.)* of AOSTA
ape *(n.f.)* bee
aperitivo aperitif
aperto *(adj.)* past participle of APRIRE
Apicio Apicius. This Roman cognomen has belonged to a number of Roman gourmets, of whom the first and most famous was M. Gavius Apicius, who lived under Augustus and Tiberius (first century A.D.). The well-known Latin cookbook *De Re Coquinaria* is attributed in the manuscripts to one Caelius Apicius and probably attained the form in which it has come down to us in the fourth century A.D.
apicultura beekeeping

apio celery; = APPIO; from *erba delle api*, or "herb of the bees"
apparecchiare (la tavola) to set (the table)
apparecchiatura table setting
apparenza appearance
apparire, *p.p.* **apparso** to appear
appassire, *p.p.* **appassito** to wither, to wilt (intransitive)
appendere, *p.p.* **appeso** to hang
appesantire, *p.p.* **appesantito** to weight, to weigh down; to become heavy
appetibile *(adj.)* desirable, appealing to the appetite
appetito appetite. It is customary for the first person at the table to lift a fork to say "Buon appetito," which cannot be translated into English, only into French "Bon appetit!" As this simple wish is an etiquette trap (similar to but more subtle and insidious than the SCARPETTA), foreigners are advised not to be the first at the table to use the phrase but to follow the lead of the host or hostess. It is not well regarded at elegant tables, but one never knows when its omission might give offense.
appetitoso *(adj.)* appetizing
appezzuta = ANGUILLA (Campania)
appiattire, *p.p.* **appiattito** to flatten
appiccatoio Tuscan beef term for what is essentially the short plate
appio celery
appio montano = LEVISTICO
appoggiare, appoggiarsi, *p.p.* **appoggiato** to lean, to rest
appoggio *(n.m.)* rest, support; **appoggiacoltello**, knife rest; **appoggiacucchiaio,** spoon rest
apposito *(adj.)* proper, special
apri– prefix for opening tools: **apribarattoli**, jar opener; **apribottiglie**, bottle opener; **apriostriche**, oyster knife; **apriscatole**, can opener
aprile April
aprire, *p.p.* **aperto** to open; cf. APRI–
aquadella = LATTERINO (Veneto)
Aquila, L' capital of the Abruzzo region and one of its four provinces, abbreviated AQ

arachide, *pl.* **arachidi** (*n.f.*) peanuts, groundnuts (*Arachis hypogaea*); **olio di arachide**, peanut oil

aragno TRACINA (Liguria)

aragosta lobster (*Palinurus vulgaris*, other Palinuridae), the clawless Mediterranean variety; rock lobster; spiny lobster; the French *langouste*

arancia, *pl.* **arance** orange, the fruit; **arancia amara**, or **di Siviglia**, is bitter orange (used for marmalade), and the same as the French *bigarde*

aranciata orange drink, orange soda. Freshly squeezed orange juice is properly called SPREMUTA *d'arancia*, but the word *aranciata* (and LIMONATA) are used loosely.

arancino (di riso) fried ball of rice bound with meat sauce (served in pizzerias); the composition varies according to region, with Lazio and Sicilia the prime exponents

arancio orange tree, orange; **acqua di fior d'arancio** is orange-flower water; the fruit is ARANCIA

arancione the color orange

aranzada a Sardinian sweet based on candied orange peel

arbada a hearty Calabrian soup based on pork and vegetables

arbore (*n.m.*), *pl.* **arbori** tree

arborela = ALBORELLA

arborio see RISO

arburela = ALBORELLA (Piemonte)

arca di Noè arkshell (*Arca noae*), a mussel-like mollusk

arca pelosa arkshell (*Arca barbata*)

arcera = BECCACCIA

Archestrato di Gela Archestratus of Gela, an ancient Greek food writer of the fourth century B.C., whose work (notably on fish) is partially preserved in the *Deipnosophistai* of Athenaeus (ATENEO)

arcigghiola = BECCACINO

ardente (*adj.*) burning

arenga = ARINGA

aretina, all' Arezzo-style; **pappardelle all'aretina** are made with duck, ham, vegetables, and nutmeg

Arezzo the name of a province and its capital city in the Toscana region, abbreviated AR. Note the ancient Roman city on the site is spelled Arretium.

arganello = SCAMPO (Marche)

argentana, argentone nickel silver

argentata, carta literally "silvered paper," hence aluminum foil

argenteria silverware

argentiera, formaggio all' cheese marinated in oil and herbs, fried or roasted, and sprinkled with vinegar; also *all'argintera*

argentina, *pl.* **argentine** argentine, smelt (Argentinidae family); = ACCIUGA (Marche)

argento *(n. and adj.)* silver; **coste d'argento** is a type of chard

argintera = ARGENTIERA

argnone = ROGNONE

aricciola = RICCIOLA (Calabria)

arigusta = ARAGOSTA

aringa, *pl.* **aringhe** herring (*Clupea harengus*). Do not confuse with *arringa*, which means speech (like harangue).

arista (di maiale) roast pork LONZA or LOMBATA, the CARRÈ; stuck with rosemary, or fennel seeds, and garlic slivers before cooking; originally a Tuscan dish, the name has caught on elsewhere as well

arlecchino *(n. used as invariable adj.)* "harlequin"; a mix of different colored pastas; potentially anything multicolored

armelline *(pl.)* apricot and peach pits used in confectionery

armleti *(pl.)* type of dumpling (Toscana)

armone part of the upper section of the beef chuck (Rome)

armonie Bolognese LASAGNE stuffed with classic TORTELLINI filling

armonioso *(adj.)* harmonious

Arneis fashionable Piedmontese light white wine with two DOC designations, Roero Arneis and Langhe Arneis

arnese, *pl.* **arnesi** tool

arnione = ROGNONE

aroma, *pl.* **aromi** *(n.m.)* aroma; in plural, = ODORI

aromatico *(adj.)* aromatic. Cf. PROFUMATO.

aromatizzare, *p.p.* **aromatizzato** to flavor

aromi aromatic herbs collectively

arpione *or* **arpone** harpoon. The best swordfish is caught this way, not in a net.
arrabbiata, all' "angry," meaning containing PEPERONCINO
arrasoias = CANNOLICCHIO (Sicilia)
arrescottu = RICOTTA
arria = BECACCIA
arricchire, *p.p.* **arricchito** to enrich, embellish
arricciare, *p.p.* **arricciato** to curl; **arricciaburro** is a butter curler
arrimbuli = ROMBO CHIODATO (Sardegna)
arriminari, *p.p.* **arriminatu** = RIMESTARE, RIMESCOLARE (Sicilia); see STRASCINARE
arromaniu = ROSMARINO
arrosticini skewers of roast sheep meat
arrostini annegati veal NODINI fried and then braised, typical of Milan
arrostino in addition to being just "a nice little roast," the term = ROSTIN in the Milanese dialect
arrostire, *p.p.* **arrostito** to roast; roasted. Note that coffee is not roasted in Italian but toasted; see TOSTATO.
arrosto *(n. and adj.)* roast, roasted; **arrosto morto**, pot roast; **arrosto segreto** is sardines with bread crumbs and lemon baked in a covered pan. *Tutto fumo, niente arrosto*—all smoke, no roast—means all show, no substance.
arrosu = RISO
arrotolare, *p.p.* **arrotolata** to roll; rolled, rolled up
arsella, *pl.* **arselle** = VONGOLA (Liguria, Toscana, Campania, Sardegna)
arsella nera = VONGOLA VERACE (Liguria, Toscana)
arsella niura = COZZA (Sicilia)
arsella pelosa = ARCA PELOSA
arsumà uncooked custard dessert (Piemonte)
artemisia mugwort (*Artemisia vulgaris*)
articiòco = CARCIOFO
artigianale artisanal; homemade or made on premises, as opposed to industrial
arzagola = ALZAGOLA

arzavola = ALZAGOLA
arzente = ACQUAVITE
arzilla = RAZZA CHIODATA (Lazio)
ascè chopped steak, *tartare*; phonetic transliteration of French *haché*
asciugare, *p.p.* **asciugato** to dry; **asciugamano**, towel
asciutti boiled meats or fish; drained pasta (see PASTASCIUTTA)
asciutto *(adj.)* dry, drained (from ASCIUGARE); see PASTASCIUTTA; for wine, it means bone dry, or drier than SECCO
ascolano *(adj.)* of ASCOLI PICENO; a **fritto misto all'ascolana** will usually include, along with various meats, a fried, stuffed olive and CREMINI; see also OLIVE ALL'ASCOLANA
Ascoli Piceno the name of a province and its capital city in the Marche region, abbreviated AP
asiago a hard white SEMICOTTO cheese from around Asiago, near Vicenza, eaten fresh or used for grating when aged; DENOMINAZIONE DI ORIGINE
asin soft, mild white cheese from Friuli, either eaten fresh or preserved in brine
asinedda = MENOLA (Sicilia)
asinello (1) young donkey; diminutive of ASINO; (2) = MENOLA
asino, asina donkey
asino, piè d' see PIÈ D'ASINO
asparagi *(pl.)* asparagus (plural of *asparago)*
asparagi selvatici wild asparagus (*Asparagus officinalis*)
asparagina various wild asparagus plants
aspettare, *p.p.* **aspettato** to wait
aspetto color, appearance, respect
aspirare, *p.p.* **aspirato** to inhale
aspiratore a fan that sucks out odors; cf. VENTILATORE
aspretto (*n.m.*) (1) slightly sour taste; (2) fruit "vinegar," which is not, properly speaking, a vinegar
asprezza asperity, harshness
asprigno *(adj.)* vinegarish, somewhat tart or sour
Asprinio white grape of Campania and Basilicata
aspro *(adj.)* tart, sour; like a lemon, as opposed to AGRO, which is like vinegar. For wine: also hard, green, sharp, dry.

assaggiare, *p.p.* **assaggiato** to taste, to sample
assaggiatore taster, as for poison or professional (e.g., for wine)
assaggiatura a (critical) tasting, as of wines
assaggio *(n.)* a taste; **assaggi** means little tastes, or small portions
assassinata pasta sauce of tomato, basil, and sharp cheese that is often served with fried eggplant on the side
asse, *pl.* **assi** board, cutting board; also ironing board (*asse da stiro*)
assemblaggio assembly, blending (of wine)
assenzio absinthe (*Artemisia absinthium*)
Asso, formaggio di small cheese of mixed cow and goat milk from Valsassina, in the province of Como (Lombardia), usually eaten fresh
assortito *(adj.)* assorted
astara syn. PINNA
Asti the name of a province and its capital city in the Piemonte region, abbreviated AT. It gives its name to the single-fermentaton method used to produce a number of low-alcohol sparkling dessert wines, including **Moscato d'Asti** and **Asti Spumante**.
astice clawed lobster of various species in the Nephropidae family, including *Homarus gammarus* and *H. americanus*
astigiano *(adj.)* of ASTI
astracio = SCAMPO (Marche, Puglia)
astrea = PANNOCCHIA (Sicilia)
astringente *(adj.)* (1) drying (of the palate); (2) astringent, young and very tannic; **astringenza**, astringency
Ateneo Athenaeus, or Athenaios, of Naucratis in Egypt (fl. ca. A.D. 200) was a writer whose only surviving work is called *Deipnosophistai*, meaning "The Learned Banquet," or really Dinner Party of Pedants. The detail, erudition, and wit with which the food, and food in general, is discussed rivals an Italian dinner party today.
attaccare, *p.p.* **attaccato** to stick (as burnt food to the pot)
attendere, *p.p.* **atteso** to wait
attesa *(n.)* wait; **ingannare l'attesa** means "to kill time while you

wait," which often involves munching bread and sipping wine till the pasta is done

attimo moment

attizzatoio poker (of the fire)

attorcigliare, *p.p.* **attorcigliato** to twist; since the usual thing that gets twisted in Italian gastronomy is spaghetti, this word is also practically synonymous, in the eye-twinkling, slightly sarcastic language of every day, with eat. One friend to another: "You'd like to twist two spaghetti, wouldn't you?" Translation: Working up an appetite, are we? (Cf. DUE.)

attorta almond cake in the form of a snake (Umbria)

attrezzatura da cucina kitchen equipment

attrezzo, *pl.* **attrezzi** utensil, tool; in plural, equipment

attuppateddi = DITALINI (Sicilia)

augella = AGUGLIA COMUNE (Lazio)

auglia = AGUGLIA COMUNE (Campania, Calabria)

augughia = AGUGLIA COMUNE (Sicilia)

aula = ALBORELLA (Lombardia)

aulivi olives (South)

auoglie = AGUGLIA COMUNE (Puglia)

aurada = ORATA (Liguria)

aurata = ORATA (Toscana, Marche, Campania)

aurora a white sauce; literally, "dawn," even though for Latin poets dawn was pink not white

Aurum orange liqueur; a proprietary name

auslese = SELEZIONATO (Alto Adige)

autunnale *(adj.)* autumnal

autunno autumn

avannotti newborn SARDINE or ACCIUGHE

avanzo, *pl.* **avanzi** leftovers, remains

avellana = NOCCIOLA

Avellino the name of a province and its capital city in the Campania region, abbreviated AV, and located in the northeastern part of the region

avemaria, *pl.* **avemarie,** *or* **avemm-** literally "Hail, Marys"; small pasta for soup named for the beads of the rosary, which they resemble

avena oats (*Avena sativa*)
avocado avocado
avola = ALBORELLA (Toscana)
avugghia = AGUGLIA COMUNE (Sicilia)
avunnu = AGNELLO (Calabria)
avvinare, *p.p.* **avvinato** to season (for wine)
avvolgere, *p.p.* **avvolto** to wrap; wrapped, rolled
axeddas wine vinegar in Sardegna
azarole fruit of rose family, eaten fresh or in pastries and candies
azienda estate, farm, company, but not "agency"; **azienda agricola** is an estate-bottling grape producer; **azienda vinicola** is a winery; **azienda vitivinicola** both grows the grapes and makes wine
azimo = AZZIMO
azoto nitrogen
azzeruola = LAZZERUOLA
azzimo unleavened; *azzima* is unleavened bread; *la festa degli azzimi* is Passover, i.e., the feast of unleavened bread
azzucchi azuki
azzurro blue; see *pesce* AZZURRO
azzurro, pesce literally, "blue fish"; includes many of the stronger-tasting, darker fleshed fish, such as TONNO, SGOMBRO, ARINGA, *pesce* SPADA, ACCIUGA, and others
azzuva = ACCIUGA (Sardegna)

babà Neapolitan pastry like a French baba
babaluscio = ARGENTINA (Campania)

babbalucci *(pl.)* = LUMACHE (Sicilia, Calabria)
bacalà = BACCALÀ
bacaro Venetian wine shop or wine bar
bacca, *pl.* **bacche** berry
baccalà salt cod, except in the northeast (Veneto, Trentino, Friuli-Venezia Giulia), where it is dried cod (what the rest of Italy calls STOCCAFISSO; salt cod they refer to as BERTAGNIN). It is used in any of dozens of regional recipes: **alla Benedettina** is baked with mashed potato; **biscaglia** is sautéed with tomato; **alla cappuccina** has parsley, garlic, milk, pine nuts, and raisins, though another version uses butter, onion, anchovy, raisins, nutmeg, cinnamon, and sugar; when **conso** it is poached and then dressed with parsley and garlic; **alla fiorentina** has tomatoes, potatoes, garlic, and rosemary; **alla vicentina** (made with STOCCAFISSO) has onion, anchovy, parsley, white wine, and a little milk and Parmesan; **in zimino** is with bread crumbs and garlic; **alla livornese**, tomato sauce; **alla napoletana** is made with tomato sauce, garlic, capers, olives, raisins, and pine nuts; **in guazzetto** is fried, then cooked in tomato sauce flavored with anchovies, pine nuts, and raisins.
baccalà mantecato Venetian specialty of boiled STOCCAFISSO beaten with olive oil into a thick cream
baccello, *pl.* **baccelli** (1) bean pod; in Toscana, immature fava beans; (2) = BOGA (Liguria)
baccellone in Toscana, a soft sheep- and cow-milk cheese eaten with fava beans; various mild cheeses suited for eating with beans
bacche plural of BACCA
bacchette chopsticks; a *bacchetta magica* is a magic wand
bacchico *(adj.)* bacchic
Bacco Bacchus. The Roman god of wine is invoked frequently, and his name alone means wine and all that goes with it.
baciato pork fillet rolled in salami paste
bacilli in Genoa, dried fava beans
bacinella basin, bowl, dishpan

bacio, *pl.* **baci** literally, "kiss"; a popular candy made famous by the Perugina company and consisting of a soft chocolate and hazelnut center topped with a hazelnut and surrounded by dark chocolate; the name is also used for a flavor of ice cream based on the candy; **baci di dama** is chocolate-covered almond or hazelnut cookies

backerbsensuppe broth with chives, parsley, and bits of egg batter

badduzzi = POLPETTINE (Sicilia)

baduzzi di cacao Sicilian almond candies rolled in cocoa

baffo, *pl.* **baffi** (1) mustache, usually in plural; *leccarsi i baffi* means "to lick one's chops"; (2) pork jowl, or potentially any product from that region of the anatomy

baggiana Umbrian soup of beans, tomato, and basil

baggianata Piedmontese ratatouille

bagia = CASSAGAI

bagigi peanuts, groundnuts (Veneto)

bagioi small snails

bagna (1) = INTINGOLO; (2) **bagna pasticceria**, diluted liqueurs used to moisten sponge cake or pie crust in certain desserts

bagna caôda, cauda Piemonte's best-known dish not involving truffles. Literally "hot bath," it is a hot, rich sauce of olive oil, butter, garlic, and anchovies served and kept warm at table, more or less like a fondue. Into it diners dip raw or parboiled vegetables, including cardoons, artichokes, peppers, celery, and Jerusalem artichokes, as well as boiled potatoes.

bagna d'infern a BAGNETTO made with hot pepper

bagnacauda = BAGNA CAÔDA

bagnapan a seafood soup thickened with bread

bagnare, *p.p.* **bagnato** to moisten, to wet; **bagnare con (vino)**, to add (wine)

bagnet a sauce, usually green (*verd*, with anchovies, garlic, parsley, and vinegar) or red (*ross*, with tomatoes), made to accompany boiled meats; also **bagnet d'tomatiche**, a tomato-based version

bagnet piemontese = BAGNET ROSS (Piemonte)

bagnetto any of various sauces to accompany meat, from the French *bagnèt*

bagno bath, in all its various meanings; also bathroom (including in restaurants), but in cooking a bath of any sort. **Mettere a bagno**, to soak

bagnomaria *bain marie*, meaning an arrangement for cooking over hot water or in a double boiler

bagnun di anciue fresh anchovy soup

bagòss, bagosso rare hard cow-milk cheese produced near the village of Bagolino, in Lombardia, in *malghe* (mountain shepherds' huts) and aged for one to four years. When cut, the cheese makes a noise supposedly resembling a small cry.

bagozzo hard, sharp GRANA cheese, also known as BRESCIANO

baicoli a type of Venetian *biscotti*

balajole young BOGA (Sicilia)

baldighera = MUGGINE (Marche)

baldonazzo a sausage of pig's blood, chestnuts, lard, raisins, and other flavorings, boiled first, then sliced and fried (Trentino)

baldone = BALDONAZZI

baldoria revelry, fun

bale d'asu sausage of Mondovì in Piemonte

bales CANEDERLI in broth

balestrin = PANNOCCHIA (Liguria)

ballerina = *pesce* CAPPONE (Campania)

ballot ed polenta POLENTA croquettes with a cheese center, either roasted over coals or sautéed in butter (Piemonte)

ballotta whole boiled chestnuts or certain dishes using them

ballotto, *pl.* **ballotti** chestnut(s)

balòn a GRANA-type cheese from around Mantova

balsamella = BESCIAMELLA

balsamico *(adj.)* balsamic; medicinal; see ACETO BALSAMICO

bambù, germogli di bamboo shoots

bamia, bammia okra

banana, *pl.* **banane** banana; the banana plant is **banano**

banchetto banquet

banco counter; **servizio al banco** is counter service, as opposed to table

bandicedde = ORATA (Puglia)

bandiera literally, "flag," hence potentially anything red, white, and green (cf. TRICOLORE), e.g., a PEPERONATA with onion (white), tomato (red), and peppers (green)

bandirolo = *pesce* PERSICO

bar bar, coffee bar, snack bar

baraccola = RAZZA CHIODATA (Marche, Abruzzo, Lazio)

baraonda chaos, hubbub (sometimes used in restaurant names)

barattolo container, jar; soda **in barattolo** is in a can; tin, canister; often used interchangeably with SCATOLA

barba beard

barba di becco = SCORZOBIANCA

barba di frate (1) in northern Italy, prickly saltwort (*Salsola soda*); also called **barba di cappuccino** or **roscano**; (2) in Central Italy (but not only), = AGRETTI

barbabietola, *pl.* **barbabietole** beet(s); **barbabietola da zucchero**, sugarbeet

Barbacarlo a light red wine from Lombardia (Oltrepò Pavese), both dry and sweet

barbaforte = CREN

barbagiuai Ventimiglia; fried ravioli stuffed with yellow squash

barbagliata *or* **barbajada** traditional Milanese hot drink of equal parts hot chocolate, milk, and coffee, sometimes served iced

barbarea = RUCOLA PALUSTRE

Barbaresco big red DOCG wine from Piemonte made from NEBBIOLO grapes

barbatella = ERBA STELLA

barbecue barbecue

Barbera the dark, acidic barbera grape gives its name to three DOC wines from Piemonte: Barbera d'Alba, Barbera d'Asti, and Barbera del Monferrato

barbine a nido *(pl.)* a long thin pasta clustered into "nests"

barbo barbel (*Barbus barbus plebejus*), fish of mountain streams, rivers, and the larger lakes

barbon = TRIGLIA (Veneto, Venezia Giulia)

barbone = TRIGLIA (Marche, Abruzzo)

barbotta cornmeal FOCACCIA of northern Toscana

barbozzo = GUANCIALE

barca, *pl.* **barche** "boat"; anything boat-shaped, usually filled, such as eggplant *barche*

barchetta barquette, boat-shaped pastry shell

bardare, *p.p.* **bardato** to bard (to protect lean meat or fish with a layer of PANCETTA or fatty PROSCIUTTO before cooking)

bardelle = LASAGNE

Bardolino a light red DOC wine from the Veneto

bardoulin = GATTUCCIO (Liguria)

bargiglio, *pl.* **bargigli** wattle, among those parts of the fowl called the RIGAGLIE

bargulle *(pl.)* boiled chestnuts in milk, white wine, or cream; a specialty of Valsesia in Piemonte

Bari the name of a province and its capital city in the Puglia region, abbreviated BA, also the regional capital and an important Adriatic port

barile cask, barrel, *foudre*

bariletto keg

barman bartender

Barolo one of Italy's most esteemed red wines (DOCG), made in Piemonte from NEBBIOLO grapes

barrique cask, usually oak, for aging wine

barucca, zucca the term is used in Milan generically for winter squash (*zucca*), but a small variety with little bumps (verrucas) is often meant specifically

base di cucina = FONDO

Basilicata an impoverished, practically landlocked region of southern Italy, lying between Calabria and Puglia, corresponding to the area known in antiquity as Lucania

basilico basil (*Ocymum basilicum*)

bassanese, alla a way of cooking asparagus (for which Bassano is famous), with a sauce of cooked yolks in oil with spices

basso *(adj.)* low, short; for coffee = RISTRETTO

bastarda, salsa *sauce bâtarde,* egg-thickened butter sauce

bastardella two-handled, round-bottomed metal bowl

bastarduni FICO D'INDIA

bastoncino, bastoncini (small) stick, straw, finger; chopsticks; small pasta for soup; actually "little stick," but for translation purposes "stick" will do. As with many suffixed words, context reveals size.

bastone stick; a pretty big stick, like a cane; a carrot stick would be a BASTONCINO

batata sweet potato

batsoà breaded and fried meat from boiled pig's feet (Piemonte)

battelmatt soft cow-milk cheese of Switzerland with a flavor somewhat like Tilsiter

battere, *p.p.* **battuto** to beat

batteria set; French *batterie*

batticarne meat tenderizer, meat mallet, meat pounder

batticolonna utensils for cutting vegetables or dough, French *boîte à colonne*

battiuova eggbeater

battuto chopped, sautéed vegetables with oil, fat, or PANCETTA—a base for soups, sauces, and stews; with oil instead of animal fat, = SOFFRITTO

batù d'oca *confit* of goose (Romagna)

batuffoli POLENTA balls with meat sauce and Parmesan, traditionally made into a pyramid

bauernschmauz an Alto Adige specialty, it is huge platter of mixed meats (sausage, smoked beef, PANCETTA) plus CANEDERLO dumpling and sauerkraut

bauletti *(pl.)* (1) literally, "little trunks," hence potentially any food stuffed and tied or rolled (usually meat); (2) Friulian ravioli

bava drool, dribble, foam (at the mouth); **gnocchi alla bava**, GNOCCHI topped with FONTINA cheese (Piemonte)

bavaglino bib

bavarese *(n.m.)* as an adjective, Bavarian; usually a dessert of flavored, molded cream, thickened with gelatin; ice-cream cake; Bavarian cream. As a feminine noun, it means a French hot drink.

bavette *(pl.)* pasta similar to LINGUINE

bavettine *(pl.)* diminutive of BAVETTE

bazzoffia a spring vegetable soup of Lazio

bazzotte, uova eggs cooked for about five minutes, harder than soft-boiled, softer than hard-boiled

bec, bek cheese similar to ROBIOLA

becanoto = BECCACCINO (South)

beccaccia, *pl.* **beccacce** woodcock (*Scolopax rusticola*)

beccaccino snipe (*Capella gallinago*)

beccafico, *pl.* **beccafichi** fig-pecker, warbler (*Sylvia borin*); **sarde a beccafico** refers to various Sicilian preparations for sardines that have nothing to do with birds

beccuccio spout

beccute, becciate cornmeal sweets from the Marche

beignet = BIGNÈ

Bel Casale soft cheese of Casalpusterlengo, near Milan

bel paese a number of popular mild, pale yellow, soft cheeses from Lombardia

bel piano a cheese similar to BEL PAESE

belga *(inv. adj.)* Belgian; **insalata belga** is Belgian endive, a type of white chicory

Bella Alpina a cheese similar to BEL PAESE

bella calda a boiled FARINATA

Bella Milano a cheese similar to BEL PAESE

Bellini a cocktail based on fresh white peach juice and sparkling wine, made famous by Harry's Bar in Venice, and now usually offered in debased versions (these days, even Harry's freezes the juice to meet off-season demand)

Belluno the name of a province and its capital city in the Piemonte region, abbreviated BL

ben cotto *(adj.)* well done

benedire (la farina) to bless (the flour), i.e., to cut a cross in the dough before leaving it to rise

Benevento the name of a province and its capital city in the Campania region, abbreviated BN

bensone, benzone a sweet FOCACCIA made with lemon rind, milk, and (sometimes) cooked fruit (Emilia–Romagna)

bere, uovo da extremely fresh egg; literally, "egg to drink"

bergamasca, alla Bergamo-style

Bergamo the name of a province and its capital city in the Lombardia region, abbreviated BG

bergamotto bergamot (*Citrus bergamia*) is a citrus fruit best known today as the characteristic flavor in Earl Grey tea

bergkäse the family of soft, Swiss-type cheeses, one of which is FONTINA

bergne goat or lamb PROSCIUTTO (Piemonte)

berlingozzo a Tuscan cookie for CARNEVALE

bernarde crumbly cow- and goat-milk cheese that is aged two months and colored yellow with saffron; also called *formagelle bernarde*

bersagliera, alla "sharpshooter style"; **maccheroni alla bersagliera** is baked in a BESCIAMELLA sauce along with cooked PROSCIUTTO, FONTINA cheese, and peas

bertagnín salt cod; = BACCALÀ in the Veneto, where *baccalà* is the name for STOCCAFISSO

bertuscell = *pesce* PERSICO (Lombardia)

besciamella béchamel, white sauce

bettelmat fontina-type cheese of Piemonte and Valle d'Aosta

bettola tavern; low-grade OSTERIA; often used humorously to name an unpretentious trattoria

beut = BECCUTE (Pesaro)

beva drinkability, drinking, "to drink"; always used with a modifier to describe wine: **pronta beva**, ready to drink; **ottima beva**, excellent drinking or very palatable; **facile beva**, easy to drink

bevanda, *pl.* **bevande** beverage(s), drink(s)

biada mainly animal fodder, but in some regions oats or rye

Bianchello del Metauro white grape and DOC wine of the Marche
biancheria da tavola table linen
bianchetto, *pl.* **bianchetti** (1) young ACCIUGHE (Liguria); (2) a sparkling white wine; (3) a type of white truffle
bianchin glass of white wine taken as an APERITIVO
bianco *(adj.)* white; but not always literally (for example, UVA BIANCA). **In bianco** usually denotes not the presence of anything white but the absence of anything red.
bianco *(n.)* white; **bianco d'uovo** is egg white; **bianco e nero d'agnello** is a mix of darker- and lighter-colored organ meats (Liguria)
Bianco di Custoza DOC white wine from the Veneto
biancomangiare (1) "blancmange"; milk or almond-milk pudding; (2) young ACCIUGHE (Calabria)
biancone a type of white truffle
biarava beet
bibanesi a type of raised cracker from bread dough
bibbin turkey
bibita, *pl.* **bibite** beverage, drinks
bicarbonato di sodio bicarbonate of soda, baking soda
bicchiere drinking glass (think of beaker); in recipes, cup
bicchierino cup (in ingredients lists); also means paper cup for ice cream; little glass or its contents
bicolore *(adj.)* two-colored
biconcentrato extra-strength tomato concentrate (CONCENTRATO)
bieda, bieta = BIETOLA
Biella the name of a province and its capital city in the Piemonte region, abbreviated BI
bietola, *pl.* **bietole** Swiss chard (*Beta vulgaris cicla*)
biffo = SCORZA A FILETTO
bigaradia = ARANCIA AMARA
bigio *(adj.)* gray; **pane bigio** is brown or whole-wheat bread
bignè *(n.m. invar.)* cream puff; beignet, fritter, puff, bun, usually made of choux pastry; **bignè** (or ZEPPOLE) **di San Giuseppe** are delicious cream-filled *bignè* made in Naples in March

for the feast of St. Joseph, March 19, the Italian Father's Day. In Rome, *bignè* is also used for the common ROSETTA bread roll.

bignolino, *pl.* **bignolini** small *bignè*

bigolaro a metal press for making BIGOLI

bigoli fat, fresh spaghetti, traditionally made by extruding the dough through a device (BIGOLARO OR TORCHIO) that leaves the center hollow. Most *bigoli* today are extruded like spaghetti (Veneto).

bigoncia wooden wine bucket, vat

bigonza, in a marinade

bigui VERMICELLI

bigutta stew-pan

bil-bol-bul a chocolate cake

bilancia scale for weighing; do not confuse with *bilancio,* which means balance sheet or budget

bilanciato *(adj.)* balanced

binu = VINO

biondo *(adj.)* light-colored, pale yellow, blonde (in reference to white wine)

biova soft, round bread (North)

birbanti *pl.* a type of Umbrian cookie

biroldo a type of Tuscan sausage with raisins and pine nuts

birra beer; *birra* ROSSA OR SCURA is dark beer, *chiara* is light

birreria beer-hall; pub

bisat, bisato = ANGUILLA (Veneto); **bisat in tecia** means sautéed with onion, wine, and tomato; **bisat sull'ara** ("on the altar") is cooked with bay leaves

bisatto flauto = LAMPREDA (Veneto)

bisatto tegrà = MURENA (Veneto)

bisciatto = ANGUILLA (Marche)

biscione snake-shaped sweet (Emilia) whose name is derived from *biscio,* a kind of snake

biscottare, *p.p.* **biscottato** to cook or bake twice; see FETTE BISCOTTATE

biscotti di cruschello = PEPATELLI

biscotti (*or* **biscottini) di Prato** = CANTUCCI

biscottiera cookie jar

biscottini essentially the same as BISCOTTI; the diminutive suffix can reflect the speaker's mood as well as the cookie's size

biscotto, pan twice-baked bread for long conservation, hard-tack

biscotto, *pl.* **biscotti** "cooked twice" cookies or biscuits; generic word for any sort of cookie (biscuit in U.K.); the Italian word "biscotti" is becoming widespread in English-speaking countries to denote particularly nice Italian baked goods, especially TOZZETTI and CANTUCCI, but in Italy, *biscotti* are also sold in packages at the supermarket.

Bismarck, (bistecca) alla (steak) topped with a fried egg

bisna POLENTA with beans, sauerkraut, and onion

bisse S-shaped lemon cookies of Venice

bistecca steak, usually of beef or veal, but may be pork, horsemeat, or virtually any meat cut to be grilled (see also FIORENTINA); **bistecchina** is sliced, boneless veal or beef, or just a small *bistecca;* **bisteccone** is large *bistecca,* usually with the bone; also used jokingly for anything big and flat, such as a huge mushroom

bisteccatrice a hamburger press. Every butcher has one.

bistecchiera grill pan, a heavy frying pan with ridged surface for cooking meats; cf. PIASTRA, GRATICOLA

bitto creamy or firm cow- and sheep-milk cheese made in the VALTELLINA, eaten at table or grated

blennio = CAGNETTA

blu blue; blue cheese

blutnudeln homemade TAGLIATELLE containing pig's blood

boba = BOGA (Venezia Giulia, Toscana, Marche, Veneto, Sicilia)

bobici corn (maize); MINESTRA *di bobici* also contains tomato, ham, pork trotters, beans, and potato

Boca a DOC red wine from Piemonte made from NEBBIOLO grapes

bocca, *pl.* **bocche** (1) mouth; (2) taste, referring to wine

bocca di dama literally, "lady's mouth"; an almond cake whose original recipe dates back to at least the seventeenth century

boccadoro *or* **bocca d'oro** meagre, shadefish, or croaker if *Argyrosomus regius*; shadefish or meagre if *Sciaena aquila*; see OMBRINA

boccale pitcher, jug; beer mug, tankard

boccetta, *pl.* **boccette** (1) small bottle, small billiard ball; (2) meatballs

bocchetta, *pl.* **bocchette** tube, tip, or nozzle (for a pastry bag)

bocconcino, *pl.* **bocconcini** potentially any bite-sized food, as the word means "little mouthful." Most often used for stewed veal; little fried rolls or balls of veal, ham, and cheese; small oval FIOR DI LATTE cheeses.

bocconotto a type of filled cookie; **bocconotti alla bolognese** are small vol-au-vents filled with giblets, sweetbreads, and truffles

bodino = BUDINO; baked veal stuffed with layers of PROSCIUTTO and vegetables

boe lamb

boei = OVOLO

boero cherry-filled chocolate candy

boga, *pl.* **boghe** bogue (*Boops boops*) is a fish of the Sparidi family (others include porgies, sea bream, ORATA, DENTICE, and SARAGO)

bogelli = BOGA (Puglia)

bogoni snails cooked in oil with onions

boldone = SANGUINACCIO DOLCE

bolè = PORCINI

boleto, *pl.* **boleti** various mushrooms of the genus *Boletus*, including PORCINI

Bolgheri, Rosé di a Tuscan rosé wine

bolla, *pl.* **bolle** bubble; cf. BOLLO

bollente boiling, very hot

bollicina, *pl.* **bollicine** pearl; (small) bubbles, perlage

bollilatte cylindrical saucepan for heating milk

bollire, *p.p.* **bollito** to boil; cf. LESSARE

bollito misto an assortment of boiled meats, usually served (in restaurants) from a special trolley that keeps the meats warm in their individual broths and accompanied by condiments, typically including SALSA VERDE OR MOSTARDA. *Bollito misto* is more likely to be found in the northern regions (famously,

Piemonte, Emilia-Romagna, and Lombardia) and is subject to regional variation.

bollitore tea kettle or any receptacle used for boiling water

bollore, portare a to bring to a boil

Bologna regional capital of Emilia-Romagna, located in Emilia, and one of its nine provinces. Its gastronomic mystique is probably greater than that of any other Italian city, and the products of the region, including PARMIGIANO REGGIANO cheese, PROSCIUTTO DI PARMA, and MORTADELLA sausage are among the best and most essential in Italy. Both the city and its region are known for enriching everything with butter, cream, and eggs.

bolognese *(adj.)* of BOLOGNA

bolognese, alla outside Bologna, and especially outside Italy, the term designates a substantial meat sauce for pasta, known in Bologna simply as RAGÙ. It is served on TAGLIATELLE, not spaghetti, except on tourist menus. **Scaloppina alla bolognese** is a veal cutlet with cheese and ham; TORTELLINI **alla bolognese** are stuffed with pork, PROSCIUTTO, MORTADELLA, turkey, cheese, and egg.

Bolzano the name of a province and its capital city, in the bilingual Trentino-Alto Adige region, abbreviated BZ, and called Bozen in German

bomba French *bombe,* a molded dessert; **bomba di riso** is roasted meat baked in mold with rice (Emilia)

bombola gas tank for stoves without a central gas supply

bombolone, *pl.* **bomboloni** a type of fritter

bombolotti a short cylindrical pasta shape

bonassai soft sheep-milk cheese from Sardegna

bonata Sicilian rolled up pizza known as "stromboli" in the U.S.

bondeina = BONDIOLA

bondella houting or whitefish (*Coregonus macrophthalmus*) is a freshwater fish found in Lago di Garda and Lago Maggiore (where it has largely been crowded out by the LAVARELLO)

bondiana = BONDIOLA

bondiola term applied to various types of SALUMI

bonet baked Piedmontese pudding of eggs, almond cookies, cocoa, and rum, with many variations

bonissima, torta a chocolate-covered pie (Emilia-Romagna)

bonnarelli thin ribbons of pasta

bopa = BOGA (Abruzzo, Lazio)

boraggine = BORRAGINE

bordatino Tuscan soup with corn flour, beans, vegetables, and (possibly) fish

bordo edge, border

bordo disco disk edge, nail (wine)

bordolese, salsa sauce bordelaise

bordrò RANA PESCATRICE (Liguria)

bordura savarin

boreto = BRODETTO (Veneto)

borghese, alla generally indicates a FRICASSEA

Borgogna Burgundy

borgognona *(n.m. inv.)* burgundy; **alla borgognona** is *bourguignon*

boricche oversize RAVIOLI, baked or fried (Veneto)

borlengho, *pl.* **borlenghi** a sort of fried wafer flavored with Parmesan (Emilia)

borlotti, fagioli red beans; cranberry beans; pinto beans

borotalco commercial name for talcum powder. Italian restaurants always have a tin handy for first aid to oil-splattered neckties.

borraccia canteen flask

borraccina sauce of fine-chopped herbs for pasta

borragine borage (*Borago officinalis*)

borrana = BORRAGINE

boscaiola, alla generally indicates the presence of mushrooms; derived from *boscaiolo,* woodsman

bosco woods; wild; **misto di bosco** is mixed berries

bostrengo a sweet rice cake (Marche)

botrite botrytis; see also MUFFA

bottaggio = CAZZOEULA

bottarga dried, pressed roe of mullet (MUGGINE), gray mullet (CEFALO), sea bass (SPIGOLA), or tuna; highly prized and very expensive. *Bottarga* comes mostly from Sicilia and Sardegna but is sold and eaten throughout Italy.

bottatrice burbot, lotte (*Lota lota*)

botte (*n.f.*) barrel, cask

bottega shop (think of boutique)

bottiglia bottle

bottigliere servant in charge of the bottles, hence the English word *butler*

bottiglieria wine shop; a place where wine can be drunk by the bottle or glass, and where bottles can be bought. Some can be quite chichi, but the institution is traditional.

boudin blood sausage (Valle d'Aosta)

bovino (*n. and adj.*) cattle, of cattle

bovoleto snail (Veneto)

bra sharp, hard white cheese of cow milk with some goat or sheep milk added, cured in brine, from Bra, in Piemonte

bracciatella, bracciatello a sort of doughnut (Emilia)

brace embers; **alla brace** means roasted over wood or charcoal embers

brachetto, bracchetto red grape from which **Brachetto d'Acqui**, a sparkling sweet red DOC wine from Piemonte, is made

braciato = BRASATO

braciere brazier

braciola chop or cutlet, usually pork but also lamb, beef, or game (and even fish). Speaking of beef, *braciola* is nearly always a synonym of COSTATA; in the Marche and other central and southern regions, *braciole* are usually INVOLTINI, as when, **all'urbinate**, they are rolled with egg, cheese, and ham and then cooked in oil, white wine, and broth. **Alla napoletana** is a *braciolone* rolled with PROVOLONE, PROSCIUTTO, egg, and raisins.

bracioletta, *pl.* **braciolette** lamb BRACIOLE cut from near the shoulder; "bracelets"; anything formed into a bracelet shape

braciolettine veal rolls *alla* BRACE

braciolona stuffed, braised rolls of beef

braciulittini arrustuti roast BRACIOLETTINI (Sicilia)

braciuola = BRACIOLA

Bramaterra red DOC wine from Piemonte made from a blend of mostly NEBBIOLO grapes

branchia, *pl.* **branchie** gill (of fish)

brand de cujun Ligurian dish of boiled STOCCAFISSO with potato, parsley, garlic, and oil; also spelled *branda cujon*

branda = GRAPPA (Piemonte)

branzi soft cheese from the Alta Val Brembana, near Bergamo (Lombardia)

branzino sea bass or striped bass (*Dicentrarchus labrax*); syn. SPIGOLA

brasà beef pot roast made with wine and served with small onions

brasare, *p.p.* **brasato** to braise; as a noun, *brasato* is usually braised beef or pot roast, often **al Barolo** (with red wine)

braschetta = CAVOLO NERO

brasciole slices of meat; rolled, stuffed veal slices; pasta sauce of oil, spices, and tomato

brasè = BRASATO

brasiera a covered baking pan for making BRASATO in the oven

brattea, *pl.* **bratte** the botanical term for the leaf of an artichoke, bracts, or scales

brazadel similar to BRACCIATELLA

Breganze a number of Veneto red DOC wines

brennsuppe traditional soup of browned flour, sometimes with broth and egg (Trentino–Alto Adige)

brenta receptacle for transporting wine

bresaola cured lean beef, lightly salted and marinated in wine, then aged; originally a specialty of the Valtellina in Lombardia, now made everywhere. It is often served sliced thin like PROSCIUTTO CRUDO and dressed with lemon and olive oil, and is quite trendy served with RUCOLA. Italian Jewish gastronomy often uses *bresaola* instead of PROSCIUTTO. Also known in some areas as CARNE SECCA.

Brescia the name of a province and its capital city in Lombardia, abbreviated BS

bresciano of Brescia; Parmesan-style cheese; = BAGOZZO

bretelline literally, "suspenders"; TAGLIATELLE made with rice flour (Friuli–Venezia Giulia)

briaco *(adj.)* = UBRIACO; cooked in wine or with spirits

Brianza fabled source of veal, especially for the most authentic COSTOLETTA ALLA MILANESE. These days it usually means about as much as "New York" when used as an adjective for sirloin.

briao = BRIACO

bricchetta briquette

bricchetti "matchstick" pasta

bricco, *pl.* **bricchi** pitcher, jug; in Piemonte and Lombardia, also means hill

briciola, *pl.* **briciole** crumb; *briciolo,* the masculine form, is used when the sense is figurative

briganti large CICERELLO (Campania)

brigata brigade

brigidini *(pl.)* anise-flavored Tuscan cookies, named for the Convento di S. Brigida, Pistoia

brik cardboard container for liquids, Tetrapak; the Tunisian *brik*

brindare, *p.p.* **brindato** to toast as in, to raise a glass

Brindisi the name of a province and its capital city in the Puglia region, abbreviated BR. Since antiquity, when it was Brundisium, at the southern terminus of the Via Appia, it has been a major Adriatic port for travel between Greece and Italy.

brindisi toast ("mud in your eye," not bread)

bringoli rustic spaghetti

brioche *(n.f. inv.)* not usually the French *brioche,* but generically breakfast pastries; see also CORNETTO and PAGNOTELLA

brioso *(adj.)* somewhat sparkling

broade = BROVADA

brocca pitcher; **in brocca** means cooked in an earthenware jug; **brocca graduata** is a calibrated measuring cup

broccio RICOTTA-type cheese of Corsica

broccoletti *(pl.)* broccoli raab or rabe (*Brassica rapa*). This is a brilliant green plant grown and eaten for its leaves and small clusters of buds; in the kitchen it is used pretty much interchangeably with its cousin CIME DI RAPA. **Broccoletti di Bruxelles** are Brussels sprouts.

broccoli siciliani broccoli (*Brassica oleracea* var. *italica*). The terms BROCCOLO, *broccoli*, and BROCCOLETTI are sometimes used loosely, but if you want "regular" broccoli, specify *siciliani*.

broccolo a light green cauliflower or broccoflower. In Rome the local variety is the BROCCOLO ROMANESCO, and the simple *broccolo* is called "the one from Naples." Cf. CAVOLO BROCCOLO and CAVOLFIORE.

broccolo romanesco or **romano** broccoflower, looks and behaves like a pale green cauliflower but the florets come to a point; this is the "broccoli" in the very Roman BRODO DI ARZILLA E BROCCOLI

brochat thick cream of milk, wine, and sugar eaten with rye bread

broculi rabi *(pl.)* = BROCCOLETTI (Sicilia)

brodera a liquidy RISOTTO, possibly cooked with pork stock that is enriched with pig's blood

brodettare, *p.p.* **brodettato** fricasseed; cooked in white wine and then enriched with yolks and lemon

brodetto (1) fish soup, any of numerous variations, especially those of the Adriatic coast; (2) **brodetto di Pasqua** is a Latian soup with broth, egg, and lemon (cf. BRODETTARE); (3) diminutive of BRODO (Lazio)

brodo broth, usually of meat, that is an essential ingredient in many dishes, most famously RISOTTO; it is not stock, which is more properly called FONDO

brodoso *(adj.)* watery, especially for sauces that should be thicker

broeto = BRODETTO; Venetian fish soup; Bellunese potato soup

brofadei Brescian broth with small squares of fried FOCACCIA

brongo = GRONGO (Liguria)

brôs, brüs, brussu fiery Piedmontese cheese fermented in GRAPPA and served with bread or POLENTA

broscia BRIOCHE, often used as a receptacle for ice cream in Sicilia

bross = BRÔS

brovada, *pl.* **brovade** turnip strips steeped in *marc* (rough brandy) for three months, served with sausage and in other Friulian dishes

bruciare, *p.p.* **bruciato** to burn; *bruciato*, the participle, can also mean toasted, browned, or roasted
bruciata (*n.f.*) roasted chestnut
brucio = SUGO D'ARROSTO (Piemonte)
brudu = BRODO (Sicilia)
Brunello di Montalcino justly famous DOCG full-bodied red wine from Tuscany, near Siena; also the name of the grape
brungo = GRONGO (Liguria)
bruno *(adj.)* brown
brüs = BROSS
brusadolis pork chop cooked in parchment or foil
bruscandoli wild hops, often boiled for use in soup or RISOTTO
bruscansi = BRUSCANDOLI
brusch pork head, tongue, and trotters in gelatine or a terrine (Piemonte)
bruschetta toasted bread rubbed with garlic and drizzled with olive oil, sometimes served with tomatoes or other toppings. The bread must have a rough texture in order to "grate" the garlic. Italian-American garlic bread is something else entirely.
brüscitt beef stew with fennel seeds or dill; similar stews with various strong spices or herbs
brusco *(adj.)* brusque, term used when speaking of a wine that is almost ASPRO
Brusco dei Barbi Tuscan red wine made with the CHIANTI GOVERNO method
bruscolino = BRUSTOLINO in Lazio
bruss = BROSS
brustengolo POLENTA-based dessert of central Italy
brustolino toasted ZUCCA seed; **brustolino americano,** = ARACHIDE
brutti ma buoni, brutti e buoni literally, "ugly but good" and "ugly and good"; drop cookies containing hazelnuts
buba = BOGA (Venezia Giulia)
bubbola mushroom (*Amanita vaginata*)
bubbolotti = RIGATONI
bublossa = BORRAGINE

bucaniera, alla literally, "buccaneer-style"; (pasta) with tomatoes, octopus, lobster, and clams

bucare, *p.p.* **bucato** to pierce, make a hole in

bucatini long, thick spaghetti bored with a small hole. They are almost always served *all'* AMATRICIANA or *alla* GRICIA.

buccellato ring-shaped dessert with a number of regional recipes. The Tuscan version is a risen dough with Marsala or anise seeds, and candied fruits or raisins; the Sicilian version uses short pastry and dried fruits; the Ligurian version is more like a pound cake.

buccia, *pl.* **bucce** peel (of fruit or vegetable); peel, crust, rind

buccina conch (genus *Strombus* or *Busycon*)

buccuni *(sing.)* = MURICE (Sicilia, Sardegna)

buco, *pl.* **buchi** hole

budella guts or intestines prepared as food; do not confuse with the innocent BUDINO.

budello part of the intestine of an animal that is used as sausage casing

budino pudding (U.S.)

bue beef, specifically a steer over four years old; these animals are virtually nonexistent on the Italian market today

bufalo, bufala water buffalo, the meat of which is eaten in some southern areas and whose milk is used for MOZZARELLA

buffet in addition to the obvious meaning, *buffet* is also used to mean cafeteria or TAVOLA CALDA

buga = ALBORELLA (Liguria); = BOGA (Liguria)

bugie literally, "fibs"; rum-flavored cookies; = CENCI (Piemonte)

buiì Piedmontese BOLLITO MISTO

bujabesa *bouillabaisse*

bulbero = CARPA (Veneto)

bulbillo = SPICCHIO (of garlic)

bulè = PROCINO

bulè réal = OVOLO

bulliente *(adj.)* very hot, boiling

bulo = MURICE

bunet = BONET

buongustaio gourmet
buono *(adj.)* good
buono *(n.)* coupon, chit
buontalenti custard-flavored ice cream
buratéli elvers (Veneto, Venezia Giulia)
buratelli eels
buridda Ligurian fish stew
buristo a Tuscan blood sausage
burlotti = BORLOTTI
burnìa, bunìja = ALBARELLO (Piemonte)
burrata delle Murge a buttery, fresh cheese from Puglia originally produced seventy years ago, near Andria. Inside a covering of fresh cheese are pieces of cow-mozzarella in cream and whey. The whole thing can be wrapped in asphodel leaves.
burrella = BUTTIRO
burrida a Sardinian fish stew made from a member of the shark family and, to be authentic, the liver of the fish (even if it is toxic)
burriello butter-rich mozzarella balls
burriera butter dish
burrini = BUTTIRI
burrino = BUTTIRO
burro butter; eggs *al burro* are fried; pasta *al burro* is sauced with plenty of sweet butter and Parmesan cheese
burro, salsa al = SALSA BASTARDA
burroso *(adj.)* buttery
burtleîna see CRESCENTINA (Piacenza)
busara, alla Veneto mode of preparing shrimp, octopus, or crab in a sauce of olive oil, garlic, white wine, parsley, bread crumbs, and possibly tomato or paprika
buseca = BUSECCA
busecca tripe, in Milano; when *in brodo,* it is a thick tripe and vegetable soup; *busecca matta* is either a fake *busecca in brodo* made using cabbage instead of tripe or a sautéed preparation like FOIÒLO, but from omelet strips in place of the tripe

busecchina dessert made of dried chestnuts
bussolai see BUSSOLANO
bussolano ring-shaped cake or cookies
butticanali = GRONGO (Sicilia)
buttiro a small, fresh cheese of PASTA FILATA with a butter center; the whey-butter for the center is itself a byproduct of making CACIOCAVALLO- or PROVOLONE-type cheeses
butto see MANTECA
buzara = BUSARA
buzzetta see MALLEGATO

~ C ~

cabbuni di mare = SCORFANO (Sardegna)
cabiette *(pl.)* Piedmontese GNOCCHI from potato, rye bread, cheese, and nettles that are baked with onion and bread crumbs
cabussun = LATTERINO (Liguria)
cacao COCOA
cacchiastrella = ANGUILLA (Puglia)
caccia = CACCIAGIONE
caccia annanz PIZZA BIANCA with oil, rosemary, and garlic
cacciagione game
caccialepre a wild green (*Reichardia pieroides*); literally, "chase hare"
cacciatora, alla literally, "hunter-style"; a highly variable method of stewing chicken, lamb, veal, and rabbit. In the North, the ingredients usually include tomatoes, while in central and southern Italy, rosemary, garlic, and vinegar are the predominant flavors.
cacciatore type of salami (literally, "hunter")

cacciucco in Toscana the word means mixture, and the name can apply to various soups or stews. The *cacciucco* par excellence, however, is Livorno's **cacciucco di pesce**, a robust and peppery fish soup.

cacciume = GATTUCCIO (Puglia)

cacciuttiello = GATTUCCIO (Campania)

cace = CACIO

cachi *(sing. and pl.)* kaki, a kind of persimmon

caciatello = CASADELLO

cacimperio = FONDUTA

cacio cheese; **cacio de Roma** is a creamy, sheep-milk cheese

cacio e pepe, (pasta) pasta, usually spaghetti or other long pasta, dressed with grated PECORINO ROMANO and black pepper

caciocavallo southern large PASTA FILATA cow-milk cheese. Hunks of curd, weighing 2 or 3 kg, are molded by hand into the characteristic shape of a large ball with a small appendage. The odd name (literally, "horse-cheese") is said to derive from the practice of tying two cheeses together and slinging them over a horizontal bar, where one might think they were riding horseback.

caciocavallo siciliano *caciocavallo* pressed in a form and possibly cured in salt or brine

caciofiore soft, buttery yellow cheese, also called CACIOTTA

caciofiore aquilano soft, fresh—or briefly-aged—sheep-milk cheese, traditionally including a blade of saffron and curdled with wild CARDO

cacioforte a very sharp cheese of Campania that is said to stimulate the appetite

cacioricotta a hard ricotta for grating (Puglia); elsewhere, = CAGLIATA, used in various ways (plain or sweetened) in desserts

caciotella di Sorrento fresh, delicate sheep-milk cheese (Campania)

caciotta various fresh or hard white cheeses, or a soft, yellow buttery cheese

caciotta pecorina fresh PECORINO SARDO

caciuni = CALCIONI

cacuociulu = CARCIOFO (Sicilia)
cadevida = GRAPPA (Trentino)
caffè coffee, in any form; in a bar, the word without further modifiers means ESPRESSO. Some of the various modifiers for this elixir: LUNGO (made with extra water, also called **americano**); DOPPIO (twice the amount of both grounds and water); **macchiato** ("stained" with a few drops, or "spot," of milk); **bollente** (very hot); **corretto** ("corrected" with a dash of spirits, such as GRAPPA or brandy); **ristretto** or **basso** (made with less water). **Caffellatte**, also spelled **caffè e latte** or **caffelatte** (and bastardized at present in America to "a latte"), is roughly equal parts of hot milk and coffee, poured from separate pitchers. A **lattecaffe** is a glass of warm milk with a shot of espresso mixed in. See also CAPPUCCINO.
caffetteria coffee service
caffettiera coffee pot
cagghiubbi home-style, hollow MACCHERONI (Puglia)
caggiune = GATTUCCIO (Sicilia)
cagliare, *p.p.* **cagliato** to curdle; curdled; cf. IMPAZZIRE
Cagliari regional capital of Sardegna as well as the name of a province and its capital city, abbreviated CA; it is located on the island's south coast
cagliata curd; a fresh, barely coagulated cheese
caglio curd, rennet
cagnetta blenny (*Blennius fluvialis*)
cagnetto = GATTUCCIO (Lazio)
cagnina = ORATA (Sardegna)
Cagnina slightly sweet red dessert wine of Romagna
cagnola = GATTUCCIO (Marche)
cagnolo = PALOMBO (Veneto)
cagnone, riso in rice with melted garlic-sage butter and Parmesan, or with melted butter and FONTINA
cagnun = CAGNON
caicc, caicco large meat-and-cheese RAVIOLI of Breno in the Val Camonica (Lombardia), served with butter and cheese

caienna cayenne
cajinci type of AGNOLOTTI
Calabria the region occupying the toe of Italy, comprising five provinces, and in antiquity called Bruttium
calamaro todero = TOTANO (Veneto)
calamaro, *pl.* **calamari** squid (*Loligo vulgaris*); nearly always seen in the plural, *calamari* are frequently linguistically and/or gastronomically confounded with the TOTANO and the SEPPIA (the resemblance to the former is fairly strong), and even to the TOTARIELLO. Mediterranean *calamari* are generally larger than either *seppie* or *totani.*
calamo aromatico = CANNELLA
calapranzi = MONTAPIATTI
calcagno hard Sicilian PECORINO for grating
calcatreppola the CARDONCELLO mushroom
calce viva pickling lime
calcinello troncato = TELLINA
calcio calcium
calcionetti sweet RAVIOLI
calcioni in the Marche, baked RAVIOLI from bread dough or *pasta frolla,* filled with fresh and aged PECORINO or RICOTTA and mixed with egg, sugar, and lemon peel; fried Abruzzese version without sugar, with cheese and ham; in Molise, fritters stuffed with nuts or with PROVOLONE, PROSCIUTTO, and RICOTTA
caldaia (1) vat, cauldron; (2) boiler, furnace
caldallessa whole boiled chestnut
caldaro = CALDAIA (1)
caldarrosta roast chestnut
calderone cauldron
caldo *(adj.)* hot (what the "C" on the faucet stands for)
calendula an herb (*Calendula officinalis*) that gives a flavor of tansy (TANACETO) in cooking
calice chalice (religious), stemmed glass, goblet
California, manzo alla braised beef with PANCETTA, onions, vinegar, broth, and cream; the reference is to a place in Lombardia, not the American state

callo del campanello rear part of the MUSCOLO POSTERIORE (Florence)

calore heat

caloria, *pl.* **calorie** calorie

calscioni baked meat- or vegetable-stuffed pasta

Caltanisetta the name of a province and its capital city in the Sicilia region, abbreviated CL

Caluso Passito Piedmontese sweet DOC wine

calvisio large, late-summer pear of the Finale Ligure area

calzagatti = CAZZAGAI

calzengiidde = CALZONI OR PANZEROTTI (Puglia)

calzinei = TELLINA (Veneto, Venezia Giulia)

calzoncelli small CALZONI (South)

calzoncini lucani = CAZINI

calzone literally, "pants"; stuffed, half-moon pizza in many regional variations; usual ingredients are ricotta, mozzarella, and salami or cracklings (CICCIOLI)

calzonicchi a stuffed pasta similar to TORTELLINI with filling of brains; it can be served in meat sauce or broth

calzuncieddi a form of fried CALZONE

cameriera maid, waitress

cameriere waiter, steward

camicia literally, "shirt"; **in camicia** means unskinned, as a baked potato; **uovo in camicia** is a poached egg

camino fireplace

camomilla chamomile, chamomile tea (popular and readily available in bars)

camoscio chamois goat

campagna the country, the countryside

campagnola, alla country-style; eggs with vegetables and cheese; RISOTTO with beans, sausage, and tomato; pasta sauce with tomatoes, mushrooms, and herbs

campagnolo *(adj.)* (1) rustic, peasant; (2) pasta sauce in Lazio with chopped meat, mushrooms, peas, and pecorino or Parmesan

campana bell; **campana coprivivande** is the French *cloche,* a bell-shaped cover for serving food

campanello (1) boneless beef from the back of the upper hind leg, used for stews; (2) handbell (for the table)

Campania the region between Lazio and Calabria on the Tyrrhenian Sea that embraces the Bay of Naples; its capital is Naples

campione, *pl.* **campioni** sample

campo field, countryside; **di campo** means "of the country," i.e., wild, not cultivated

Campobasso regional capital of Molise and the name of a province and its capital city, abbreviated CB

Campofilone, pasta di long, thin, egg-pasta strands

can bianco = PALOMBO (Venezia Giulia)

canadese type of bottle

canarini small artichokes (Venice)

canarino infusion made yellow with lemon peel

canasta a lettuce with red-edged green leaves

canavesani agnolotti pasta stuffed with rice, beef cooked in red wine, cheese, truffles, cabbage, and garlic

canavrola = BECCAFICO

candela candle

candeliere candle holder

candire, *p.p.* **candito** to candy (fruit)

candito, *pl.* **canditi** candied fruit

canederli type of GNOCCHI (Trentino-Alto Adige)

canêna red NOVELLO wine drunk between November and Easter

canescioni ricotta-stuffed RAVIOLI

canestrato heavily salted sheep cheese of southern Italy, aged in a basket (*canestro*)

canestrel, *pl.* **canestreij** = CANESTRELLO

canestrello, *pl.* **canestrelli** (1) = CUORE (Marche); scallop, variegated scallop (*Chlamys varius*); (2) **canestrelli di pasta di mandorle**, Ligurian or Piedmontese cookies

canestriello = CAPASANTA (Puglia)

canestrini *(pl.)* small pasta for soup; potentially anything shaped like a small basket

canestro, *pl.* **canestri** basket

canevera, alla capon with herbs, boiled in a pig's or cow's bladder

canina see ROSA

caniscione like a large CALZONE, stuffed with a mix of cheeses, egg, salami, and PROSCIUTTO; a version dubbed MAGRO will be stuffed with beets, anchovies, and olives

canna cane; pipe, tube, anything tubular. All the cylindrical *cann-* foods (e.g., CANNELLONI, CANNOLI) derive from this. **Canna da zucchero** is sugarcane.

cannaiola young ANGUILLA (Toscana)

cannamela sugarcane

cannarozzetti = DITALINI

cannarozzoni = RIGATONI

cannaruozzoli Calabrian egg pasta cut in small squares and rolled around a stick

cannella cinnamon; also a type of hammer or a spigot (see CANNA)

cannellino, *pl.* **cannellini** (1) elongated white beans; (2) a very pale, light white wine of the CASTELLI ROMANI

cannelloni tubular stuffed pasta or crêpe filled with meat or RICOTTA (literally, "big tubes"), usually topped with a sauce, or sauces, and cheese, and then baked

canneroni = CANNARUOZZOLI

cannistreddu type of Sicilian BUCCELLATO

cannolicchio, *pl.* **cannolicchi** (1) grooved razor, razor clam (*Solen vagina* or *Ensis minor*); their elongated shells look like the case of an old-fashioned barber's razor; (2) a tubular pasta

cannolo, *pl.* **cannoli** literally, "tubes," and potentially any food shaped like a large tube and filled; **cannolo alla siciliana**, a crisp pastry tube filled with ricotta and candied fruits (note that the word *cannoli* is plural, and it is possible, even advisable, to eat them in the singular); **cannoli di tuma**, breaded and fried slices of TUMA enclosing veal RAGÙ (Sicilia)

Cannonau di Sardegna robust red grape variety and DOC wine from Sardinia
cannoncino filled tubular pastry whose name means "little cannon"
cannulicchio, *pl.* **cannulicchi** (1) = DATTERO DI MARE (Sicilia); **cannulicchio ferraro**, = CANNOLICCHIO (Campania); (2) = DITALINI
canocchia mantis shrimp, squill (*Squilla mantis*); syn. PANNOCCHIA
canovaccio dish towel, tea towel
cantalupo melon, canteloupe
cantarello chanterelle mushroom (*Cantharellus cibarius*)
cantina cellar, hence also wine cellar; wine shop; winery; **cantina sociale** is a wine-making cooperative
cantinetta diminutive of CANTINA; wine rack
cantorello = TANUTA
cantucci, cantuccini *(pl.)* Tuscan almond cookies that look like cooked slices from a larger cake (which they more or less are), traditionally dunked in VIN SANTO; cf. BISCOTTO
canzanese, (tacchino) alla (turkey) in gelatin
cao di lat a type of MASCARPONE cheese
capa margarote = CUORE (Veneto, Friuli)
capare, *p.p.* **capato** to trim (a vegetable), to choose; Roman dialect for MONDARE and SCEGLIERE
caparossolo, caparozzolo = VONGOLA (Venezia Giulia)
capasanta scallop (*Pecten jacobaeus*); **capasanta piccola**, = CAPASANTA or CANESTRELLO (Veneto)
cape de morte = CAVOLO RAPA (Puglia)
capelletto a pork sausage eaten boiled
capellini very fine pasta strands (literally, "fine hair"), usually for soup
capello, *pl.* **capelli** strand of hair of the head, hence anything very thin; **capelli d'angelo** is angel-hair pasta, usually shaped into birds' nests for soup
capelomme smoked and aged pork
capelvenere = CAPELLI D'ANGELO
capesante *pl.* of CAPASANTA

capeto offal
capetune = ANGUILLA (Puglia)
capicollo = CAPOCOLLO
capignaro = SARAGO (Puglia)
capillari young ANGUILLE (Marche, Veneto)
capitone large female ANGUILLA (Lazio) whose destiny is to be cooked in vinegar and eaten on Christmas Eve
capitune = ANGUILLA (Sicilia, Calabria)
capo head, also used in many compound words
capocchione = GHIOZZO (Marche)
capocollo meat, usually cured pork, from the top of the neck
capocuoco chef, head cook
capomazzo = ANGUILLA (Puglia)
caponata a relish usually made with eggplants, onions, and other vegetables to which seafood is sometimes added (**caponata ricca**); Sicilian dish of mixed fried vegetables sprinkled with sweetened vinegar sauce; **caponata povera** is olive oil and onion (and possibly some anchovies) on a biscuit
caponatina baked vegetables, something like a CAPONATA but without the sweetened vinegar sauce (Sicilia)
capone = *pesce* CAPPONE; = LAMPUGA (Puglia)
caponet Piedmontese cabbage or zucchini-flower rolls stuffed with meat and fried
capovolgere, *p.p.* **capovolto** to turn upside down (as a mold, to turn out the food)
capozzone = MUGGINE (Campania)
cappa chione = FASOLARO
cappa gallina = VONGOLA
cappa verrucosa = TARTUFO (DI MARE)
cappalunga syn. CANNOLICCHIO
cappel di prete = CAPPELLO DEL PRETE
cappelasci large Genovese LASAGNE
cappella, *pl.* **cappelle** (1) chapel; (2) mushroom cap
cappellaccio, cappellacci literally, "shabby old hat"; large stuffed pasta, like big TORTELLINI, from Emilia-Romagna
cappelletti little hats, = TORTELLINI; **di grasso**, with meat filling; **di magro** (typical of Romagna), with cheese

cappello, *pl.* **cappelli** hat, used metaphorically (with suffixes) for a number of stuffed pastas

cappello (da gendarme) literally, "(gendarme's) hat"; conical Pugliese TIMBALLO of MACCHERONI within a crust of PASTA FROLLA and filled with fried eggplant and zucchini with meat, egg, tomato sauce, and cheese

cappello da prete part of the beef outer shoulder (Milan)

cappello del prete pork sausage of Emilia-Romagna

cappelloni large CAPPELLETTI filled with braised beef and SALAMINO conserved in lard

cappero, *pl.* **capperi** capers, which may be bought in SALAMOIA or SOTTO SALE. This plant—of which capers are the flower buds—can be seen throughout Italy climbing on cliffsides, walls, and even urban ruins and churches, but the best for eating come from the southern islands, most famously Pantelleria.

cappidu d'ancilu = CAPPELLI D'ANGELO

cappieddi 'i prieviti Calabrian egg pasta formed into a tricorn shape

capponalda salad made on top of moistened crackers or bread; a version of CAPPON MAGRO (Liguria)

capponata = CAPPONALDA

cappone (1) capon, a castrated male chicken, weighing about 5½ lb; (2) = SCORFANO (Veneto); (3) **pesce cappone**, sea-hen, gurnard, gurnet; Triglidae family

cappuccina watercress; a type of Bibb or Boston lettuce

cappuccino (1) ESPRESSO with steam-frothed milk; sometimes served with cinnamon or chocolate sprinkled on top, but less often in Italy than abroad, and occasionally a free dollop of fresh whipped cream (PANNA). If CHIARO, it is made with extra milk, if SCURO, with extra coffee. It may also be requested BOLLENTE OF TIEPIDO. (2) = SARAGO (Marche, Abruzzo).

cappuccio (1) hood; (2) CAPPUCCINO to its friends; (3) type of cabbage (CAVOLO); see also LATTUGA

capra goat; **formaggio di capra** is goat cheese; the diminutive, meaning kid, is CAPRETTO

caprese *(adj.)* (1) mozzarella and tomato salad with basil; (2) of Capri

caprettato something else (e.g., lamb) cooked in the manner of kid
capretto kid
Capri fabled island in the Bay of Naples and its DOC white wine
capriata slow-cooked beans with olive oil, rice, or pasta, and boiled chicory on the side
capricciosa, pizza pizza topped with various ingredients, supposedly chosen at whim, typically artichoke hearts, hard-cooked eggs, prosciutto, and mushrooms
capriccioso *(adj.)* literally, "capricious" or "whimsical," hence chef's choice and used to describe something with a number of ingredients. However, they are almost always the same, as, famously, on PIZZA CAPRICCIOSA, and so there is nothing capricious about it.
caprifoglio honeysuckle
caprino generic word for any of various goat cheeses
capriolo roe deer, venison (*Capreolus capreolus*); in **capriolo alla caprilese**, the haunch is marinated and cooked with veal liver, PANCETTA, and sage; in **capriolo** (or CAMOSCIO) **alla valdostana**, the meat is marinated in red wine, browned, splashed with GRAPPA, and then braised in the marinade
capsico capsicum
capsula bottle cap; the metal foil on the wine bottle, capsule
capuliatu chopped meat (Sicilia)
capuzzelle lamb or kid head baked in a casserole with garlic, oregano, and potato (Puglia, Basilicata)
carabaccia Florentine onion soup; Tuscan onion soup
caraceju = PICCIONE (Calabria)
caraffa decanter, carafe; carafes usually come as *litro* (liter), *mezzo* (half-liter) and *quarto* or *quartino* (quarter-liter); **caraffa da decantazione** is a (wine) decanter, though the English word is often heard
caraffa graduata calibrated measuring cup
carafoi fried strips of sweetened dough
caragoi = GARAGOLI
caramei Veneto sweet: skewers of nuts and dried fruits coated in hard caramel and arranged in the shape of a fan
caramella (1) caramel; toffee; (2) almost any kind of small (usually) non-chocolate candy

caramellare, *p.p.* **caramellato** to caramelize; caramelized
caramello caramel
caramelloso *(adj.)* caramel
carapigna or **carapina** the rectangular or cylindrical stainless-steel tub in which ice cream is kept at the GELATERIA counter; the name is from the Spanish *garapiña,* which means *sorbettiera*
carasau Sardinian flatbread with olive oil, similar to, but thinner and crisper than CARTA DA MUSICA
caratello small wooden barrel in which VIN SANTO is made
carattere character, but if you hear about the chef's *carattere,* his temper is being discussed, not his morals
caratteristico *(adj.)* characteristic, typical
caratterizzato *(adj.)* **da** characterized by
carboidrati = IDRATI DI CARBONIO
carbonade not usually the classic French stew, but salt or fresh beef stewed with onions and wine (Valle d'Aosta); = CARBONATA
Carbonara, agnello alla lamb pieces baked slowly in a dish lined with baking paper to absorb the fat and seasoned only with salt. In this case Carbonara is the name of a town, near Bari, and is not related to *pasta alla* CARBONARA.
carbonara, pasta alla pasta (usually spaghetti) with egg yolks, GUANCIALE, PECORINO ROMANO or (less traditionally) Parmesan cheese, and black pepper. Variations from these few ingredients are common, but they are not called *carbonara,* at least not in Italy. Cream is not an ingredient of true *carbonara;* it is an aid to inexperienced cooks who have trouble getting the eggs to the right consistency without it.
carbonata the French *carbonade*
carbone coal; **carbone di legna** is charcoal
carbonica carbonic
carcadé hibiscus; a red infusion made from the plant
carcassa the whole animal carcass after being bled, skinned, boned, and plucked
carciofini *(pl.)* preserved artichoke hearts; small artichokes often marinated in olive oil
carciofo artichoke; **alla giudia** (Jewish-style) means fried whole in olive oil with resulting crisp leaves and soft heart; **alla**

romana means slow-cooked with olive oil, garlic, MENTUCCIA, and/or parsley; **alla matticella** means crushed flat between two bricks and cooked in an open fire

carciofo del Giappone = STACHYS

carciù big RAVIOLO filled with ricotta and spinach

cardamomo cardamom (*Elettaria cardamomum*)

cardinale, alla anything with a red sauce or garnished with something bright red like a cardinal's cloak

cardo, *pl.* **cardi** cardoons

cardoncello type of mushroom (*Pleurotus ferulae*)

cardone broth with cardoons, meat, and cheese

carida = MUGGINE (Liguria)

Carignano del Sulcis Sardinian grape and red wine

cariota a wild green

carlaccia rolled omelet stuffed with cheese and served on a bed of potatoes

carlino a variety of SARAGO called *sarago dell'anello* (*Diplodus annularis*)

Carmignano Tuscan DOCG red wine of Chianti grapes with some cabernet

carne meat, flesh (of anything); **carne macinata** is ground meat; **carne nera** is "black meat," indicating game (SELVAGGINA), as distinguished from red meat (**carne rossa**) and white meat (**carne bianca**, such as veal and chicken)

carne 'ncantarata pork aged and preserved in salt along with hot pepper and fennel seeds

carne aglassata = CARNE ALLA GLASSA

carne alla glassa "glassy" sauce obtained from beef braised slowly in wine; the sauce goes either over the sliced meat or on pasta (Napoli, Sicilia)

carne alla pecorara (1) pork with olive oil and onions, covered with melted PECORINO; (2) veal, chicken, or lamb cooked with oil, garlic, oregano, and tomato (Calabria)

carne secca *or* **carnesecca** = GUANCIALE (Toscana); beef COPERTINA, salted and aged 2–3 weeks (Rome); in some places in the Valtellina, a synonym for BRESAOLA

Carnevale Carnival, the period of festivities just before Lent (QUARESIMA) that ends with the bash on *Martedì grasso* (Shrove Tuesday, better known as Mardi Gras). Certain sweets are typical of the Carnevale period, and the name itself presages the period of fasting (i.e., meatlessness) to follow. It comes from Old Italian *carnelevare*, from *carne* (meat) + *levare* (remove).

Carnevale, lasagna di in Campania, a pre-Lenten dish of square LASAGNA baked in layers with small sausages and meatballs (POLPETTINE), MOZZARELLA, RICOTTA, and hard-boiled eggs

carnia pale yellow Friulian cheese of cow milk and possibly some sheep milk as well

carnoso *(adj.)* meaty, fleshy

caro *(adj.)* dear, expensive

carota selvatica = GALLINACCIO (3)

carota, *pl.* **carote** carrot(s)

carpa carp (*Cyprinus carpio*)

carpaccio originally, thin-sliced raw beef with a mayonnaise dressing, invented and named at Harry's Bar in Venice; this word is now also used for thin-sliced raw fish or other meats

carpellese fried fish marinated in vinegar and must, and served with pickled fruits and vegetables

carpiò = CARPIONE

carpionata food prepared IN CARPIONE

carpione freshwater fish found (not so often these days) only in Lago di Garda (*Salmo trutta carpio*); **in carpione** describes food (usually fish) fried and then marinated in vinegar, herbs, and spices

carpiù = CARPIONE

carpium = CARPIONE (Piemonte, Lombardia)

carrati, gnocchi made of wheat flour, served with egg, PECORINO, and PANCETTA

carrè roast loin or saddle; rack, e.g., rack of lamb

carrello cart; trolley, as for antipasto or dessert; **carrello per la spesa** is a shopping cart

carrettiera, (pasta) alla a sauce for pasta hearty enough to keep a wagon driver's (*carrettiere*) strength up; it is subject to much local variation but usually contains some form of tomatoes and garlic

carrobisi sweet Sicilian RAVIOLI whose dough contains lemon peel and almonds, stuffed with dried figs, and then cooked in red wine with cinnamon

carrozza, mozzarella in mozzarella between slices of bread, floured, dipped in egg and fried; anything similarly prepared can be called *in carrozza*

carruba carob

carsenza = CRESCENZA

Carso DOC reds and whites from Friuli–Venezia Giulia

carsolina broth with addition of fried egg batter

carta (1) menu; **carta dei vini** is a wine list; (2) paper; **carta da forno** is baker's paper; **carta paglia** is brown paper, like a grocery bag

carta da musica Sardinian flatbread used to make *pane* GUTTIAU and *pane* FRATAU

cartamo safflower (*Carthamus tinctorius*)

cartilagine cartilage

Cartizze a DOC PROSECCO

cartoccio improvised paper (*carta*) cone for carrying food; **al cartoccio** means *en papillote*; the word should mean parchment, but is now widely used for aluminum foil

carvi caraway (*Carum carvi*)

casa house; **della casa** (of the house), e.g. **vino della casa**, house wine; **casa vinicola** is a winery that buys its grapes; **fatto in casa** means homemade

casalinghi *(pl.)* housewares

casalingo *(adj.)* home-style; as a noun (**casalinga**) it means "housewife"

casareccio *or* **casereccio** *(adj.)* homemade or home-style; **pane casareccio** is the basic loaf of chewy, crusty good-quality bread

casaro cheesemaker

casatella rich cow-milk cheese of the Veneto
casatelle *(pl.)* half-moon-shaped filled pasta of Sicilia
casatiello type of savory CIAMBELLA containing cheese and salami
cascà Sardinian couscous with chopped meat, vegetables, and saffron. The recipe's Arabic origin is said to be owed to the villagers of Carloforte, originally Genovesi, who left there in the sixteenth century for the island of Tabarca, off the Tunisian coast, and brought the dish to Sardegna two centuries later.
cascina farm, dairy
caseificio a place where cheese is made
caseina casein
caseo curds
casereccio = CASARECCIO
Caserta the name of a province and its capital city in the Campania region, abbreviated CE, and located in the northern part of the region; it is famous both for its mozzarella and for the Versailles-like royal palace
casher kosher
casigiolu Sardinian cheese of CACIOCAVALLO family
casoncelli = CASONSEI
casonsei Lombardian pasta stuffed with meat, spinach, egg, cheese, and bread crumbs
casonziei Veneto RAVIOLI with various stuffings according to locale
cassa "cashier." Signs in bars will advise you to get a receipt (*scontrino*) at the *cassa* before ordering. The receipt is then tendered at the counter. Italian law (not always followed) requires that patrons carry the receipt with them when they leave, or they are otherwise subject to a fine.
cassagai POLENTA with beans (Emilia-Romagna)
cassata molded mix of ice creams; cream tart or Sicilian *pan di Spagna* filled with almond paste, chocolate, candied fruit, and ricotta cream; the most famous version is the **cassata siciliana**
casseruola saucepan; brazier (two-handled low pot), braising pan
cassetta, pane a bread baked in a loaf pan to be sliced for sandwiches

cassis black currant

cassoeula, cassoeûla see CAZZOEULA

cassola (1) casserole; (2) a fish soup (Sardegna); (3) a dessert: RICOTTA omelet flavored with cinnamon

cassôla = CAZZOEULA

cassolla, a Sardinian ZUPPA DI PESCE

cassuola casserole; fish soup

castagna, *pl.* **castagne** chestnut; **pesce castagna** is sea bream or pomfret; **castagna d'acqua**, water chestnut; **castagno** is a chestnut tree

castagnaccio flat cake made of chestnut flour and decorated with pine nuts

castagnole, *pl.* chestnut-shaped fritters, usually filled; sweet GNOCCHI of Friuli

Castel del Monte DOC red, white, and rosé wines from northern Puglia, named for Frederick II's fabulous octagonal castle

Castelfranco see RADICCHIO DI TREVISO

castellana, *pl.* **castellane** literally, *châtelaine*, but (1) peppers rolled up with PROSCIUTTO and FONTINA; (2) in plural, a short pasta

castellano see RADICCHIO DI TREVISO

Castelli Romani the hill towns around the volcanic lakes Albano and Nemi, southeast of Rome, including Castel Gandolfo (site of the Pope's summer residence) as well as FRASCATI and MARINO and other towns producing the wines collectively known in Rome as *vino dei Castelli*

castello castle, château

castelmagno rich, ivory-colored cheese of Piemonte from cow milk with a little sheep milk added; it is traditionally aged with an *erborinatura* (see ERBORINATO) to create mold, along the lines of a GORGONZOLA; today, this is often omitted and the cheese eaten younger

castradina smoked, dried lamb stewed and served in RISOTTO, or with cabbage and potatoes; it is made in and around Venice during the November festival for Santa Maria della Salute

castrato mutton; older lamb that will never be a ram

castraure (*pl.*) small wild artichokes available in spring (Veneto)

casunziei type of RAVIOLI (Veneto)

catalogna Catalan chicory, a crisp green vegetable that comes in a head with spiky leaves; in Rome it is eaten as a salad (see PUNTARELLE), but elsewhere can be cooked

cataluzzo = LAMPUGA (Veneto, Friuli, Toscana)

catanesella short, thin, hollow pasta

Catania second city of Sicily and the name of a province and its capital city in the Sicilia region, abbreviated CT

Catanzaro the name of a province and its capital city in the Calabria region, abbreviated CZ

cattas = ZEPPOLE

cattivo *(adj.)* bad, gone bad, nasty-tasting

caussano = *pesce* CAPPONE (Liguria)

cavaglia = SGOMBRO (Sardegna)

cavallo horse

cavatappi (1) corkscrew; (2) in the plural, corkscrew pasta

cavatello southern handmade short pasta, something like ORECCHIETTE

cavatiddi = CAVATELLI

cavatieddi = CAVATELLI

cavaturaccioli = CAVATAPPI

cavedano chub (*Leuciscus cephalus*)

cavezzale = CAVEDANO

caviale caviar

cavolbroccoli broccoli

cavolfiore usually cauliflower, but in some southern areas it means broccoli

cavoli, cavolini, cavoletti di Bruxelles, Brusselle Brussels sprouts

cavolo cabbage; **cavolo cappuccio** covers various varieties of what in the U.S. is simply called "cabbage"; **cavolo rapa** (literally, "cabbage turnip") is kohlrabi; **cavolo verde** and **cavolo riccio** are both kale-like; **cavolo marino** is sea kale; **cavolo nero** is a dark green cabbage, typical of Toscana, closely related to curly kale; **cavolo palmizio**, **cavolo Toscano**, and **cavolo a penna** are other names for **cavolo nero**. **Cavolo verza** or **cavolo verzotto** belong to the family of Savoy cabbages.

cavolo broccolo = BROCCOLO ROMANESCO

cavolo romano = BROCCOLO ROMANESCO
cavolrapa = CAVOLO RAPA
Cavour, alla sliced meat served over fried or baked polenta slices, perhaps also with chicken liver purée or grilled mushrooms; roast meat served with semolina croquettes
cavreti = CAPRETTO; **cavreti di Gambellara** is herb-stuffed, spit-roasted *capretti bianchi* (kids weighing less than 4 kg) (Vicenza)
cavriolo = CAPRIOLO
cavroman mutton browned in a BATTUTO with cinnamon clove and possibly some tomato sauce, served with onion and boiled potato (Veneto)
cazini small stuffed pasta from Puglia filled with ricotta, sugar, and spices, and sauced with lamb RAGÙ (Matera)
cazzagai POLENTA with beans
cazzarielli PEPERONCINI (Abruzzo)
cazzilli fried potato croquettes, sometimes with cheese and PROSCIUTTO COTTO (Sicilia)
cazzimperio = PINZIMONIO
cazzmar lamb innards, closed in a pig's peritoneal sac, baked or grilled (Puglia, Basilicata)
cazzoeula Milanese casserole of various pork cuts and cabbage, usually served with POLENTA
cazzola = CAZZOEULA
cecatelli = CAVATIEDDI
cecenielli tiny fish that is typically battered and fried, or used as pizza topping
cecesale dried, cooked garbanzo beans baked with salt
ceci chickpeas, garbanzo beans
cecino = FARINATA
cedevole *(adj.)* yielding
cedioli elvers (Veneto, Venezia Giulia)
cedrata citron-based soft drink
cedrina lemon verbena (*Lippia triphylla*)
cedro citron (*Citrus medica*)
céc young ANGUILLA (Toscana)

cefalo gray mullet (*Mugil cephalus*) and other members of the Mugilidae family; syn. MUGGINE
cegala di mari = PANNOCCHIA
cémicé = *pesce* SAN PIETRO (Puglia)
cena supper, dinner; the Last Supper is *l'Ultima Cena*, but Leonardo's painting is known as *il Cenacolo*
cenci literally, "rags"; fried pastry ribbons; = FRAPPE or CHIACCHIERE
cenere, *pl.* **ceneri** *(n.f.)* ash(es)
centerbe an herbal liqueur
centinara, maccaruni a = JACCOLI
cento hundred; **maccaruni a cento**, = JACCOLI
centopelli = OMASO
centrale *(adj.)* central
centrifugato fresh vegetable or fruit juice made in a centrifuge
centrone = GATTUCCIO (Puglia)
cepa = CHEPPIA (Piemonte, Lombardia, Marche)
ceppa, maccheroni alla see CEPPE
ceppatello = PORCINO
ceppe, maccheroni al a kind of homemade BUCATINI
ceppo (1) butcher block; (2) vine; (3) tree trunk
cera wax, candle
ceroso *(adj.)* waxy
ceraselle *(pl.)* cherry peppers
cerasuolo *(adj.)* cherry red; wines so called are darker than rosé but lighter than true red; DOC rosé version of MONTEPULCIANO D'ABRUZZO
cerchio circle, hoop
cereghin fried egg
ceresa cherry
ceresolini a version of TAJARIN
cerfoglio chervil (*Anthriscus cerefolium*)
ceriola = CIRIOLA (Lazio)
ceriole thick spaghetti or TAGLIATELLE
cerna = CERNIA (Venezia Giulia)
cernia grouper, various members of the genus *Epinephelus*
certosa a Carthusian monastery

certosina, alla RISOTTO made with frog broth, peas, shrimp, seafood, and mushrooms, sometimes tiny frogs as well (Lombardia); **pasta alla certosina** is pasta with a sauce based on fish broth with prawns and crayfish, sometimes with tomatoes

certosino Bolognese Christmas fruitcake

cervela see HIRN–PROFESEN

cervella brains, as a food (*cervello* in anatomy); **alla napoletana**, baked with olives, capers, and bread crumbs

cervelland type of sausage

cervellata name given to various sausages

cervo stag, venison (like Latin *cervus*)

cervone chocolate-covered, marmelade-stuffed, serpentine Christmas dessert of the Abruzzo

cesena (1) thrush-like bird; (2) Cesena, city in Emilia-Romagna

ces<u>oi</u>e (*pl.*) shears

cesta basket and numerous basket-like objects. This word, which derives from the Greek *kiste* (box, chest), can have any number of suffixes, but any time you see the root *cest–*, think basket.

cestello (small) basket; **cestello a vapore**, steamer

cestino (1) bag lunch, often sold at railroad stations or prepared by hotels on request; (2) wastebasket; (3) various small baskets; cf. CESTA

cetra, pisci = *pesce* SAN PIETRO (Puglia)

cetriolini very small cucumbers, usually pickled (SOTTACETO)

cetriolo cucumber. The same word is often used for cucumber pickles (SOTTACETO). **Cetriolo di mare** is sea cucumber.

cev<u>a</u>pcici fresh pork, beef, and lamb sausage of Friuli

champignon the ordinary button mushroom, the cultivated cousin of the wild PRATAIOLO; cf. FUNGO

charaduzza = MAIALINO (Calabria)

charlotte a common ice-cream cake

checca, alla (spaghetti) (spaghetti) with raw tomatoes

chenelle (*pl.*) quenelles

cheppia shad (*Alosa fallax nilotica*); cf. AGONE, ALOSA

cherna = CERNIA (Venezia Giulia)

cheunao = LATTERINO (Liguria)
chiacchia = LUCERNA (Veneto, Friuli–Venezia Giulia)
chiacchiere *(pl.)* strips of fried or baked pastry dusted with powdered sugar; it is traditional during Carnevale and is known by various names
chiancarelle small pasta shells
Chianina race of Tuscan beef from the Val di Chiana. Chianina VITELLONE is the source of choice for the classic BISTECCA ALLA FIORENTINA, but the cattle themselves are fighting a losing battle against other, more profitable breeds.
Chianti a celebrated Tuscan DOCG red wine from near Florence, first recorded in 1398. In this century it was once considered the typical Italian wine, not for its taste but for its characteristic straw-covered FIASCO, but since the 1970s it has been taken seriously as a dry, tannic wine to drink young. **Chianti Classico**, from a restricted zone within the Chianti region, ages better.
chiara raw egg white; see CHIARO
chiaretto pale red wine, either a claret or rosé
chiaro *(adj.)* light (in color), clear
chiavari cheese from soured cow milk (Liguria)
chicce sweets
chicco, *pl.* **chicchi** single grain, grape, coffee bean, or similar item
chierna = CERNIA (Venezia Giulia)
Chieti the name of a province and its capital city in the Abruzzo region, abbreviated CH
chifel Tyrolean breadstick
chìfferi type of small MACCHERONE
chilo, *pl.* **chili** kilo, kilogram (2.2 lb), abbreviated kg
chinino quinine
chinoso *(adj.)* cinchonaceous
chinotto citron; these days it often refers to a carbonated beverage flavored with bitter orange
chinu = RIPIENO (Sicilia)
chinulille = PANZEROTTE
chiocciola (1) snail (see also LUMACA); a **chiocciola di mare** (sea

snail) is a periwinkle; (2) anything snail-shaped, from pasta "shells" to spiral staircases and the symbol @

chiodini small mushrooms that look like little nails, the literal meaning of the name (*Agrocybe aegerita, Armillaria mellea*)

chioggiotto *(adj.)* from Chioggia

chioppa = BOTTATRICE

chirimoia cherimoya

chiscioi type of SCIATT using mixed white and buckwheat flour that is made into rounds and boiled along with potatoes, and then served with cheese

chiscioul variant version of SCIATT

chisolini = CRESCENTINA

chisülein = CRESCENTINA

chitarra literally, "guitar"; a wire apparatus for cutting sheets of fresh pasta to make square-cut MACCHERONI or SPAGHETTI; typical of ABRUZZO and the CIOCIARIA

chiudere, *p.p.* **chiuso** to close; closed

chiusura closing, closure; **chiusura ermetica**, hermetic seal

chizze = CRESCENTINA

ciabatta literally, "slipper"; something flat and floppy, a flat bread. The metaphorical possibilities of this word can extend even to an electical outlet strip.

ciabotta vegetable stew

ciacapreti traditional pasta similar to BUCATINI (Lazio); **ciacapreti alla ciociara** is made with goat-meat sauce and PECORINO

ciacci chestnut-flour fritters filled with RICOTTA or other mild cheese; **ciacci di ricotta** are made with regular flour, the ricotta is mixed in and they are served with PROSCIUTTO

ciaccia = CARNE (Calabria)

ciaffagnoni = CANNELLONI

cialda, *pl.* **cialde** (1) a delicate wafer, often served with ice cream; (2) wafer-shaped cartridge, as for coffee-making machines

cialdiera iron utensil for making CIALDA

cialdone large CIALDA used as a container for whipped cream

cialledda FRISELLA biscuit with a topping

cialòta, in stewed in a pot

ciambella ring-shaped cake, doughnut, or practically anything round with a hole in the middle. Can be large (**ciambellone**) for a cake or small (**ciambellina**) for cookies.
ciambotta vegetable stew with potato, tomato, eggplant, onion, and peppers
ciambrotta = CIAMBOTTA
ciammotta vegetables fried and then combined, similar to CIAMBOTTA
cianchettone = LINGUATTOLA
cianfotta mixed cooked summer vegetables; vegetable RAGÙ
ciaudedda vegetable stew
ciauscolo soft, spreadable, lightly smoked pork SALUME (Marche)
ciausculu = CIAUSCOLO
ciautella in Abruzzo, stale bread boiled and dressed with oil, vinegar, and basil
ciavarra a sterile or barren ewe-goat for braising with tomato and herbs (Abruzzo, Molise)
ciavattoni a dried pasta
ciavusculu = CIAUSCOLO
cibo food; *un cibo* is a foodstuff
ciboreia chicken RAGÙ with onion and potato
cibreo classic Tuscan dish made from chicken livers, coxcombs, and giblets with egg yolks and lemon
cicala di mare = PANNOCCHIA (Toscana)
cicatelli = ORECCHIETTE
cicc type of cornmeal FOCACCIA with cheese, or a sweetened version for dessert
ciccerello = CICERELLO (Lombardia)
cicche *(pl.)* thick pieces of meat
ciccia any edible meat
ciccioli cracklings
cicciolo = CARDONCELLO
ciccirumirri = GRONGO (Sicilia)
cicerbita wild plant of the *Sonchus* genus; young leaves can be used in soup, and the leaves or cooked roots can go into salad
cicerchia, *pl.* **cicerchie** chickling (*Lathyrus sativus*), a legume used in

traditional Latian cooking and an ingredient in the Abruzzese soup LE VIRTÙ. It is becoming difficult to find. According to the system of naming foods for other foods they resemble superficially, the word is also used for various small sweets and, due to similarity of appearance, is found in the Umbrian **cicerchiata**, small fried pastry-balls made into a ring- or heart-shaped honeycake.

cicerello smooth sand lance, sand-eel (*Gymnammodytes cicerellus*)

ciceri chickpeas; **ciceri e ttria** is Pugliese chickpea soup with short noodles

cichetti, cicheti little snacks served in a BACARO (Venice)

cicinella = CICERELLO (Calabria)

cicinielli see CICERELLO; AVANOTTI DI PESCE

ciciones = MALLOREDDUS

cicireddi = CICERELLO (Sicilia)

cicoria chicory, endive, in many varieties; **cicoria di Bruxelles** is Belgian endive; see also RADICCHIO

cicoriella wild chicory, sometimes served in broth

cicorietta = TARASSACO

cieche *(pl.)* young ANGUILLA (Toscana)

ciffe ciaffe pork stew with herbs

cilantro coriander leaves

ciliegia, *pl.* **ciliege** cherry

ciliegina, *pl.* **ciliegine** small round units ("cherries") of various foods, such as mini-mozzarellas; cherry tomatoes

ciliegioso *(adj.)* (of wine) cherry

cima, *pl.* **cime** (1) top, tip of anything, including vegetables, as in CIME DI RAPA, turnip greens; (2) veal breast, which can be roasted or stuffed **alla Genovese**, with eggs, nuts, herbs, chopped meats, spinach, and peas

cimarolo *(adj.)* from the top (CIMA); used to describe vegetables (notably artichokes) from the top of the plant, considered of superior quality

cime di rapa turnip greens. In cooking they are virtually interchangeable with BROCCOLETTI, but the plant differs in two important aspects: the presence of a turnip (RAPA) at the root of the one, and that of the small buds among the leaves of the other

cinese *(adj.)* Chinese

cinesini small pasta for soup

cinestrata festive Tuscan chicken soup with yolks, sugar, and spices

cinghiale wild boar

cinnamomo the plant from which cinnamon (CANNELLA) is obtained

cioccolata chocolate; a chocolate drink

cioccolatino piece of chocolate candy, praline

cioccolato chocolate. Note that the word is always used as a noun; a prepositional phrase, **al cioccolato**, is used when an adjective is needed. **Cioccolato al latte** is milk chocolate; **fondente** is bittersweet or baker's chocolate.

ciociara, alla in the style of the CIOCIARIA

Ciociaria a mountainous area of LAZIO's hinterland, southeast of Rome, whose cooking has much in common with that of Abruzzo. The name comes from the characteristic footwear of the area's shepherds, the same ones who can still be seen in Rome at Christmastime playing bagpipes.

cioffa cauliflower

cioncia braised veal or beef muzzle, lips, ears, and other head parts with peppers, spices, and black olives, a specialty of Pescia in Tuscany

ciotola bowl, basin, cup

cipolla onion

cipollaccio = LAMPASCIONE

cipollata baked or stewed onion condiment for fish or meats (Sicilia); Sienese onion soup with pork

cipollato *(adj.)* layered

cipollina, *pl.* **cipolline** generically, small or young onions, or specifically, pearl onions; **cipolline verdi** are scallions; **cipolline in agrodolce** are sweet and sour pearl onions

cipollotto scallion

cipudazzi = LAMPASCIONE

cipudda = SCORFANO (Sicilia)

circelle = TAGLIATELLINE

cirenga = CERNIA (Sicilia)

ciribusla = CASSAGAI

cirimbirru = CICERELLO (Calabria)

ciriola, *pl.* **ciriole** (1) a small eel; (2) a type of bread shaped like a small football; (3) = UMBRICI

cisrà vegetable soup with chickpeas (Piemonte)

citula = *pesce* SAN PIETRO (Lazio)

ciuffo sprig, tuft

ciufulitti homemade FUSILLI

ciuppin Ligurian fish soup, the ancestor of San Francisco's cioppino, which was first made by Genoese immigrant fishermen

civè = CIVET

civet, in game marinade; fried, marinated hare (LEPRE), deer, or kid

cixireddu = CICERELLO (Sardegna)

cjalzons *or* **cjalzons** Friulian AGNOLOTTI filled with spinach, chocolate, candied citron, sultanas, and rye bread. Other versions (and there are many) are filled with meats, ricotta, and herbs, though almost always sweetened or containing sweet ingredients. There are also dessert versions. The *c* is hard (the word is Friulian and not Italian, but is obviously related to the Italian CALZONE).

cjarsons = CIALZONS

classico classic; on wine labels, this means it was produced in the oldest, most traditional DOC area

clementina, *pl.* **clementine** clementine; small citrus fruit

clone clone

clorofilla chlorophyll

coanello = PAVONCELLA

coatto stewed ewe leg with herbs, white wine, tomatoes, and spicy peppers

coccetta, al see COCCIO

coccio (1) earthenware, clay; **al coccio** means cooked in earthenware; (2) a fish (red gurnard), which is red-skinned, firm, and white-fleshed and often served in Neapolitan ACQUA PAZZA or grilled; = *pesce* CAPONE LIRA (Campania, Basilicata)

cocco, noce di coconut

cocomero watermelon

cocone = OVOLI

cocoro = NOCE

cocotte egg poacher; round or oval casserole dish (pronounced as French)

cocuzza = ZUCCA, squash

coda tail of anything (hence its meaning as a concluding part of a piece of music, and also line or queue); **coda di bue** is oxtail; **coda di rospo** is the tail of the RANA PESCATRICE; **coda alla vaccinara** is braised oxtail in tomato sauce, a classic Roman dish from the QUINTO QUARTO repertory

codeghi small COTECHINO sausages

codine sprinkles, jimmies

codino tail of a pig, as opposed to CODA

codognà = COGNÀ

cofacce dessert FOCACCIA stuffed with with banana or apple

cogliere, *p.p.* **colto** to gather, to grasp

coglioni di mulo = MORTADELLINE DI CAMPOTOSTO; literally, "mule's balls"

cognà fruit sauce for boiled meats (Piemonte)

cognolo = PALOMBO (Puglia)

coi with the (contraction of *con i*)

cola type of Pugliese cauliflower

colabrodo chinois, pointed colander

colapasta colander

colarda = SCAMONE

colatura anything filtered, sieved, or strained

colazione sometimes lunch but usually breakfast, which is correctly *prima colazione*

colino small sieve, small strainer

colla di pesce, foglio di literally, "fish glue"; isinglass—sheet or leaf gelatin from fish (these days from other souces as well)—used in making some desserts, such as PANNA COTTA

collaggio sizing (for wine)
colle, *pl.* **colli** hill
collina, *pl.* **colline** hill, slope
collinare *(adj.)* hill
collo neck; from quadripeds, the neck meat is typically used for stewing and braising
colmare, *p.p.* **colmato** to fill to the brim, to top up
colmo *(adj.)* full to the brim
colomba (1) wood pigeon; (2) dove-shaped cake with orange peel and almonds
colombo dove, pigeon
colorante, *pl.* **coloranti** coloring agent
colorare, *p.p.* **colorato** to color, to take on color, to brown
colore color
colostro colostrum, the first milk from a cow after it has given birth
coltello knife; further specified by adding *da* + the thing to be cut or place where the knife is to be used, e.g., *coltello* (or the diminutive **coltellino**, when appropriate) *da* PANE, *da* TAVOLA, *da* PESCE
coltivato *(adj.)* cultivated, as opposed to wild
coltivatore grower
coltivazione, *pl.* **coltivazioni** cultivation, crop
colza colza, a subspecies of *Brassica napus,* normally used for a vegetable oil
commensale, *pl.* **commensali** an extremely useful word whose translation, "table companion," does not begin to express how useful. It means the person eating (and the prefix *con-*, transformed to *com-* before the *m,* implies that nobody eats alone), or, in the plural, everybody at the table.
commercializzare, *p.p.* **commercializzato** to market; **commercializzazione** is marketing (also called "il marketing")
commestibile *(adj.)* edible
Como (1) the name of a province and its capital city in Lombardia, abbreviated CO; (2) Lake Como
companatico from CON and PANE, it is anything eaten with bread
completare, *p.p.* **completato** to complete, to finish

completo *(adj.)* complete; as a noun it can mean a set; when ordering breakfast at a hotel, you may be asked if you want your coffee or tea *completo*, i.e., with rolls and jam; when the restaurant is *completo*, you can't get a reservation—it's fully booked.

composto *(adj.)* "composed" of several ingredients; an INSALATA *composta* is assembled, not tossed; as a feminine noun, it means stewed fruit or compôte

compreso *(adj.)* included

con with

conca de moru = GHIOZZO (Sardegna)

concavo concave

concentrato *(adj.)* concentrated

concentrato (di pomodoro) *(n.)* (tomato) paste (but see also CONSERVA); can be DOPPIO (double) or TRIPLO (triple) strength, with, respectively, 500 and 600 g of tomatoes to 100 g of concentrate. Single-strength *concentrato* (called simply that) has 300 g tomatoes to 100 g of paste.

conchiglia, *pl.* **conchiglie** shells, pasta shells; shellfish

conciare, *p.p.* **conciato** to cure (among many other meanings, including to tan leather)

concorrere, *p.p.* **concorso** the first meaning is "to compete," but the literal meaning (from *con*, "with," and *correre*, "to run") is intended when this verb is used to describe grapes going into blends. A *concorso* is a competition.

condiggion = CONDIMENTO (Liguria)

condijun = CONDION (Liguria)

condimento condiment, dressing, sauce; the word is much more general than the meaning of condiment in English

condion Genovese salad of tomato, peppers, pickles, olives, celery, onion, and basil

condire, *p.p.* **condito** to dress, to season; see also CONDIMENTO

condito *(adj.)* dressed; seasoned, pickled; treated with one or more CONDIMENTI, or flavorings. "Dressed" in the case of a salad.

Condorelli brand name of much-loved Sicilian TORRONCINI

confetti (1) sugar-coated, or Jordan, almonds, traditionally presented to guests at weddings, most famously produced in the town of Sulmona (birthplace of the Roman poet Ovid), in Abruzzo; (2) anything that looks anything like confetti, in the English sense (i.e., small and multicolored, including small chopped up vegetables used as a garnish)

confettura jam; sweetmeat

confezionato pre-packaged, industrial; as opposed to ARTIGIANALE or homemade

confezione (1) package; (2) anything ready-made, especially clothing, hence uniforms and work clothes for kitchen and dining room staff

congelare, *p.p.* **congelato** to freeze (usually industrially), deep freeze; see also SURGELARE. *Congelare* is also used when freezing something metaphorically is intended, as in assets. **Congelatore** means deep freeze.

congelato *(adj.)* frozen; by law, Italian menus must indicate frozen products

coniglio rabbit. Figuratively, *coniglio* means chicken, in the sense of cowardly.

cono (ice-cream) cone

conserva generic term for a preserved food, but virtually always refers to *conserva di pomodoro*, a dense, highly concentrated and nearly black product made by drying strained tomatoes in the sun. Needless to say, this is a specialty of southern regions, especially Sicilia.

conservante *(adj. and n.)* preservative (Beware: *preservativo* is Italian for condom)

conservazione, a lunga long-life (usually referring to milk), UHT (ultrahigh temperature)

consigliato *(adj.)* recommended

consistente *(adj.)* of a certain consistency, thick

consistenza substance, consistency

conso *(adj.)* = CONDITO; see POLENTA CONSCIA

consorzio consortium, an association of growers or producers that ensures quality control over a particular food and controls use of its name

consum dumplings

consumare, *p.p.* **consumato** to eat, to drink, to consume, to use; **consumare entro** means use by (a certain date)

consumo, al according to consumption; the term indicates that you will be charged for wine by how much disappears from the bottle or how much you take from the antipasto table

contadina, alla country-style, peasant-style

contenere, *p.p.* **contenuto** to contain

contenitore container

contenuto content, contents (from CONTENERE)

conto bill, check

contorno side dish; vegetable or salad; it also means outline

controfiletto = LOMBATA; regional variations

controgirello a cut of beef and veal round that lies along the GIRELLO and is used for roasting and braising

controllare, *p.p.* **controllato** to check, to control

convesso *(adj.)* convex

conza stuffing

conzo = CONDITO (Veneto)

copata almond brittle

coperchio lid, cover

copertina part of the beef chuck (including the tender) that lies along the outside face of the shoulder blade and extends from the FESONE DI SPALLA to the GIRELLO DI SPALLA

coperto place setting; cover charge; **pane e coperto** means "bread and cover," a now obsolete (but not yet extinct) cover charge applied in restaurants. It originated as sort of corkage for food brought to a wineshop, where the landlord, who sold wine not food, would put a covering and a basket of bread on the table.

coppa (1) cup, bowl, Champagne glass, dish for ice cream; (2) head cheese: pork head meat boiled, pressed, and sliced

coppetta the diminutive of COPPA (1), often used for ice cream as an alternative to the CONO

coppiette *(pl.)* literally, "little couples"; strips of salted, dried, and ginger-seasoned smoked meat

coppo (1) terra-cotta container, pot; (2) a custard pudding (Emilia-Romagna)

coppone pork neck (Emilia–Romagna)
coprire, *p.p.* **coperto** to cover; *copri–* as a prefix
coque, uova alla coddled eggs
corada lungs of beef, sheep, or pork
coralli *(pl.)* small pasta for soup
corallina (1) a type of salami eaten in Lazio at Easter; (2) an alga, eaten raw; (3) small pasta for soup
corallo see FAGIOLINI
corallo, fagioli al see FAGIOLI
corata (1) heart, lungs, and liver; (2) syn. CORADA
coratella pluck (i.e., heart, liver, and lungs), usually of lamb, possibly also of pork, classically cooked chopped up with artichokes
corbello = OMBRINA (Toscana, Marche)
corbezzolo a white berry shrub (*Arbutus*); see MIELE AMARO
corcorighedda zucchini in Sardegna
cordone alla faentina stewed or grilled beef stomach
cordula in Sardegna, lamb or goat guts prepared variously
coreda = CORADA
coregone powan, whitefish (*Coregonus lavaretus*), a delicate white-fleshed lake fish; see LAVARELLO and BONDELLA
coriandolo (1) coriander (*Coriandrum sativum* L.L.), both leaves (cilantro) and seeds; the name comes from *koris*, Greek for bedbug, because of the nasty smell supposedly produced by both bug and herb when squashed; (2) usually in the *pl.*, **coriandoli** means confetti (in the English sense; cf. CONFETTI)
coriandro = CORIANDOLO
corifena = LAMPUGA
coriglianese, agnello alla lamb covered with PANCETTA and a mixture of crushed garlic, oregano, and vinegar, then roasted (Calabria)
corinedda = LATTERINO (Sicilia)
cornetto (1) croissant, roll; a *cornetto* is crescent-shaped like the croissant, but the dough is not necessarily the French-style flaky pastry; see BRIOCHE; (2) tip for pastry bag
cornetto di mare = MURICE SPINOSO (Toscana)

corniola, *pl.* **corniole** cornel, cornelian cherry (*Cornus mas*)
corpo body; **di corpo** means full-bodied
corposo *(adj.)* full-bodied, thick
correggere, *p.p.* **corretto** to correct; used most often for ESPRESSO, "corrected" with a splash of GRAPPA, brandy, or liqueur; **correggere di sale** is a recipe instruction to "correct" the salt to taste
correzione correction or "correction" (a drop of alcohol); i.e., added to something else, usually coffee
corta, pasta short pasta shape(s). RIGATONI, PENNE, and similar pastas are thus placed in a different category from the long pastas, such as SPAGHETTI or FETTUCCINE, or the stuffed pastas, such as RAVIOLI.
corteccia rind
cortile courtyard, barnyard, yard; **animali da cortile**—literally, "courtyard animals"—is a generic term covering poultry and rabbits
corto *(adj.)* short; see *pasta* CORTA
corvina corvina (*Corvina nigra*) is a Mediterranean fish of the Sciaenidae family, which includes the OMBRINA
corvo syn. CORVINA; crow
corzetti multi-colored Ligurian disk- or figure-8-shaped egg pasta, usually served with butter, marjoram, and PINOLI
coscetta in poultry, the leg up to just before the hip joint
coscia (1) thigh, haunch or, by extension, the whole leg, usually when still attached to the animal (cf. COSCIO); (2) variety of pear; *coscie delle monache* ("nun's thighs") are a variety of plum
coscia doppia in fowl, the entire breast with the legs and tail still attached
coscio butchered thigh, haunch, or leg
cosciotto diminutive of COSCIO, used for thighs or legs of smaller animals (e.g., chicken, baby lamb)
Cosenza the name of a province and its capital city in the Calabria region, abbreviated CS
cospargere, *p.p.* **cosparso** to sprinkle
cospeton = ARINGA (Veneto)
cossöla mixed meats and vegetables in a little broth

costa, *pl.* **coste** (1) rib; sirloin (= COSTOLA); (2) = BIETOLA DA COSTA; (3) a rib of anything, e.g., celery

costardella, costardello Atlantic saury, saury pike (*Scomberesox saurus*)

costarelle *(pl.)* chops, baby lamb chops (ABBACCHIO); there is one recipe for pork cutlet that uses this term: *costarelle di* MAIALE *con la* PANUNTELLA

costata beef rib steak from the LOMBATA; see FIORENTINA

costato (1) rib cage; flank; (2) as an adjective, garnished

costicine *(pl.)* spareribs

costine *(pl.)* rib tips; small chops

costola rib, in beef, goats, and sheep, the *costole* are thirteen pairs of bones that make up the rib cage. Sliced apart, some of these are used to make COSTATE.

costoletta (1) cutlet, but as the name implies, from the rib. The *costoletta* par excellence is the **costoletta alla milanese**, pounded till it covers a dinner plate, then breaded several times and sautéed in butter. (2) Veal (but not beef), lamb, mutton, pork, or game sliced from the LOMBATA

cotechino a large-diameter pork sausage (of Emilian origin) served boiled and sliced, usually with lentils; the name derives from the presence of COTICHE in the mixture

cotenna pork rind, usually skin cut away from the PROSCIUTTO before slicing; cooked rinds are called COTICHE

cotica, *pl.* **cotiche** pork rind(s) to be used for cooking (the raw material is called COTENNA); **fagioli con le cotiche** are CANNELLINI beans cooked with tomatoes and pork rinds

cotogna quince

cotognata quince marmalade, quince cheese

cotoletta most simply, cutlet (veal unless not otherwise specified), usually breaded and fried, though geographic attributions indicate a variety of preparations. The famous *milanese* is known as both COSTOLETTA and *cotoletta*, possibly depending on whether the speaker is emphasizing the cut of meat or the preparation. **Cotoletta alla bolognese** is breaded thin-sliced veal with prosciutto and Parmesan.

cotronese sheep-milk cheese of Calabria

cotto *(adj.)* cooked (also for wine); **cotto adagio** literally means "cooked slowly," meaning braised. **Formaggio cotto**—"cooked cheese"—means hard cheese heated during manufacture to temperatures exceeding 48°C (more than 100°F).

cotto *(n.)* (1) a type of sausage; (2) a type of floor tile often found in rustic and faux rustic kitchens

coturnice pheasant-like bird (*Alectoris graeca*)

coulis sauce (French)

couregun = LAVARELLO (Piemonte)

covata, zuppa = SOPA COADA

coviglia mousse-like Neapolitan dessert variant of the SEMIFREDDO, made in numerous flavors

cozza mussel (*Mytilis galloprovincialis* and *Mytilis edulus*); **cozza pelosa**, bearded horse mussel (*Modiolus barbatus*); **cozza gignacula** or **pellegrino**, = CAPASANTA (Puglia)

cozzola = TELLINA (Sicilia)

crapiettu = CAPRETTO (Calabria)

crauti sauerkraut

cravaoa = MALLOREDDUS

crema (1) anything creamy or very smooth ("È una crema!" is a compliment reserved for foods of unexpectedly voluptuous texture); (2) the basic ice cream flavor (instead of vanilla, which is rare). **Crema di latte** is actual dairy cream (see PANNA). **Crema cotta** is cream and milk thickened with gelatin and usually flavored. **Crema inglese** is custard sauce used as a dessert topping. **Crema pasticciera** (often called simply *crema*) is custard or custard sauce; chunks of it can be breaded and fried as **crema fritta**.

crema bruciata crème brûlée

cremeria milk bar and/or place that sells dairy products

cremino, *pl.* **cremini** (1) cocoa-colored ordinary mushroom (CHAMPIGNON) with slightly more texture and flavor, sometimes known in the U.S. as Roman mushrooms. The so-called portobello, or portobella, mushroom is nothing more than an overgrown *cremino*; the term portobello and its variations may sound Italian but are not. (2) Deep-fried pieces of CREMA PASTICCIERA (syn. CREMA FRITTA). (3) Four-layer chocolate candy with nuts.

cremolata = GREMOLADA

Cremona the name of a province and its capital city in Lombardia, abbreviated CR. Best known as the home of Stradivarius and other great violin makers, it is still a center of violin making but is also known for its characteristic MOSTARDA.

cremore di tartaro, cremortartaro cream of tartar

cremoso *(adj.)* creamy or thick, as opposed to liquid or runny

cren horseradish, horseradish sauce

cresc tajed pasta from corn and wheat flours

crescente fried dough squares, usually served with cheese or salami

crescentina fried pasta squares of Emilia, stuffed with cheese or vegetable; in Toscana, stuffed with salami

crescenza a soft, buttery white cheese

crescia a yeasty pizza; **crescia di Pasqua** is an Easter cake with cheese; **crescia al panaro** is a bread baked on a stone slab and served with sausages and salami

crescione cress; **crescione inglese**, *Lepidium sativum, Nasturtium sativum* Medik, garden or pepper cress

cresciuta, pasta yeast-raised dough; a yeasty pizza

cresctajat = CRESC TAJED

crespedde di nunnata Sicilian fried balls of tiny fish

crespella, *pl.* **crespelle** crêpe

crespigno syn. CICERBITA

crespolini small filled crêpes

crespone pork intestine used as casing for the salami of the same name

creste di gallo *(pl.)* cockscombs; pasta in that shape

creta clay; **alla creta** means cooked wrapped in clay (like Chinese Beggar's Chicken) or in a clay pot

crispeddi fried pasta stuffed with ricotta or anchovies, and fried

cristallino *(adj.)* crystalline

cristallizzare, *p.p.* **cristallizzato** to crystalize

critmo sea fennel, a seaside plant

croccante *(adj.)* crunchy; as a noun, nut (usually almond) brittle

croccantino potentially anything crunchy and yummy; ice cream with crunchy bits

croccolone great snipe (*Capella media*)
crocette = MURICE SPINOSO (Marche, Lazio)
crochetta, *pl.* **crocchette** croquette(s); croquettes of mashed potatoes are staple snacks on the pizzeria menu
crogiolato *(adj.)* simmered
crognolo sardinaro = LATTERINO (Toscana)
crongo = GRONGO (Puglia)
crosetti disk-shaped pasta, the Emilian version of *corzetti*
crosta crust; cheese rind; pastry crust. **Crosticina**, the diminutive, can be used for the nice brown crust that forms when certain foods are cooked.
crostata fruit-covered tart
crostino, *pl.* **crostini** (1) toast with toppings; (2) croutons
crostoli strips of fried or baked pastry dusted with powdered sugar
crostone, *pl.* **crostoni** crouton, fried bread, or piece of dry bread to put in a soup bowl
Crotone ancient Croton, the name of a province and its capital city in the Calabria region, abbreviated KR
crotonese strong sheep- and goat-milk cheese
crovello = OMBRINA (Liguria, Toscana, Puglia, Sicilia)
crovetto = TINCA (Liguria)
crudaiola, alla with a sauce of raw vegetables
crudo *(adj.)* raw, rare; for salami and fish, it often means "cured." **Formaggio crudo** describes hard cheese heated during manufacture to less than 35°C (95°F).
crumiri *(pl.)* Piedmontese butter cookies
crusca bran
cruschello type of fine bran (CRUSCA) containing some flour
crusetti closed, stuffed pasta tubes
cubbaita almond-sesame brittle
cubetti *(pl.)* dice
cuccagna abundance, plenty; with capital *C*, Cockaigne, a mythical land of plenty
cucchiaiata a good spoonful
cucchiaino teaspoon, coffeespoon; in recipes: teaspoon
cucchiaio tablespoon, dessert spoon, any spoon larger than a

teaspoon and smaller than a serving spoon; in recipes: tablespoon. **Dolci al cucchiaio** are the class of sweets soft enough to require a spoon, e.g., custards or a pudding, as opposed to those you can pick up in your fingers and dunk in your wine or coffee. **Cucchiaio di legno**, wooden spoon; **cucchiaio forato**, slotted spoon.

cucchiaione serving spoon or large kitchen spoon

cuccìa cooked wheatberries (the word derives from CHICCO). Typical of the far South, it may be a PRIMO PIATTO containing meat or a dessert.

cucculli = CUCULLI

cuccuma = BRICCO

cucina (1) kitchen, the room; (2) stove, range; **cucina a gas**, gas range; **cucina elettrica**, electric range; (3) cuisine, style of cooking, as in **cucina regionale**

cucina creativa creative cuisine, usually glossed as the Italian equivalent of the French *nouvelle cuisine*, but it is not so much a specific cooking style or movement as a non-traditional approach. Creative chefs usually follow the time-honored practices (as those of eating pasta or rice before meat or fish), but have a lighter hand than NONNA did and like daring combinations of ingredients. A felicitous offshoot of the creative approach has been the rediscovery, rehabilitation, and bringing up to date of many dishes belonging to regional cuisines.

cucinare, *p.p.* **cucinato** to cook, to prepare food

cucire, *p.p.* **cucito** to sew, to stitch

cuculli various Ligurian fritters flavored with marjoram and made of potato or chickpea flour

cucuna = OVOLO

cucurdia = POLENTA (Calabria)

cucuzella = ZUCCHINA (Sicilia)

cucuzza = ZUCCA (Sicilia, Calabria)

cucuzzedda, cucuzzella zucchini

cudugna = COGNÀ

cuffia (1) = RETICOLO; (2) various things to put on the head, such as a showercap or similar protective/hygienic gear, or even earphones

cuggiune = GHIOZZO (Puglia)

cugnà = COGNÀ

cugoli GNOCCHI made of bread crumbs

culatello cured pork butt, the lean "heart" of the PROSCIUTTO; the most prized is **culatello di Zibello** from a town near Parma

culatto rump

culingiones Sardinian RAVIOLI

culo butt. It is not a word for polite company. Colloquially, the *culo* of a loaf of bread is the heel.

culurjones, culurzones CULINGIONES

cumino cumin (*Cuminum cyminum*), not much used in Italian cooking; **cumino dei prati, cumino tedesco**, = CARVI

cuncia see POLENTA CONCIA

Cuneo the name of a province and its capital city in the Piemonte region, abbreviated CN

cuneo wedge

cunigghiu = CONIGLIO (Sicilia)

cunscia see POLENTA CONCIA; **pasta cunscia**, = PASTA CONDITA

cuocere, *p.p.* **cotto** to cook

cuoco cook, chef

cuoioso *(adj.)* leathery

cuore (1) heart; (2) **cuore edule**, cockle, heart shell; various mollusks of the *Acanthocardia* species

cupeta almond brittle

curadduza small cylindrical pasta for soup

curcuma turmeric (*Curcuma longa*)

curegun = LAVARELLO (Liguria, Piemonte)

curinedda = LATTERINO (Sicilia)

curnale = LATTERINO (Puglia)

cuscinetto see CUSCINO

cuscino, *pl.* **cuscini** cushion, pillow; either literally or, often in the plural diminutive, **cuscinetti**, as a fanciful name for various food preparations involving stuffing; **cuscinetti di vitello**, braised veal stuffed with cheese and ham

cuscus, cuscusu Sicilian or Livornese version of couscous

cuticùsu mashed beans with anchovy, oil, and tomatoes

cutturiddu lamb and vegetable stew

cutturiello pasta sauce of stewed lamb

cutturo = PAIOLO; **agnello a cutturo**, lamb with herbs and hot pepper served over bread slices (Abruzzo)

cuzzutella = ANGUILLA (Campania)

cvapcici = CEVAPCICI

≈ D ≈

dadini small dice

dado cube, bouillion cube; **brodo di dado**, bouillion made with a cube

dadolata diced food used as a garnish

daino fallow deer (*Dama dama*)

damigella hollow, elongated MACCHERONE; literally, "damsel"; also bridesmaid

damigiana demijohn, a large glass bottle with wide body and narrow neck, encased in wicker or plastic and used for transporting liquids, usually 50 liters. Assume it is larger or smaller according to its suffix, e.g., **damigianetta**, **damigianina**, **damigianona**.

dariola = TIMBALLO

data date; **data di scadenza**, expiration date or sell-by date

dattao de ma = DATTERO DI MARE (Liguria)

dattero di mare literally, "sea date"; date shell (*Lithophaga lithophaga*)

dattero nero = COZZA (Liguria, Lazio)

dattolo di mare = DATTERO DI MARE (Veneto)

decaffeinato decaffeinated, caffeine-free

decalitro decaliter (10 cc)

decantazione decantation
decongelare, *p.p.* **decongelato** to thaw; cf. SCONGELARE, SBRINARE
decorazione, *pl.* **decorazioni** decoration
decorticare, *p.p.* **decorticato** to strip off the hull or husk, as rice or grain; to shell (a crustacean); to strip a tree of bark
deficeira, pasta alla MACCHERONI cooked slowly in wine
definito *(adj.)* definite
defrutum *(Lat.)* grape must boiled until it is reduced to one half or one third its volume. It was used as a sweetener in place of the much more expensive honey.
deglassare, *p.p.* **deglassato** to deglaze (a pan); French *déglacer*
degustare, *pp.* **degustato** to taste (critically); cf. ASSAGGIARE
degustatore professional taster
degustazione tasting, sampling; **una degustazione di vino** is a wine tasting; a **menù degustazione** is a tasting menu with several small portions
delizia, *pl.* **delizie** delicacy; literally, "delight"
delizioso *(adj.)* delicious
denominazione name, designation; **denominazione commerciale**, trade name, trade description; **denominazione d'origine**, designation of origin; **denominazione dei prodotti**, list of products; **denominazione d'origine protetta**, protected designation of origin (often applied to cheeses)
denso *(adj.)* thick, dense
dentade = DENTICE (Puglia)
dentale = DENTICE (Toscana, Marche, Abruzzo, Lazio)
dentato = DENTICE (Campania)
dente, al of pasta—still firm enough to be resistant to the bite, not overcooked. The degree of resistance rises the farther south in Italy you travel.
dente di cane = DENTE DI LEONE
dente di leone dandelion (*Taraxacum*)
dentesgi = DENTICE (Liguria)
denti di cavallo an industrial pasta shape similar to RIGATONI but smaller; literally, "horse's teeth"
dentice dentex, dog's teeth (*Dentex dentex*), a saltwater fish of the Sparidae family

denticuozzo = DENTICE (Campania, Sicilia)
dentile = DENTICE (Toscana)
dentissi = DENTICE (Sardegna)
dentixi = DENTICE (Sardegna)
dentro inside, within
dentul = DENTICE (Sardegna)
deperibile *(adj.)* perishable
desco table, dining table
desinare, *pp.* **desinato** to dine, to eat the principal meal of the day; as a noun (*m.*), the dinner itself
destra right (direction)
destrosio dextrose
detere = DENTICE (Puglia)
detersivo detergent
diavola, alla literally, "devil style"; can have two meanings, the obvious one of highly spicy, and the slightly more imaginative one of grilled, an allusion to the Infernal method of treating sinners. **Pollo alla diavola** is a chicken, split, flattened under a weight, brushed with oil (sometimes containing a chili pepper), and grilled.
diavoletto hot chili pepper
diavolicchio hot chili pepper
diavolillo hot chili pepper
dic. abbreviation of December
dicembre December
dieta diet, in all its meanings; **a dieta**, on a diet
Dietor® brand name of a popular artificial sweetener
difetto defect
differente *(adj.)* different
digestivo a liqueur, AMARO OR GRAPPA (or even herbal tea) taken after eating in the belief that it will aid the digestion; the principle is dubious, the custom delightful. As an adjective, it means digestive.
digiuno (1) state of fasting; **a digiuno**, on an empty stomach; **digiunare**, to fast, to go without food; (2) part of the intestine
diliscare, *p.p.* **diliscato** to bone (a fish); see LISCA

diluire, *p.p.* **diluito** to dilute
dimezzare, *p.p.* **dimezzato** to halve
diminuire, *p.p.* **diminuito** to reduce, to diminish (trans. and intrans.)
dindanella = TACCHINELLA
dindo turkey (see TACCHINO); from the French *dinde*, meaning *(coq) d'Inde*, or Indian cock
dintatu = DENTICE (Sicilia)
dintici = DENTICE (Sicilia)
diplomatica, salsa white sauce with lobster butter, cayenne, truffles, and cognac; also called **salsa Riche**
diplomatico dessert of custard, cake, and candied fruit; also called **torta diplomatica**
Dipnosofisti *Deipnosophistai;* see ATENEO
diradamaneto (dei grappoli) thinning (of [grape] bunches)
dismaturo *(adj.)* unripe (for wine)
disossare, *p.p.* **disossato** to bone
dispensa pantry, and many other meanings not pertinent to the kitchen
disponibile *(adj.)* available; **disponibilità**, availability
disporre, *p.p.* **disposto** to arrange, to place (a frequent instruction in recipes)
disposizione disposition, arrangement
dissanguare, *p.p.* **dissanguato** to bleed (an animal)
distendere, *p.p.* **disteso** to spread (the cloth on the table; cf. SPALMARE), to stretch out
distillato, *pl.* **distillati** *(adj. used as noun)* distillates, hard liquor, e.g., whisky, cognac, grappa; syn. SUPERALCOLICI
distributore automatico vending machine
ditalo, *pl.* **ditali** short tubes of pasta; literally, "thimble"; **ditalini** are smaller versions, usually for soup, **ditaloni** larger
dito, *pl.* **dita** finger, including as a unit of measurement (as in add three fingers of water); **maccheroni a tre dita** (three-finger MACCHERONI) is a Sicilian egg-pasta dish with meat sauce, eggplant, sugar, cinnamon, and cheese
diverso *(adj.)* different; **diversamente**, differently

D.O.C. *or* **DOC** **Denominazione d'Origine Controllata** is a limited geographic zone of distinction and registered designation of origin. It is a governmental designation for wines produced from specific grapes, grown in limited areas, and vinified according to certain standards. Some hams, cheeses, and olive oils are also DOC. Italians have taken to extending the term popularly to describe almost anything quasi-official, of high quality, or done *come si deve* (French *comme il faut*). **D.O.C.G.** or **DOCG** (**Denominazione d'Origine Controllata e Garantita**): the same plus "guaranteed."

doga stave (of a barrel or keg)

dolce *(n. and adj.), pl.* **dolci** sweet, mild; dessert; **(di) acqua dolce**, freshwater

dolceforte *or* **dolce e forte** sweet and sour (Toscana); game sauce of vinegar, sugar, spices, raisins, and chocolate

dolcelatte a mild cheese, related to gorgonzola

dolcetta = VALERIANELLA

Dolcetto grape variety and red DOC wines of southern Piemonte, usually drunk young

dolcetto, *pl.* **dolcetti** diminutive of DOLCE; sweet tidbit, petit fours, and other little sweet confections

dolcezza sweetness

dolcificante sweetener, used popularly to mean artificial sweetener. In a bar you can ask for *un dolcificante* for your coffee.

dolciume, *pl.* **dolciumi** usually plural; sweets collectively, confectionery

dolico synonym of FAGIOLI DALL'OCCHIO

domani tomorrow

domenica Sunday

donzelle = CENCI

donzelline *(pl.)* various types of fried pastries

d.o.p. (denominazione d'origine protetta) a legal designation that assures a product name is used only for foods produced in a specific geographical area

dopo after; sometimes used informally as a noun to mean SECONDO PIATTO

doppio *(adj.)* double

dorare, *p.p.* **dorato** to brown lightly; literally, "to gild"; **fritto dorato**, dredged in flour and dipped in egg, then deep fried

dorata = ORATA (Toscana, Lazio)

dorso back

dosare, *p.p.* **dosato** to measure out

dose *(n.f.), pl.* **dosi** amount, quantity (in a recipe), dose

dotto = DENTICE (Puglia); but **pesce dotto** = CERNIA (Sicilia). The word means "learned."

dottori = DENTICE (Puglia)

dozzina dozen, but not used quite as much as in English; *decine*, tens, is more usual to indicate unspecified quantities. It is usual to ask for six or twelve eggs rather than for a half dozen or dozen. However, *dozzinale* means cheap or second-rate, in other words, a dime a dozen.

dracina ragna TRACINA

dragoncello tarragon (*Artemisia dracunculus*)

dragone TRACINA (Toscana, Lazio)

droga, *pl.* **droghe** spice

drogheria originally a spice (DROGA) shop, it is a small grocery store, like the French *épicerie*. Its proprietor is the **droghiere**.

drömesa a typical PRIMO PIATTO of Albanian Calabria consisting of small dumplings with a tomato and onion sauce

due literally, "two"; metaphorically, "just a little." Waiter: "Would the signora like some more spaghetti?" Customer: "*Due!* I'm on a diet." Don't forget pasta names are usually plural and construed as true plurals, thus spaghetti could be counted, if anyone cared.

dunderet potato gnocchi made with egg and nutmeg, a specialty of Cuneo

durello, durone poultry stomach

duro *(adj.)* hard, hard-boiled

≈ E ≈

e and

ebbrezza intoxication, inebriation

ebbro *(adj.)* drunk

ebollizione, portare ad to bring to the boil

ebraico *(adj.)* Jewish; **all'ebraica**, Jewish-style. Does not mean anything specific (except for the obvious absence of pork) but refers to any of the traditional recipes of the Jewish ghettoes of Italy.

ed and (used before a vowel)

edulcorare to sweeten

edule, cuore = CUORE

effervescente *(adj.)* effervescent

einbrennsuppe gruel with wine and potatoes

Eisacktaler Valle dell'Isarco

elefante elephant, meaning anything huge, such as an enormous platter of mixed boiled, fried, grilled, roasted, and smoked meats atop rice pilaf. **Elefante di mare** is a large lobster. **Elefante** or **orecchio d'elefante** (elephant's ear) can also indicate a huge steak or a flattened veal chop.

elefante di mare = ASTICE *(Homarus gammarus)*

elettrodomestico appliance; large ones, such as dishwashers, are called *elettrodomestici*; small ones, such as toasters and blenders, are *piccoli elettrodomestici*; really small ones are sometimes called *gadget* (singular and plural)

elettromescolatore = PAIOLO ELETTRICO

eliche helical pasta (plural of *elica*, helix)

elicoidali *(pl.)* helical tubular pasta
elisir elixir
emiliano *(adj.)* Emilian; as a noun, it is a hard, Parmesan-type grating cheese
Emilia-Romagna a region in the Po valley in northeast Italy just south of Lombardia and the Veneto, of which Bologna is capital. More than any other region of Italy, Emilia-Romagna is associated with fine food products and food production.
emmental Emmenthaler cheese
energia energy, in all its meanings
Enna the name of a province and its capital city in the Sicilia region, abbreviated EN
enogastronomico *(adj.)* relating to food and wine. English cannot express it all in one word.
enologia oenology, enology
enoteca wine "library," "oenothèque"; wine store; restaurant with wine cellar; wine bar with snacks
enula campana elecampane (*Inula helenium*), a wild herb whose bitter but aromatic roots are used to flavor alcoholic drinks; also called **elenio**
eporediese *or* **eporediense** *(adj.)* relating to Ivrea; **eporediesi al cacao**, a local sweet
equilibrato *(adj.)* balanced (used in wine tasting)
equilibrio balance
equino *(adj.)* equine: horse, donkey or mule; *carne equina*, horsemeat
erba, *pl.* **erbe** the basic meaning is "grass"—more than, but not to the exclusion of, "herb"; it becomes herb in the presence of an adjective, as **erba aromatica**. See individual entries, and see also ERBETTA. Can also mean "spinach."
erba acciuga a kind of SANTOREGGIA
erba amara = ERBA DI SAN PIETRO
erba barbara = RUCOLA PALUSTRE
erba brusca = ACETOSA
erba canina = ALCHECHENGI
erba cimicina = CORIANDOLO (*cimice* is Italian for bedbug, and for that matter also a small electronic listening device)

erba cipollina chive or other thin grass with mild onion flavor (*Allium schoenoprasum*)

erba gatta catnip (*Calamintha officinalis*), a wild mint-like herb much used by the ancient Romans and highly attractive to cats

erba lucina = ARTEMISIA

erba Luigia *or* **Luisa** = CEDRINA

erba noce salad burnet

erba stella if you meet this word, ask for a local synonym; it seems to be a catchall name for a number of edible plants of the species *Plantago coronopus*, including ALCHIMILLA, BARBA DI CAPPUCCINO, CERFOGLIO, and SALVASTRELLA

erbaceo *(adj.)* herbaceous

Erbaluce Piedmontese white grape variety and DOC wine

erbazzone pie from spinach, pancetta, eggs, and Parmesan; pizza with herbs; dessert version made with beets, ricotta, almonds, and sugar

erbetta, *pl.* **erbette** in Rome, usually parsley; but in Emilia, = BIETOLA

erborinato *(adj.)* said of cheeses that develop a mold, such as GORGONZOLA, roquefort, or other blue cheeses

ermeticamente hermetically; **chiusura ermetica**, hermetic seal

esattore see OSSOBUCO

escabecio see SCAPECE

escluso *(adj.)* excluded; except (as a preposition)

esercizio pubblico food service; a restaurant, bar, or similar establishment

espadon = *pesce* SPADA (Liguria)

esperto *(adj.)* expert

espresso the life-blood of Italy; the essence and truth of coffee; for the variations, see CAFFÈ. Note that properly speaking, espresso is made in a bar with a high-pressure machine; stove-top Italian coffee is CAFFÈ.

essenza extract, juice, broth, essence

essicare, *p.p.* **essicato** to dry (out), dehydrate; **essiccazione**, dessiccation, dehydration

est (1) east; (2) Latin third person singular of the verb "to be," which gives us Est! Est!! Est!!!, a white wine from Montefiascone, near Lake Bolsena in northern LAZIO

estate summer

estero *(adj.)* foreign, imported

esteticamente aesthetically

estivo *(adj.)* summer

estragone = DRAGONCELLO

estratto extract; **estratto di carne**, meat extract

estroso *(adj.)* whimsical, imaginative

estrudere, *p.p.* **estruso** to extrude; **estrusione**, extrusion. Pasta dough is shaped in two basic ways: rolled out and cut, or extruded through a device, which can range from a handheld potato ricer to industrial equipment.

età age

etanolo ethanol

etere = DENTICE (Puglia)

etichetta label, not etiquette

etrusco *(adj.)* Etruscan

etto, *pl.* **etti** hectogram(s), 100 grams, 3.5 oz. This is the basic unit of food purchases, the practical equivalent of the quarter pound.

eugubino *(adj.)* of Gubbio or Gubbio-style; **cappelletti all'eugubina** is said to be the richest egg pasta in Italy, using approximately 7 eggs per pound of flour (14 per kilo). They are traditionally made at Christmas and eaten until Epiphany.

eviscerare, *pl.* **eviscerato** to eviscerate, to gut

evoluto *(adj.)* developed

extravarietale *(adj.)* extravarietal

F

facoltativo *(adj.)* optional

fagiana = *pesce* CAPPONE (Calabria)

fagianello young pheasant

fagiano pheasant (*Phasianus cochicus*)

fagiolata (1) sort of a Piedmontese *cassoulet*, or pork-flavored bean stew; (2) potentially any bean dish

fagioliera bean pot

fagiolini string beans, green beans, haricots, or any bean eaten casing and all; **fagiolini** (or **fagioli**) **a corallo**, broad green beans usually cooked with tomatoes and onion (Lazio)

fagiolo, *pl.* **fagioli** beans; **fagioli dall'occhio** are black-eyed peas, cowpeas; **fagioli di Spagna** are large white beans; see also BORLOTTI, CANNELLINI

fagiuolo bean, kidney bean

fagopiro = GRANO SARACENO

fagottino, *pl.* **fagottini** "little bundle," hence dough or meat stuffed and/or wrapped, but also used for real bundles, lunch-bags, packages, and similar items

Falerio DOC white wine from the province of Ascoli Piceno

Falerno much as its producers would like you to think this was Horace's Falernum, there is, unfortunately, no continuity. Falerno today is the name of a red and white wine produced in southern Lazio and northern Campania.

faloppe young SARDINA (Puglia)

falsomagro = FARSUMAGRU

fame *(n.f.)* hunger, appetite; *sciopero della fame*, hunger strike; famine, however, is *carestia*

fango mud

faraona guinea fowl; guinea hen

farcia stuffing, filling

farcire, *p.p.* **farcito** to stuff

fare, *p.p.* **fatto** to do, to make; often used as a sort of auxiliary with the infinitive of an instruction, e.g., **far rosolare**—literally, "to make to brown"—means simply to brown

farecchiata (1) flour made from ROBIGLIO, called FARINA *di* ROVEIA; (2) Umbrian polenta-like dish made from such flour and topped with sáutéed garlic and anchovy

farfalla, *pl.* **farfalle** butterfly or anything shaped like one, including a bow-tie; in the plural, bow-tie pasta; **a farfalla**, butterflied

faricella a soup made of FARRO

farina flour; **farina gialla**, cornmeal (cf. POLENTA); **farina 00** is all-purpose flour; **farina 0** is cake flour; **fior di farina**, highly refined flour; **farina lattea**, powdered milk

farina di pesce fish meal

farinata (1) FOCACCIA-like crust of chickpea flour; a Tuscan variant is made from corn with vegetables and legumes; (2) cornmeal mush, porridge; **farinata d'avena** is cooked oatmeal; near Lucca, it can indicate INFARINATA soup

farinella a liquidy POLENTA

farinoso *(adj.)* mealy, floury

fario see TROTA

farricello = FARRO broken into pieces

farro in modern cookery, emmer (*Triticum dicoccum*), a grain used to make excellent soups as well as porridges, pasta, and just about anything else cereals are used for. The name is also found applied to various spelt-like grains, including the older *Triticum spelta* (spelt), on which the Roman army marched.

farru (*or* **su farru**) a FARRO soup (Sardegna)

farsi, da on a menu, made to order

farsumagru dialect for *falsomagro*, classic Sicilian stuffed, braised veal or beef roll; spelled so many ways that probably any four-syllable word containing *f, s, m,* and *g* is probably another spelling of this dish.

fasan = FAGIANO

fascetto, *pl.* **fascetti** little bunch, bundle

fascio, *pl.* **fasci** bunch, sheaf, bundle, as in the Latin *fasces,* the bundle of rods that was the symbol of the Roman Republic and became the emblem of Fascism

fasciul = FAGIOLI

faseui = FAGIOLI

fasiola = TELLINA (Lazio)

fasoi = FAGIOLI

fasolaro Venus clam (*Callista chione*)

fassone breed of beef from Piemonte

fastoso *(adj.)* sumptuous

fasui = FAGIOLI

fatto *(adj.)* made, ready (past participle of FARE)

fattoria farm (not factory, which is *fabbrica*); sometimes, = AZIENDA VITICOLA

fattura (1) manufacture; (2) invoice, as opposed to a simple receipt

fava, *pl.* **fave** broad bean, pigeon bean, fava bean (*Vicia faba*). *Fave* can be eaten dried all year round, but in spring are eaten fresh (e.g., stewed with GUANCIALE) or, if young and tender, eaten raw with fresh pecorino cheese.

favata Sardinian bean stew with tomato, pork, and cardoons

fave 'ngrecce a traditional FAVA salad of Macerata, in the Marche, made from boiled beans with marjoram leaves, oil, and garlic

fave dei morti literally, "beans of the dead"; almond cookies for All Souls Day (November 2), also called, more pleasantly, **fave dolci** (sweet beans)

favetta, *pl.* **favette** (1) small fava beans; (2) polenta-like gruel or thinner soup from FAVA bean flour (Liguria); (3) in plural, sweet fritters for Carnevale, or potentially anything small and bean-shaped

favollo large GRANCHIO of the Venetian lagoon

favorire to favor. If you are inviting somebody to join you at table, you might politely say, "Vuole favorire?"

feagallo = GRONGO (Liguria)

febbraio February

feccia, *pl.* **fecce** dregs, lees; **fecce nobili**, noble lees
fecola flour, but **fecola di patate**, potato flour, is usually meant, even when not specified
fedelini a very thin spaghetti-like pasta
fegatelli small livers (always plural), usually of pork but sometimes of chicken, often cooked wrapped in caul (see RETE)
fegatini livers of fowl or small animals, such as chicken or rabbits
fegato liver, usually calf's. It is most famously served **alla veneziana**, sautéed with onions; **fegato grasso** is *foie gras.*
felat = GRONGO (Liguria)
Felino, salame di much-respected salami named for the town of Felino, near Parma (nothing to do with cats)
fenescecchie hollow, Pugliese MACCHERONE
fenoci = FINOCCHIO
feria, *pl.* **ferie** holidays, vacation
ferièda = SARAGO
feriale *(adj.)* any non-holiday weekday (including Saturday); **giorni feriali**, weekdays
ferlenghi = FINFERLI
fermentare to ferment (both transitive and intransitive)
fermentazione fermentation
fermenti lattici vivi active milk cultures (as in yogurt)
Fernet-Branca proprietary name of a very strong-tasting, quasi-medicinal DIGESTIVO
Ferrara the name of a province and its capital city in the Emilia-Romagna region, abbreviated FE
ferri, ai grilled, broiled
ferritus, maccherones a long pasta twisted around a knitting needle (*ferritus*). This name is Sardinian, but the concept exists in many other locations.
ferro (1) iron, the metal; (2) tool; **ferro di cavallo**, horseshoe, horseshoe shape; **ferro da calza**, knitting needle; **ferro da stiro**, iron (the appliance)
ferse rolls of pork liver and pork meat mixed with wine-marinated sultana raisins and rolled in netting
fesa rump of beef or veal; meat from the extreme hindquarter, part

of the top round, from the inner part of the COSCIA. It is typically used to make veal SCALOPPINE, roasts, or slices of beef for INVOLTINI. Use of the name has spread to other boneless cuts, such as skinless turkey breast (**fesa di tacchino**). **Fesa della spalla** is part of the cross rib.

fesone di spalla most of the cross rib, part of the beef shoulder, essentially between the upper foreleg and the shoulder joint, used for ground beef and also for BISTECCHE

festivo *(adj.)* festive; **giorni festivi** are Sundays and holidays

festonati rectangular pasta with V ridges

fetta, *pl.* **fette** slice (of anything); **le fette** is a soup of dark green cabbage and slices of dark, toasted bread rubbed with garlic; **fette biscottate** are slices of bread dried in the oven; see also AFFETTARE

fettina, *pl.* **fettine** thin or small slice; if otherwise unqualified in a list of second courses, it most likely means a large but thin slice of veal to be grilled simply

fettuccine literally, "little ribbons"; the basic flat egg noodles as known in the southern half of the country, TAGLIATELLE in the northern half; **fettuccine alla papalina**, with prosciutto, eggs, and Parmesan (a CARBONARA variant favored by Pope Pius XII while he was still free to go out to eat); **fettuccine alla romana**, with tomatoes and dried mushrooms; **fettuccine al triplo burro**, the correct name of "fettuccine Alfredo," with a sauce of butter, cream, and Parmesan, is possibly the most enduring product of the golden age of Hollywood on the Tiber

fettunta, fett'unta in Toscana, bread slices rubbed with garlic, charcoal-grilled and brushed with olive oil or fried therein (from FETTA and UNTO); cf. BRUSCHETTA

fezze, maccheroni a = JACCOLI at Rieti in the Lazio region

fiaccheraia spaghetti with tomato, cress, and spicy peppers

fiacco *(adj.)* flaccid, tired

fiadone a stuffed sweet, with versions in Trentino and ABRUZZO

fiamma flame; **alla fiamma** is flambé

fiammeggiare, *p.p.* **fiammeggiato** to singe over an open flame

fiammiferi (1) matches; (2) anything cut into matchsticks or julienned

fianchetto triangular section of beef hindquarter, made up of side tensor muscle, often attached to the SCAMONE and/or NOCE. Used for ground or boiled beef; veal filet mignon, for medallions or tenders.

fiandolein Aostan form of ZABAGLIONE made with milk, rum, and lemon rind

Fiano di Avellino white grape and DOC wine of Campania

fiapon sweet cornmeal fritter (Mantova)

fiaschetteria traditionally an establishment for the sale of wine in *fiaschi* (see FIASCO), hence a very informal sort of OSTERIA

fiasco, *pl.* **fiaschi** flask, bottle; straw-covered Chianti bottle; glass bottle, traditionally covered with straw for Chianti; in Toscana, FAGIOLI (beans) are sometimes cooked **al fiasco** (in the bottle) and then dressed with oil. *Fare fiasco,* as in English, means to lay an egg.

fibra dietary fiber

ficello "string"; tied

fichi plural of FICO; **fichi mandorlati**, almond-stuffed figs

fico d'India, *pl.* **fichi d'India** prickly pear (*Opuntia ficus-indica*). The cactus is plentiful in the southern regions and islands, and the fruit is a fixture of Italian markets in late summer and early fall. It is also used fresh to flavor ice cream.

fico, *pl.* **fichi** fig, both the tree and the fruit

ficodindia = FICO D'INDIA

fidei thin spaghetti, VERMICELLI

fidelini = FEDELINI

fieno literally, "hay"; homemade TAGLIATELLE

figà = FEGATO; **figà garbo e dolce** is liver, breaded and fried, with a touch of vinegar and sugar; **figà col radeselo** is cut up, wrapped in caul along with sage leaves, and fried in butter (Venice)

filante *(adj.)* for wine, oily; for cheese, stringy, ropey when melted

filare, *p.p.* **filato** literally, "to spin" (thread); **zucchero filato** is spun sugar, or cotton candy. The term is used (**a pasta filata**) to describe certain soft cheeses with an initial plastic consistency, e.g., MOZZARELLA, SCAMORZA, PROVOLA, CACIOCAVALLO, PROVOLONE.

filato see FILARE

filatu thin, homemade spaghetti

fileja Calabrian hand-rolled pasta, like MACCHERONCINI, incised on the surface with an instrument like a knitting needle

filetto tenderloin, filet mignon, found just under the lumbar and dorsal vertebrae

filigrana filigree

filippu = LEPRE (Calabria)

fillossera *or* **filossera** phylloxera

filo, *pl.* **fili** thread, including metaphorically, as in *un filo d'olio*—a "thread" of olive oil—which is what you might pour over a bowl of soup or a fish as a finishing touch; **filo gastronomico** is thread for use in the kitchen

filone, *pl.* **filoni** (1) long loaf of bread, as opposed to PAGNOTTA; (2) in plural, = SCHIENALI

filotrotta = ANGUILLA (Sardegna)

filtrare, *p.p.* **filtrato** to filter, to strain

filtrazione filtration

filtro filter, strainer

filú e ferru Sardinian *grappa*

finanziera veal sweetbreads with chicken liver, mushrooms, and Marsala, used as a sauce to accompany various dishes or on its own to top RISOTTO or pastry shells; cheese crêpe

fine *(adj.)* fine

fine *(n.f.)* end, finish. Note that the word exists also in the masculine, meaning end in the sense of goal.

finferlo chanterelle, = GALLINELLA OF GALLINACCIO

fino see RISO

finocchiella = FINOCCHIO SELVATICO, but only if fresh; occasionally found as a synonym of MIRRIDE

finocchio fennel; **finocchio fetido**, **finocchio bastardo**, = ANETO

finocchio marino = CRITMO

finocchio selvatico wild fennel (*Foeniculum vulgare,* var. *dulce, sativum,* and others); the green leaves are used as a herb

finocchiona Tuscan salami flavored with fennel seeds

finochietto herbal fennel variety, sometimes called "wild fennel"
finto *(adj.)* false, fake, pretend, bogus, mock; **sugo finto**, "pseudo-sauce," is a sort of poor man's meat sauce, containing only pork fat in the way of meat
fiocca for egg whites, **montare in fiocca** means to beat until stiff
fiocchetto, *pl.* **fiocchetti** (1) the front thigh part of a prosciutto, which remains after the CULATELLO has been removed; (2) in plural, pasta squares made with lemon peel and nutmeg
fiocco, *pl.* **fiocchi** (1) bow (*con i fiochi* means "with bells on"), bow pasta; (2) flake (e.g., *fiocchi di* MAIS, *di* AVENA); (3) the fore part of beef or veal breast; in pork, part of the thigh (see FIOCCHETTO); **fiocco di punta**, breast of veal tip, also called **fiocco di petto**; (4) various other meanings that seem to be assigned on an ad hoc basis
fiore (*or* fior), *pl.* **fiori** flower; **fior di** ..., "the best part of ..."; **acqua di fior d'arancia**, orange-blossom water; **fior di latte**, mozzarella-like cheese made from cow milk; **fiori di zucca** are squash or zucchini blossoms, which may be used in RISOTTO or stuffed and/or batter-dipped and then sautéed or fried
Fiore Sardo a hard raw sheep-milk cheese from Sardegna, which can be grated after six months
fiorentina, la the famous Florentine beefsteak, a thick T-bone from the LOMBATA, ideally from CHIANINA beef, grilled very rare over coals; in Toscana the cut is referred to just as BISTECCA
fiorettino a salami of Reggio Emilia
fioretto fresh cheese of the Veneto, also called *grasso monte*
fiorilli = FIORI DI ZUCCA (Campania)
fiorito *(adj.)* literally, "flowered"; said of cheese with a powdery efflorescent crust or mold
fiorrancio = CALENDULA
Firenze Florence. Major art center, regional capital of Toscana as well as the name of a province and its capital city, abbreviated FI.
fischietti = FUSILLI (Calabria)
fischione species of duck
fitascetta ring-shaped Lombardian onion bread
fitto *(adj.)* thick
fiuchett = STRICCHETTI

fiumarola = ANGUILLA (Lazio)
fiume river; as adjective, freshwater
flambare = INFIAMMARE
flan in Italian, = SFORMATO
flisse (*or* frisse) similar to GRIVE
floreale *(adj.)* flowery
flûte long, tall glass for sparkling wine; **flûttino**, small *flûte*
fluviale *(adj.)* from a river
focaccia basically a flat bread, usually flavored with oil and herbs, but subject to huge variation in flavoring, fillings and toppings, and thickness of dough; can also refer to bread-like cakes, e.g., a homestyle PANETTONE. Note that the word has three syllables, not four (fo-ca-ccia).
focolare hearth, fireplace
fogghie = CATALOGNA
Foggia the name of a province and its capital city in the Puglia region, abbreviated FG
foggiana, alla Foggia-style, after a provincial capital in the Puglia region
foglia, *pl.* **foglie** leaf (of a plant); very thin slice, potentially anything very thin and flat; *foglio* is a leaf (sheet) of paper
fogolar Friulian open cooking hearth
foiolo honeycomb tripe
folaga moorhen, coot
folpo = POLPO (Veneto, Venezia Giulia)
fondamentale *(adj.)* basic, indispensable, important
fondente flourless cake; baking chocolate, bittersweet chocolate; French *fondant*
fondere, *p.p.* **fuso** to melt
fondo (1) bottom, of anything (the pot, the artichoke); (2) short for **fondo di cottura**, translation of French *fond de cuisine*, stock and pan juices; **fondo bruno**, brown stock
fonduta fondue, usually of cheese, sometimes white truffle, characteristic of Piemonte
fongadina stew from pluck (heart liver and lungs) of veal and/or lamb or kid, mushrooms, and spices (Veneto)

fonghi = FUNGHI

fontana fountain. When recipes say to make a *fontana* of the flour, it means to make a mound with an indentation, or crater, into which to put the eggs.

fonte *(n.f.)* spring (for water), source

fontina various white and yellow cheeses with delicate flavor, of which the one considered the real *fontina* is from Valle d'Aosta, protected by a Consortium

foraggio fodder

foralattina can opener (the kind that makes a triangular hole in the can)

forare, *p.p.* **forato** to pierce, to perforate

forato *(adj.)* perforated, slotted

forbici scissors

forcella various forked instruments; wishbone

forchetta table fork. The epithet **una buona forchetta** is applied to people who enjoy eating good food.

forchettone serving fork, pot fork, any large fork

Forlì capital of the province of Forlì-Cesena, one of the nine provinces of the Emilia-Romagna region, abbreviated FO

forma (1) form, mold; (2) whole cheese. Cheeses, FORMAGGI, are made in a mold, so a form of cheese can mean not only the utensil but the whole cheese itself. In Emilia-Romagna, the word is also used for grated Parmesan.

formagé = FORMAGGIO (Piemonte)

formagella soft, fresh cow-, sheep-, or goat-milk cheese, sometimes salted

formagetta = FORMAGELLA; **formaggetta di Capua**, sheep-milk cheese of Capua (Campania) with a touch of PIMPINELLA

formaggino di Lecco syn. ROBIOLINO

formaggino, *pl.* **formaggini** (1) various small cheeses, e.g., *formaggini di Lecco* (a dessert cheese) or *formaggini di Montpellier*, curdled with rennet paste that contains white wine and thistle blossoms; (2) processed cheeses, e.g., in foil-wrapped wedges or disks

formaggio, *pl.* **formaggi** cheese, but it's not that simple. Strictly speaking, *formaggi* are cheeses aged in a FORMA, or mold. Free-form fresh cheeses, made by pulling the solids from the whey with the bare hands in whatever shape comes out, are properly called LATTICINI. The word *formaggio* used alone usually means The Cheese, PARMIGIANO REGGIANO.

formaggio a pasta dura any hard cheese, defined as having less than 40 percent water

formaggio a pasta molle any soft cheese, defined as having more than 40 percent water

formaggio del caglio a near-mythical Calabrian aged PECORINO, very strong tasting, which contains live small worms

formaggio di fossa sheep, goat, or mixed cheese of EMILIA-ROMAGNA and the MARCHE that is wrapped in leaves and aged in special tufa caves, where the characteristic mold that forms is said to improve the flavor (*fossa* means ditch or trench)

formai de mut soft cow-milk cheese from Lombardia

formare, *p.p.* **formato** to form, to shape; as a noun, *formato* means not only format but size

formentino = GRANO SARACENO

formentone = GRANTURCO

fornaio, fornaia baker, *boulangère*

fornara, vitello alla veal breast cooked with herbs and potatoes (Rome). *La fornara* means the (female) baker, and La Fornara was a famous mistress of the painter Raphael.

fornel, lasagna da from the northern part of Belluno province (Veneto), homemade LASAGNA dressed with butter, nuts, sultanas, grated apple, and dried figs—a sort of lasagna strudel

fornello, *pl.* **fornelli** burner (of a kitchen range); *ai fornelli* means "at the stove"

forno (1) oven; **al forno**, baked or oven roasted; (2) bakery (= PANIFICIO). Ovens may be: **a convezione**, convection; **elettrico**, electric; **a gas**, gas; **a legna**, wood-burning, considered essential for good pizza because of the high temperature it is able to reach; **a microonde**, microwave; **a vapore**, steam-injection.

fortaia = FRITTATA (Veneto)

forte *(adj.)* loud, strong, even heavy in senses other than literal weight

forza strength

forzare, *p.p.* **forzato** to force

fozze Piedmontese peasant bread from whole-wheat flour and cream, cooked on a griddle

fracaja fried patties of tiny fish (Puglia, Basilicata)

fracassà = FRICASSEA

fracchiata chickpea-flour gruel, often served with fried herring (Abruzzo, Molise)

fragola, *pl.* **fragole** strawberry

fragoline *(pl.)* **di bosco** tiny wild strawberries, in season in early summer and usually served with fresh lemon juice and sugar, but also with whipped cream or CREMA-flavor ice cream

fragolino (1) red sea bream, any of several species of the genus *Pagellus*; see PAGELLO; (2) see UVA FRAGOLA

fraina = GRANO SARACENO

frammentare, *p.p.* **frammentato** to break into pieces

Franceschiello, alla (chicken) sautéed with garlic, rosemary, and olives

francese *(adj.)* French

Francia France

Franciacorta excellent DOC METODO CLASSICO sparkling wines from Lombardia

francolino grouse (*Francolinus francolinus*)

frangere, *p.p.* **franto** to break, to crush

franto *(adj.)* mashed, crushed, broken, *p.p.* of FRANGERE

frantoiana, zuppa soup from Toscana with BORLOTTI beans and olive oil

frantoio olive-press, any mention of which in oil denominations implies that the oil is not merely first-pressing but artisanally produced

frantumare, *p.p.* **frantumato** to crush, to break up into pieces

frappe strips of fried dough with powdered sugar; = CHIACCHIERE, CENCI

frascarelli a liquid polenta (central Italy)

Frascati DOC white wine from the Castelli Romani

fratau, pane Sardinian flatbread, softened in broth and covered with tomatoes, egg, and PECORINO

frattaglie *(f. pl.)* variously translated animal or bird parts, possibly inclusive, at any given moment, of the giblets, entrails, tripe, brains, heart, tongue, tail, marrow, lights, liver, lungs, and chitterlings

frattau = FRATAU

fratti stuffed lettuce leaves (Liguria)

frecola = FREGULA

freddo *(adj.)* cold; cf. FRESCO

fregnacce thin pasta crêpes served with cheese (Lazio) or rolled around various fillings and baked (Abruzzo). The name means "trifles," in the sense of something unimportant.

fregolata a POLENTA shortbread

fregolotta kind of hard biscuit from Treviso

fregoloz di jerbis Friulano for GNOCHETTI DI ERBE

fregula Sardinian dish consisting of tiny balls of dough cooked in broth; there are meat and cheese as well as seafood versions

Freisa Piedmontese FRIZZANTE red wine

fresa mild, soft Sardinian cow-milk cheese

fresco *(adj.)* cool, fresh; name is sometimes used to indicate particular foods, e.g., MILANO cheese; **al fresco**, outdoors

fresina flat pasta strands, wider than TAGLIATELLE

friabile *(adj.)* crumbly, friable (nothing to do with frying)

friarielli in Naples, = (the local) BROCCOLETTI

fric dal marghé = FRITTO MISTO ALLA PIEMONTESE

fricandeau astigiano type of beef stew (Asti)

fricandò (1) meat, regional; (2) pot roast of veal larded with ham, carrot, and celery; (3) French *fricandeau*

fricassea any of various meat dishes enriched with yolks and lemon juice, fricassee

fricc = FRICO

friccioli the little bits of meat that remain after rendered lard is sieved through a cloth

friccò duck, lamb, rabbit, or chicken stewed with wine and herbs; lamb fricassee with egg-bound sauce

fricia, friccia = FRITTO MISTO ALLA PIEMONTESE

friciule fritters; of fried bread dough (Piemonte)

frico typical dish of the Carnia section of Friuli; MONTASIO, LATTE-

RIA, or other young cheese is melted and fried, and served either crisp like a thick cracker or, as a hot dish, with potatoes and other ingredients

fricon Piedmontese fried sardine

frienno magnanno Neapolitan FRITTO MISTO

friggere, *p.p.* **fritto** to fry, to deep-fat fry

friggione slow-cooked onion and tomato sauce served with meats or vegetables (Emilia-Romagna)

friggitoria fry shop; a storefront where foods are deep-fried and sold to take out

friggitrice deep-fat fryer (the appliance)

frigo "fridge," short for FRIGORIFERO

frigobar minibar, the little refrigerator in hotel rooms

frigorifero refrigerator

frigulozzi a type of pasta made from bread dough, typical of northern Lazio

frisceu = FRITTELLE (Liguria)

frisciolata = FARINATA

frise = FRISELLA

frisedda = FRISELLA

frisella, *pl.* **friselle** ring-shaped hard biscuits made of flour, water, and olive oil; they are moistened with water to soften and topped with tomatoes and oil, or other vegetables

frisuli stewed pork parts with spicy peppers used to enrich soup, stuff PITTA, or serve with PAGNOTELLA

frisulimiti = FRISULI

fritole type of FRITELLA for Carnevale (Veneto)

fritolìn fried fish sold from a cart (now rare)

frittata an omelet that has been turned over, not folded in half. It is usually filled with a vegetable, sometimes eaten in a sandwich. The potential for variety is enormous. **Frittata rognosa** ("mangy") contains bits of ham, sausage, or similar items; the Neapolitan **frittata di maccheroni** contains not only pasta and egg but cheese, meats, tomatoes, and any number of other ingredients; **frittata alla trentina** contains sardines, cheese, mushrooms, and artichokes.

frittatina FRITTATA or nonsweet crêpe when used as an ingredient
frittedda Sicilian dish of fava beans, peas, and artichokes; similar to the Latian VIGNAROLA
fritteddi = CRISPEDDI
frittella, *pl.* **frittelle** fritter, pancake
fritto (*p.p.* of FRIGGERE) fried, deep-fried; **fritto misto** is a mix of batter-fried meats and sometimes other ingredients (vegetables, eggs, cheese, custard). The exact ingredients and fat used may vary in the many regional interpretations, but the principles are the same. No sauce is served, just lemon, and salt is added at table.
frittola = FRITTELLA
frittuli pork parts, seasoned and cooked in lard
frittura any fried dish; **frittura piccata** is what English menus usually call "veal piccata," i.e., sautéed with lemon, parsley, and butter
Friuli–Venezia Giulia the modern region, in northeast Italy, that comprises two distinct zones, Friuli, to the northwest, known for its acidic white wines, and Venezia Giulia, to the southeast. Its gastronomic traditions draw not only from Italy but from Slovenia and Austria-Hungary; its capital is the much fought-over Trieste.
frize, frizze = CICCIOLI
frizòn = FRIGGIONE
frizzante *(adj.)* effervescent, lightly sparkling, semisparkling, *pétillant*
frizzantino *(adj.)* slightly effervescent
frocia = FRITTATA (Sicilia)
frolla, pasta = PASTAFROLLA
frollare, *p.p.* **frollato** used for game (transitively and intransitively): to hang, to soften, to become high
frollini shortbread cookies
Frosinone the name of the southernmost province and its capital city in the Lazio region, abbreviated FR
fruffella a kind of vegetable soup (Molise)
frullare, *p.p.* **frullato** to process in a blender
frullato *(n.)* Italy's version of the milkshake, which is made of milk and fresh fruit, and not to be confused with a thick shake. The

word is the past participle of FRULLARE and has nothing to do with FRUTTA and LATTE except by coincidence.

frullatore blender

frullino whisk, beater

frumento wheat (*Triticum vulgare*)

frusta literally, "whip," the term can be used metaphorically for anything long and narrow, such as certain types of PANINI. In the kitchen the *frusta*, or depending on size, **frustino**, is a wire whisk. The **frusta elettrica** is an immersion blender.

frustingu Christmas sweet from Ancona (Marche)

frutta fruit. Note that the form *frutto* also exists, but is used more for metaphorical fruits, as those of your labors or of the sea (see FRUTTI DI MARE), rather than those from a fruit tree.

frutta alla Martorana little fruits made of marzipan

frutteto orchard

fruttiera fruit dish

fruttificare to bear fruit (as a tree)

fruttini marzipan fruits (Toscana), like FRUTTA ALLA MARTORANA

fruttosio fructose

fufulloni large, mild red peppers

fugassa, fugazza dialect form of FOCACCIA (Liguria, Veneto); in Venice, a dessert *focaccia*

fuiade = TAGLIATELLE

fuje strascinate sautéed cabbage with white wine and herbs

fula bread GNOCCHI of Gorizia with raisins, herbs, and chopped corn cooked in the water used for boiling a ham and dressed with fried lard

fumare, *p.p.* **fumato** to smoke (a cigarette); **vietato fumare**, no smoking

fumetto fish stock

fumicato = AFFUMICATO

fumo smoke; *il punto di fumo* of an oil is its smoking point

fumoso *(adj.)* smoky (tasting)

fungetiello pasta sauce with black olives and capers

funghetto, al = TRIFOLATO

funghi cremini see CREMINI
funghi di bosco wild mushrooms
funghi porcini Boletus mushrooms
fungo, *pl.* **funghi** mushrooms. The word applies to all mushrooms, but is especially used in contradistinction to CHAMPIGNONS.
fuoco fire
fuori out, out of, outside
fuori stagione out of season
furmagghiu du quagghiu = FORMAGGIO DEL CAGLIO
fusaglie see FUSAIE
fusaie *(pl.)* in Rome, = LUPINI, soaked in salt water and eaten as a snack
fuscaldese, alici alla ALICI baked in layers with staled bread, hot pepper, oregano, lemon, and olive oil (Calabria)
fusiddi = FUSILLI
fusilli helical short pasta
fusilloni long FUSILLI
fuso (1) drumstick (from the meaning of *fuso* as "spindle"); (2) *p.p.* of FONDERE
fusto barrel keg, cask; stem; **fustino** is the large box with handles that powdered detergents come in. The original meaning is shaft, like that of a Greek column, or tree trunk, and in this sense is sometimes used to describe a fine figure of a man.

gaddarana = SCORFANO (Sicilia)
gaddina = GALLINA (Sicilia)

gaddu, pisci gaddu = *pesce* SAN PIETRO (Sicilia)
gaggia wild BIETA (Liguria)
gaggiardella = COSTARDELLA
galani = CHIACCHIERE
galantina galantine, fowl paté
galitola = CANTARELLO
galletta, *pl.* **gallette** cracker; **gallette da marinaio** are ship's biscuits, hard-tack
galletti = CUCULLI
galletto (1) young cock; (2) = CANTARELLO
gallina stewing hen
gallinaccio (1) turkey (popular); (2) = CANTARELLO; (3) a wild carrot
gallinazzu = TACCHINO (Calabria)
gallinedda = *pesce* CAPPONE (Puglia, Sardegna)
gallinella (1) chanterelle mushroom (also spelled *gallenella*); (2) = *pesce* CAPPONE; type of mullet; (3) lamb's lettuce or corn salad, = VALERIANELLA; (4) pullet; **gallinella d'acqua**, water-hen, moorhen
gallo (1) cock, rooster; (2) box crab. **Gallo d'India** is turkey; **gallo cedrone** is a capercaillie, or wood grouse.
gallo = *pesce* SAN PIETRO (Sicilia)
galluccio = CANTARELLO
gallucieddo = CUORE (Puglia)
gambero shrimp or, less often when unmodified, crayfish of various species belonging to the Penaeidae, Palaemonidae, Crangonidae, and Astacidae families
gambero di fiume crayfish, either *Astacus astacus* (also called GAMBERO EUROPEO) or *Astacus pallipes*
gambero europeo European crayfish, crayfish (*Astacus astacus*)
gambero rosa a light-colored shrimp (*Parapenaeus longirostris*)
gambero rosso various shrimps of several species belonging to the Penaeidae and Palaemonidae families. The Louisiana crayfish (*Procambarus clarkii*) is farm-raised to a limited extent in Italy and marketed under this name.
gambetto = GAMBUCCIO
gambo, *pl.* **gambi** stem, stalk

gambuccio the narrow end of the PROSCIUTTO, usually minced and used in cooking

ganascione a savory pie

ganassino GUANCIALE of ASINA (Emilia-Romagna)

gancio, *pl.* **ganci** hook

ganiotellus = GATTUCCIO (Sardegna)

garagoli = TORRICELLA (Marche)

garajuni = MURENA (Sicilia)

garal = LATTERINO (Veneto)

garao = LATTERINO (Veneto)

garbo charm or courtesy

garfagnini, maccheroni PASTA STRACCIATA with beef RAGÙ

garganelli a handmade short pasta consisting of ribbed, rolled squares of dough made of flour, water, and Parmesan

gargotta a greasy spoon, dump, dive

garitula = CANTARELLO

garizzo = MENOLA (Veneto, Friuli)

garmugia spring soup of Lucca with peas, asparagus, artichoke, chopped beef or veal, and PANCETTA

garofano clove (spice); **chiodi di garofano**, cloves, literally, "nails of clove"

garofolato (1) preparation in which the predominant spice is cloves; (2) type of beef pot roast with red wine and cloves (Rome)

garum *(Lat.)* ancient Roman fish-based condiment much-maligned by posterity, probably as a result of a remark by Pliny the Elder to the effect that it was "the liquid of rotting fish." However, *garum* was made much the way anchovies are today preserved in salt.

garusolo = MURICE SPINOSO (Veneto, Friuli)

garza cheesecloth, gauze

gasare, gasato = GASSARE, GASSATO

gassare, *p.p.* **gassato** to carbonate (a liquid)

gassato *(adj.)* carbonated, bubbly, aerated, charged

gasse *(pl.)* "bow-tie" pasta (Liguria)

gassosa the name of a lemon-flavored fizzy drink

gassoso *(adj.)* bubbly, aerated, charged

gastaurello = COSTARDELLA (Toscana)

gastodella syn. COSTARDELLA

gastronomia gastronomy in all its aspects, but the word is also seen in shops and bars to signal the sale of prepared foods, usually more snacks than meals

gatta = GATTUCCIO (Venezia Giulia)

gatta, pesce = GATTUCCIO (Veneto)

gattafuin TORTELLI stuffed with vegetables, onion, cheese, and egg, fried in oil

gattò phonetic spelling of the French GATEAU—it has nothing to do with cats (*gatto*). The name covers a wide ground, often meaning some sort of timbale. The best-known *gattò*, however, is the Neapolitan potato cake made with egg, cheese, and prosciutto.

gattopardo = GATTUCCIO (Toscana)

gattu de mari = GATTUCCIO (Sardegna)

gattuccio dogfish, rough hound, species of small shark, including *Scyliorhinus stellaris, S. canicula,* and *Galeus melanostomus*

gattusso = GATTUCCIO (Liguria)

Gavoi myrtle- and juniper-smoked sheep-milk hard cheese from the village of Gavoi, in Sardegna

gazzosa = GASSOSA

gefülltes gemüse stuffed vegetables

gelateria ice-cream shop; look for the ones that say *produzione propria* or *artigianale* (made on premises). Plastic tubs are an obvious sign that the ice cream is of industrial manufacture.

gelatina aspic, gelatine

gelato *(adj.)* iced, frozen

gelato *(n.)* ice cream; see also MANTECATO

gelato di ricotta not a true GELATO, but a traditional Roman frozen dessert made with RICOTTA and eggs

gelette wine cooler

gelo (1) cold, ice; (2) chilled gelatin dessert, often made with watermelon (**gelo** *di* ANGURIA or *di* **melone** or **jelu i mulini**) plus chocolate, candied pumpkin, vanilla, cinnamon, and other flavorings. Other versions are made with lemon, jasmine, and carob or coffee.

gelso mulberry

gelsomino jasmine

gemma bud, germ

gen. = GENNAIO

genepì wormwood (*Artemisia*); genepi liqueur

gennaio January

Genova Genoa, regional capital of Liguria and one of its four provinces, abbreviated GE

genovese, alla Genoa-style; expect olive oil, garlic, and herbs; classic RAVIOLI **genovesi** are stuffed with wild greens and a curdled-milk cheese (PREBOGGION and PRESCINSOEA)

genovese, carne alla Neapolitan beef stew with onions and tomato sauce, often used as a pasta sauce

genziana gentian; **radice di genziana**, gentian root

geretto veal shank, hind (*posteriore*) or fore (*anteriore*)

germano reale wild duck, mallard

germe *(n.m. sing.)* germ, bud

germinare, *p.p.* **germinato** to sprout

germoglio, *pl.* **germogli** sprout, shoot, germ, bud; **germogli di soia** are bean sprouts

gernia = CERNIA (Sardegna, Sicilia)

Gerstensuppe soup with barley, SPECK, onion, and parsley (Trentino–Alto Adige)

gesminus Sardinian sweets

gg. days, abbreviation of *giorni*

gghiuni = ANGUILLA (Sicilia)

gheriglio, *p.p.* **gherigli** kernel

ghiacciato *(adj.)* frozen, iced

ghiaccio ice

ghianda acorn

ghiandola gland

ghiggiun = GHIOZZO (Liguria)

ghiotta dripping pan; **alla ghiotta** indicates merely that something is particularly flavorful, though it can have a more precise regional connotation. In Abruzzo, a *ghiotta* is a sort of vegetable pie. It can also be a stew or sauce (e.g., of tomatoes, olives, and capers in Sicily). There is also a kind of Sicilian fish soup called **ghiotta**—or **agghiotta—di pesce**, and Sicilian **ghiotta di patate** is a thick potato and vegetable soup. A similar sauce in Calabria adds raisins and is often paired with dried cod. An Umbrian version combines red and white wines with ham, chicken liver, black olive, lemon rind, garlic, vinegar, rosemary, juniper, and other herbs, as an accompaniment for game. See LECCARDA. **Pesce alla ghiotta** is usually cooked with white wine and olives.

ghiotta, salsa sauce for game

ghiotto *(adj.)* of a person, gluttonous; of a food, toothsome

ghiottone gourmand, glutton

ghiozzo goby (Mediterranean); various fish of the Gobidae family, including *Gobius cobitis, Gobius niger,* and *Gobius paganellus*; **ghiozzo di fiume**, goby (*Padagobius martensi*), a freshwater fish

ghiro dormouse

ghisa cast iron

ghisau beef stew with tomato, onion, and potato

già already

gialletti cookies containing cornmeal (northeast Italy)

giallo *(adj.)* yellow

giambars freshwater shrimp

giambonetto stuffed chicken or turkey thigh, French *jambonet*

gianchetti *(pl.)* young ACCIUGA OR SARDINA (Liguria)

gianduia, gianduja a combination of chocolate and hazelnut used as an ice-cream flavor or to make **gianduiotti**, candy logs of *gianduia*. The name derives from Gianduja, a character from Torino in the commedia dell'arte.

gianfottere = CIAMBOTTA

gianfrèta = LAMPREDA (Puglia)

giardiniera (1) vegetable pickles; (2) vegetable soup made without beans or lard; (3) mixed vegetables

ginepro juniper; a juniper-based liqueur. Juniper berries are **bacche di ginepro**.

ginestrata = CINESTRATA

ginevrina, alla with wine and anchovy
giornaliero *(adj.)* daily
giornata, di of the day
giorno, *pl.* **giorni** day
giovane *(adj.)* young
giovedì Thursday
giral = LATTERINO (Venezia Giulia)
girandola pinwheel
girare, *p.p.* **girato** to stir, to turn
girarrosto rotisserie; **al girarrosto** means spit-roasted
girasole sunflower
girato *(adj.)* "turned," as on a spit
girello eye round, both of leg and shoulder; in the hindquarter, it is the extreme rear of the COSCIA in beef and veal, a single, very lean muscle; the **girello di spalla** lies along the upper part of the shoulder and is used for roasting and boneless cutlets
Girone sesto the sixth circle of Dante's Purgatory, the one for GOLOSI
giudia, alla Jewish-style; most famously refers to artichokes (CARCIOFI)
giuggiola, *pl.* **giuggiole** jujube, the fruit of the *Zizyphus jujuba-sativa.* **Brodo di giuggiole** is a syrup of these and other fruits used as a topping for dry cake. The expression *andare in brodo di giuggiole* means to display complete and utter delight; to gush. A specialty of Desenzano (Lombardia), *brodo di giuggiole* is becoming very hard to find.
giugno June
giuncata junket
gius a phonetic spelling of the French *jus;* = SUGO
glassa icing
glassato *(adj.)* glazed, frosted
gli plural form of "the"
glicerina glycerine; **glicerinoso**, glycerineous
gliomarieddre = GNUMMERIEDDI (Calabria)
gnervitt = NERVITT
gnocarei chicken soup with polenta and egg

gnocchetti small GNOCCHI; see also MALLOREDDUS
gnocchi al raschera MALTAGLIATI with sausage sauce (Piemonte)
gnocchi alla romana little patties of semolina, usually with scalloped edges, baked in a cream, cheese, or tomato sauce and served as a pasta course
gnocco, *pl.* **gnocchi** essentially dumplings of any kind, but usually small potato and flour dumplings (properly called **gnocchi di patate**), but they can be made of SEMOLINO, POLENTA, or other ingredients. **Gnocchi alla bava** are dressed with FONDUTA cheese and sometimes cream and egg yolk; **all'Ossolana** are made from flour with cheese and nutmeg, sauced with butter and sage; **alla cadorina** are served with butter and smoked ricotta; **alla lariana** are light gnocchi from flour, egg, and milk; **gnocchi carrati** are made from flour and dressed with scrambled egg, pecorino cheese, and PANCETTA. In Rome, Thursday is *gnocchi* day.
gnomirelli = GNUMMERIEDDI
gnudi see IGNUDI
gnummerieddi lamb innards rolled in caul fat, generally roasted or baked (Puglia)
gò de mar = GHIOZZO (Veneto)
goatto sassardo = GHIOZZO (Marche)
gobbein RAVIOLI stuffed with beef, veal, pork, cheese, egg, and nutmeg
gobbo, pesce = CARPA (Lombardia)
gobbo, *pl.* **gobbi** cardoons; in Piemonte, sometimes slang for AGNOLOTTI
gobetto, *usually pl.* **gobetti** shrimp of the genus *Plesionika*
gobione gudgeon (*Gobio gobio*), the French call it *goujon*
goccetto "a little drop"
goccia drop; **vino di goccia**, first pressings; cf. GOCCIO
goccio a metaphorical drop, as in "just a drop"
gocciolare to drip
goffa see BOMBA
goletta cured meat from under the pig's chin
golosità (*pl. invar.*) gluttony; tasty tidbits

goloso *(n. and adj.)* gluttonous, but not quite that bad; the person who is *goloso di dolci*, for example, has a sweet tooth

golosone *(n.m.)* epicure; glutton

gommoso rubbery, gummy

gonfiare, *p.p.* **gonfiato** literally, "to swell"; to puff up or increase in size

gorgonzola blue-veined cheese of Lombardia and Piemonte (the coloring is due to the introduction of a mold of the *Penicillium* genus); a fuller name is *Stracchino di Gorgonzola. Gorgonzola bianco* or *dolce* is a fast-ripened, white version. The true, naturally ripened *gorzonzola* is usually sold as *gorzonzola naturale.*

Gorizia the name of a province and its capital city in the Friuli–Venezia Giulia region, abbreviated GO

governo wine-making technique involving a second fermentation, which softens the wine and allows it to be drunk young

grado, *pl.* **gradi** grade, degree; in plural, degrees of alcohol (percentage of volume)

gramigna (1) dog's tooth (*Cynodon dactylon*), couch-grass (*Triticum repens*); (2) thin, short, pasta strands, sometimes hollow

gramolare, *p.p.* **gramolato** to knead

gramolata (1) a cold drink similar to GRANITA but using frozen fruit pulp instead of juice; (2) = GREMOLATA

gran premio (1) literally, "grand prize"; (2) in Sardegna, a horse-meat steak with bone

grana *(m.sing.)* any number of hard, sharp grating cheeses, including PARMIGIANO REGGIANO, GRANA PADANO, PECORINO ROMANO, ASIAGO, LODIGIANO, and others. Note that the gender is masculine despite the ending.

granaglie *(f.pl.)* grain, wheat, cereal

granatina, *pl.* **granatine** (1) grenadine, pomegranate syrup; (2) usually in plural, small balls, as of meat or rice

grancevola = GRANSEOLA

granchiessa = GRANCHIO (Toscana)

granchio small trapezoidal-bodied crab with enlarged front claws (*Carcinus mediterraneus*); **granchio di fiume**, freshwater crab (*Potamon fluviatile fluviatile*); other crabs, large and small

granciporro large, oval bodied crab with enlarged front claws (*Cancer pagurus*)

grande *(adj.)* large

grandinine *(pl.)* literally, "small hailstones"; small pasta for soup

granelli veal testicles, when **alla maremmana** they are breaded and fried in butter or oil. However, according to the Italian practice of using the same name for things that look alike, the name is also used for some preparations of meatballs.

granita frozen and crushed coffee or fruit juice

granitte grated pasta cooked like POLENTA and usually served with beans and onions

grano grain, wheat (*Triticum vulgare; Triticum durum*). **Grano saraceno** and/or **grano nero** is buckwheat or whole wheat, depending on where you are and who you ask. **Grano tenero** makes a soft flour milled from the heart of the kernel. **Grano duro** is durum, hard grain wheat.

grano dolce *or* **di S. Lucia** = CUCCÌA

granoturco sweet corn, maize

granseola large, round bodied crab with small front claws (*Maja squinado*)

granso = GRANCHIO (Veneto)

granzo = GAMBERO (Venezia Giulia); = GRANCHIO (Veneto, Abruzzo); = GRANSEOLA (Venezia Giulia)

granzo tenere = GRANCHIO DI FIUME

grappa (1) *marc*, pomace (residue after grapes are crushed), (2) grape distillate, *eau de vie*; a generic term for various aquavits, some of extremely high quality but all gullet-singeing

grappolo bunch (of grapes)

grascia lard, fat

graspo = GRAPPOLO

grassatu pieces of lamb or kid with potato and white wine, served on its own or as a pasta sauce

grasso *(n. and adj.)* fat, rich

gratè, al phonetic spelling of *au gratin*

gratella grill; **gratellato**, grilled

graticola grill, broiler; gridiron, as in the martyrdom of San Lorenzo

gratinare, *p.p.* **gratinato** to gratin
gratinato *(adj.)* au gratin; with bread crumbs and/or cheese crust
grattachecca crushed ice with flavored syrup that is an alternative to GELATO and very Roman. It is traditionally sold at street stands, which are fast disappearing.
grattare, *p.p.* **grattato** (1) to grate; (2) to scratch
grattata (una) (a) grating, a unit of measurement for truffles, for example
grattugia grater
grattugiare, *p.p.* **grattugiato** to grate
gravidanza, in "pregnant," a humorous way of saying "stuffed"
graviuole large RAVIOLI stuffed with MACCHERONE, PANCETTA, peas, and mushrooms
greca, alla *à la grecque*
Grechetto white grape and wine of Umbria
Greco di Bianco Calabrian sweet white DOC wine
Greco di Tufo fruity white DOC wine from Campania enjoying enormous popularity
greggio *(adj.)* raw; **zucchero greggio** is brown sugar
grembiule apron
gremolada mix of grated lemon rind, parsley, and garlic, used to top OSSOBUCO
gricia, alla ALL'AMATRICIANA without the tomato; pasta sauce made with pork jowl and PECORINO cheese
griesnocken nutmeg-flavored dumplings
grifi veal muzzle, sautéed and stewed with spices and tomato paste
grigette small snails
grigio *(adj.)* gray
griglia grill; **alla griglia** means grilled or broiled
grigliata mixed grill
Grignolino light red wine from Piemonte
grigole crisp pieces of fried goose skin
grissini breadsticks
grive Piedmontese meatballs of calf's brains, pork, and pork liver, mixed with cheese, bread, and egg, enclosed in caul fat, and sautéed with juniper berries in butter and oil

grolla multi-spouted drinking vessel from Valle d'Aosta

gronco = GRONGO (Venezia Giulia, Lazio)

grongo conger eel (*Conger conger*), not related to the ANGUILLA

groppa = SELLA

Grosseto the name of a province and its capital city in the Toscana region, abbreviated GR; it is the main town of the Maremma, the southern coastal part of Tuscany

grossezza size

grosso *(adj.)* big

grossolanamente coarsely (as in chopped)

gröstl potato slices, onion, and meat (or sometimes fried pig's blood) fried into a TORTINO; boiled beef with fried potato

grotta cave, grotto, wine cellar; see LATTE

groviera Gruyère cheese, though the name is sometimes applied to Emmenthal. The name is also used figuratively—"una groviera" can be anything full of holes.

gruenche = GRONGO (Puglia)

grugnale = LATTERINO (Puglia)

grugno = MUSO

grumo, *pl.* **grumi** clot, lump, as in what you don't want in sauces

grumolo heart (of a fruit or vegetable)

gruneu = GRONGO (Sicilia)

grunghiddu = GRONGO (Sicilia)

grungu = GRONGO (Sicilia)

gruonco = GRONGO (Abruzzo, Puglia)

guamaldi wild spinach

guancia cheek, jowl

guanciale cured fat from the hog's jowl; can be sliced thin and eaten on bread or FOCACCIA, or cut in small pieces and fried to flavor other dishes; sometimes used for other types of cheek meat

guantone (da forno) (oven) mitt

guarnina = ARGENTINA (Campania)

guarnina vera = LATTERINO (Calabria)

guarnito *(adj.)* garnished

guarnizione garnish; also gusset, washer, and various hardware items

Guastalla Sicilian roll from bread dough, often filled with cheese, PANCETTA, and spleen

guastedde = GUASTELLA

guasto *(adj.)* literally, "broken"; off, gone bad; of wine, unsound

guato de mar = GHIOZZO (Veneto, Venezia Giulia)

guazzetto, in cooked in a light tomato sauce

gubana Friulian coffee cake or pastry with candied fruit and nuts

gueffus Sardinian almond sweets

guggiuni = GHIOZZO (Sicilia)

gulasch goulash; can mean either the Italo-Hungarian version with paprika and tomatoes, or simply "stew"

guscio shell, pod, hull; eggs **al guscio** are soft-boiled

gustare, *p.p.* **gustato** to taste, to enjoy; cf. ASSAGGIARE, DEGUSTARE

gusto flavor (e.g., of ice cream); taste; pleasure

gustoso *(adj.)* tasty, but literally, in the sense of "full of taste"

guttiau, pane CARTA DA MUSICA dressed with olive oil and salt

~ H ~

Hag® brand of decaffeinated coffee; the name is used generically, like Sanka®

hamburger the same as in English, but note where the accent falls

hamin Ferrarese specialty of TAGLIOLINI baked with goose fat, raisins, and pine nuts

hipposelino = LEVISTICO

hirn-profesen slices of bread covered with layer of brains, battered and fried in butter, essentially CERVELLA in CARROZZA

~ I ~

i the (masculine plural)
iadduzzu = GATTUCCIO (Sicilia)
iatte de scuglio = GATTUCCIO (Puglia)
iattopardu di scogliu = GATTUCCIO (Sicilia)
ibrido hybrid
idrati di carbonio carbohydrates
idromele a drink of water, honey, wine, and spices
igname yam, genus *Dioscorea*
ignudi, RAVIOLI "naked" RAVIOLI, a spinach-ricotta-egg "filling" without the pasta, boiled as dumplings and sauced usually with butter and cheese, sometimes with meat RAGÙ (Toscana)
IGP/Indicazione Geografica Protetta literally, "protected geographical indication" (similar to D.O.P.), a legal designation that assures a product name is used only for wines or foods produced in a specific geographical area. The designation provides a measure of freedom and prestige for winemakers who wish to make wines of quality without the restrictions of the DOC and DOCG designations.
IGT/Indicazioni Geografiche Tipiche literally, "typical geographic indications"; new European Union designation roughly equivalent to the French *vin du pays*
il the (masculine singular)
imballaggio packaging
imbevibile *(adj.)* undrinkable
imbianchire, *p.p.* **imbianchito** to blanch
imbiondire brown lightly

imbottato *(adj.)* put in barrels (wine)

imbottigliare, *p.p.* **imbottigliato** to bottle, to "can" (in the sense of home preserves); bottled; **imbottigliato all'origine**, estate bottled; **imbottigliato dal viticoltore**, bottled by the grower

imbottito *(adj.)* stuffed

imbrecciata thick soup of mixed vegetables and grains

imbrogliata of eggs, "scrambled"; **imbrogliata di carciofi** is scrambled eggs with artichokes

imburrare, *p.p.* **imburrato** to butter

imbuto funnel

immondizia garbage

impanadas type of Sardinian CALZONE

impanados small pasta TIMBALLI filled with meat and baked

impanare, *p.p.* **impanato** to bread; the act and the substance is **impanatura**

impanata food , often fish, wrapped and cooked in bread dough, a specialty of Sicily

impastare, *p.p.* **impastato** to knead, to mix thoroughly

impastatrice electric mixer for dough

impasto dough, mixture

impastoiata POLENTA with beans cooked in tomato sauce

impazzire, *p.p.* **impazzito** literally, "to go crazy," meaning, for a sauce to curdle or separate

impepata a Neapolitan dish of shellfish (classically COZZE), heated just to open the shells, and served in their own juices with plenty of pepper (PEPE, hence the name), parsley, and lemon

Imperia the name of a province and its capital city in the Liguria region, abbreviated IM

impuro, pesce = GATTUCCIO (Lazio)

inacetire, *p.p.* **inacetito** to turn into vinegar (of wine)

inacidito *(adj.)* pricked (of wine), turning to vinegar

incaciato *(adj.)* sprinkled with cheese

incanestrato any of various cheeses that are pressed in wicker molds, leaving an imprint; literally, "embasketed"

incannulate = FUSILLI

incapriata = 'NCAPRIATA

incartato *(adj.)* wrapped in parchment or foil

incasado *(adj.)* = INCACIATO
incassare, *p.p.* **incassato** to encase, used of appliances that are built-in or foods that are encased in a crust
incavare, *p.p.* **incavato** to scoop out, to hollow out; **incavo**, a hollow, a groove
incavolata Versilian soup based on cabbage, beans, and cornmeal. *Incavolato*, as an adjective, means angry.
inchiostro ink, in pen or squid
incoperchiare to cover, put a lid (COPERCHIO) on
incorporare, *p.p.* **incorporato** to mix well, to fold in, to add and mix
indiana, all' with curry
indiavolato *(adj.)* deviled, i.e., spicy
indivia endive, frisée; endive, chicory; **indivia belga**, Belgian endive; **indivia riccia**, curly endive; **indivia scarola**, escarole
indivia selvatica wild endive
indiviola a wild endive
infarinare, *p.p.* **infarinato** to dredge with flour
infarinata hearty vegetable-bean soup thickened with cornmeal
inferigno *(adj.)* referring to bread, "brown," containing bran
Inferno DOC red wine from Lombardia
inferrettati *(pl.)* pasta rolled around a metal rod to leave a hole at the center
infiammare, *p.p.* **infiammato** to "flambé," the French *flamber*
infiammato *(adj.)* aflame
infornare, *p.p.* **infornato** to bake; literally, "to put in the oven"
infusiera infuser
infuso infusion (*infusione*); a beverage made by steeping
inglese, all' English-style; usually means boiled or poached, with perhaps the addition of butter and cheese
ingresso entrance
inossidabile *(adj.)* see ACCIAIO; stainless
inox stainless steel
inquinamento pollution
insaccati *(pl.)* sausages and salamis; refers to the group of all meats stuffed into a casing, whether cooked, raw, fresh, or aged

insalata salad, also used for lettuce; **insalata Belga** is Belgian endive or chicory

insalata a taglio at least in Rome, various types of tender lettuce sold as cut leaves, not in a head

insalata caprese sliced tomato and mozzarella with fresh basil

insalata di mare seafood salad, almost invariably an appetizer of tepid (ideally) boiled or steamed seafood, including at least some squid or octopus (cut in chunks) and mussels or clams, dressed with oil or lemon and some chopped celery

insalata russa Russian salad; cooked vegetables with a great deal of mayonnaise and sometimes gelatin

insalatiera salad bowl; often used generically for a large bowl

insaporire, *p.p.* **insaporito** to flavor, to let the flavors blend; the participle means flavored. This is a basic concept in Italian cooking, usually achieved by heating food over low heat or by leaving foods to rest, whereby ingredients share their flavors and lose any sharp distinctions to form a harmonious whole. Occasionally it means simply to season. **Fare insaporire**, to let the flavors blend.

inserire, *p.p.* **inserito** to put in, insert

insieme *(adv.)* together; as a substantive it means set, whole or *ensemble*

integrale *(adj.)* (1) whole, complete; (2) whole wheat, whole grain

interiora *(pl.)* offal

intero *(adj.)* whole, entire

intiepidire, *p.p.* **intiepidito** to become tepid, lukewarm; also, to come to room temperature

intingolo sauce, dip; flavorful meat or fish sauce for dipping bread; gravy; stew; any particularly tasty dish

intruglia = INFARINATA

invecchiamento aging, seasoning

invecchiare, *p.p.* **invecchiato** to age, to season

invernale *(adj.)* winter

invernengo grating cheese made in winter

inverno winter

involtino, *pl.* **involtini** virtually any food rolled into a cylinder, preferably with something inside. The rolls are usually thin slices of meat, but eggplant and swordfish slices are also used (notably in Sicilia).

involucro cover, coating, outer wrapper

inzimino, all' see ZIMINO

inzuppare, *p.p.* **inzuppato** to dunk; also, to drench, to imbue

iota = JOTA

iper– hyper– (prefix), high

ipercalorico *(adj.)* high–calorie

ipermercato large SUPERMERCATO, often outside of town

ipo– hypo– (prefix), low

ipocalorico *(adj.)* low–calorie

iridea, trota see TROTA

irinate vegetable and grain soup

iris unsweetened doughnut–type dough filled with meat RAGÙ and peas, and then deep–fat fried

irrorare, *p.p.* **irrorato** to pour (liquid) over

Isernia the name of a province and its capital city in the Molise region, abbreviated IS

issolone = FASOLARO (Veneto, Friuli)

issopo hyssop (*Hyssopus officinalis*)

isspessire = ADDENSARE

italico a soft, mild, white cheese similar to BEL PAESE

ittico– prefix denoting something to do with fish (from the Greek *ichthos*)

~ J-K ~

jàccoli thick, homemade spaghetti, usually served with meat sauce and PECORINO

jaral = LATTERINO (Veneto)

javal = LATTERINO (Veneto)

jelu i muluni = GELO DI MELONE

jeur hare (Friuli)

jiritaleddi = DITALINI

jota Friulian minestrone whose ingredients include beans, sauerkraut, and pork

juganega = LUGANEGA

kaki = CACHI

kanostrelle type of waffle

karkadé = CARCADÉ

kasher kosher

kiwi kiwifruit

knoedel = CANEDERLI

knolle type of cornmeal GNOCCHI

krapfen ball- or ring-shaped fritter, often with a variety of sweet fillings; also spelled *crafen* and *krafen;* syn. BOMBA

krenfleisch pork shoulder boiled with wine and vinegar, served with potatoes and horseradish

kuscus sweet semolina and pistachio cake

kuskus = CUSCUS

L

la the (feminine singular)

La Spezia the name of a province and its capital city in the Liguria region, abbreviated SP

laane = LAGANE

labbro, *pl.* **labbra** lip

labirinto literally, "labyrinth"; hollow, helical pasta

laccato *(adj.)* (1) lacquered; (2) coated with a honey-based sauce prior to roasting, so as to produce a "lacquered" crust

laccètt veal sweetbreads (Lombardia)

laccia = CHEPPIA (Puglia)

lacciola = ALACCIA (Lazio)

lacerto (1) mackerel, syn. SGOMBRO; (2) of beef, part of the hindquarter

laciada typical sweet of Lombardia

laciaditt apple fritters for Carnevale (Lombardia)

lacustre *(adj.)* lacustrine, from a lake

lagana, *pl.* **lagane** = LASAGNE

laganedde = LASAGNE (Calabria)

laganelle narrow LASAGNE noodles, often served in soup with beans, hot peppers, and PECORINO

laganon large TAGLIATELLE

lago lake

lagone sardaro = LATTERINO (Campania)

Lagrein grape variety as well as red and rosé wines from Trentino–Alto Adige

laianelle ricotta-filled, moon-shaped RAVIOLI made completely by hand, without even a rolling-pin. They are usually stuffed with RICOTTA and covered with kid-meat RAGÙ (Abruzzo, Molise).

lama blade

lambarda = GATTUCCIO (Liguria)

Lambrusco sparkling red DOC wine from Emilia-Romagna, dry to sweet. The dry is traditional with the region's BOLLITO MISTO.

lamella, *pl.* **lamelle** (1) literally, "razor blade"; (2) anything extremely thin; very thin slice; (3) (mushroom) gill

Lamon town in the Dolomites (Veneto), source of prized cranberry-type beans; **alla lamonese** usually indicates the presence of these beans

lampagione = LAMPASCIONI

lampascione, *pl.* **lampascioni** a specialty of Puglia, for which there are possibly more spellings than recipes. This is the grape hyacinth bulb, which looks something like a shallot. It is inedibly bitter unless subjected to a long process of washing and soaking, after which it can be baked or boiled for salad, or stewed and puréed to spread on bread.

lampasciuolo = LAMPASCIONI

lampi e tuoni "lightning and thunder," spicy Neapolitan pasta with chickpeas

lampone, *pl.* **lamponi** raspberry

lampreda lamprey; **lampreda di mare**, sea lamprey (*Petromyzon marinus*); **lampreda di fiume**, freshwater lamprey (*Lampetra fluviatilis*)

lampredotto (1) Tuscan tripe with vegetables; (2) young lamprey eel

lamprua = LAMPREDA (Liguria)

lampuca = LAMPUGA (Campania, Puglia)

lampuga mahimahi, dolphinfish (*Coryphaena hippurus*)

lampusa = LAMPREDA (Puglia)

lanache homemade Pugliese hard-wheat pasta strands like thin TAGLIATELLE, often sauced with stuffed mussels and PECORINO

lancette small pasta for soup

Langhe, le the Langhe; area of Piemonte famous for its foods and wines

Langhirano town near Parma (Emilia-Romagna) in the heart of the prosciutto area, known for its particularly sweet PROSCIUTTO DI PARMA

lanzardo = SGOMBRO (Veneto)

lappola burr, burdock (*Xanthium strumarium*)

lardare, *p.p.* **lardato** to lard

lardellare, *p.p.* **lardellato** to lard; **lardellatore**, lardoir, larding needle

lardo cured pork fat; fat bacon, fatback. It is not lard (see STRUTTO). Once you stop thinking of it as pure cholesterol, LARDO is delicious, sliced thin and served on warm bread or FOCACCIA. **Lardo rosa di Colonnata** is a particularly prized type of *lardo*, as is **prosciutto bianco friulano**.

lardone salt pork or bacon

larghezza width

largo *(adj.)* wide; **per largo**, crosswise

lasagna di Carnevale see CARNEVALE, LASAGNA DI

lasagna, *pl.* **lasagne** broad ribbon-shaped pasta, usually in plural. Note that the ribbons can be narrower or wider, and that the narrower ones are often served in a bowl with sauce; **lasagne al forno**, layered sheets of pasta baked with fillings and cheese in dozens of variations.

lasagnette narrow LASAGNE

lastra slab

Latina the name of a province and its capital city in the Lazio region, abbreviated LT, located south of Rome in the reclaimed area called the Pontina

latta tin, can; **in latta**, tinned, canned

lattaiolo (1) baked sweet custard dessert; (2) a mushroom (*Lactarius deliciosus*)

latte milk; **da latte** means "milk-fed" or "baby"; **latte di pesce** is the seminal fluid of fish, used smoked, salted, poached, or as an omelette filling; **latte alla grotta**, = MERINGA (Liguria). The word *latte* used alone has absolutely nothing to do with coffee (see CAFFÈ).

latte di mandorle literally, "almond milk"; milky liquid extracted from almonds and used in sweets

latte fritto fried custard dessert
latte inacidito sour milk
lattemiele sweetened whipped cream drink, or whipped cream
latteria (1) dairy; name for various fresh cheeses; place to buy milk products and/or a bar that serves dairy products and coffee; (2) a young cheese of Friuli
latterino smelt, silverside (*Atherina hepsetus*, *A. boyeri*, *A. mochon*, and *A. lacustris*); in plural, young ACCIUGHE (Marche)
lattesiol = PASSERA (Veneto, Venezia Giulia)
latticello buttermilk
latticini fresh cheeses; milk products
lattico *(adj.)* lactic
lattiera milk pitcher or special pan for heating milk
lattina can, especially for beer or soft drinks; diminutive of LATTA; see also SCATOLA
lattonzolo suckling pig or calf
lattosio lactose
lattosità milkiness
lattoso *(adj.)* milky
lattuga certain types of lettuce; in Rome, it refers almost exclusively to romaine lettuce, elsewhere called **lattuga romana**; **lattuga a cappuccio** is Bibb. Note that the catchall term for salad greens is not *lattuga* but INSALATA.
lattuga a taglio see INSALATA A TAGLIO
lattughella, lattughino lamb's lettuce or corn salad, = VALERIANELLA
lattume = LATTE DI PESCE
lauro laurel (*Laurus nobilis*); bay leaf; **foglia di lauro**, bay leaf; syn. ALLORO
lauto *(adj.)* lavish, sumptuous
lavanda (1) lavender, the herb plant, *Lavandula angustifolia* (*L. officinalis* or *L. spica*); (2) a washing (from LAVARE); a *lavanda gastrica* is a stomach pumping
lavandino sink, washbasin
lavapiatti dishwasher
lavarello powan or whitefish (*Coregonus lavaretus*), a delicate white-fleshed lake fish; see COREGONE
lavaret = LAVARELLO (Veneto)

lavastoviglie dishwasher (the machine)
lavello sink, washbasin
lavone = LATTERINO (Campania)
Lazio the large region of central Italy of which Rome is the capital. The translation "Latium" is an archaic usage that is ambiguous and inaccurate. Latium should be used only for the ancient Roman region, whose boundaries were much different from present-day Lazio's. Lazio contains five provinces: Roma in the center, Rieti and Viterbo to the north, Latina and Frosinone to the south. The southern provinces have much in common gastronomically with Campania, the northern with Umbria and Toscana, while eastern (Appennine) Lazio shares tastes with Abruzzo.
lazzeruola azarole (*Crataegus azarolus*), a small orange-yellow or red fruit that looks like a small apple
le the (feminine plural)
lebernocken liver dumplings
lecca-lecca lollipop
leccapentola di gomma rubber scraper
leccarda, alla dripping-pan, drippings; served with the sauce made from drippings of a roast; syn. *alla* GHIOTTA
leccare, *p.p.* **leccato** to lick; **leccarsi i baffi**, to lick one's lips (literally, "mustaches") in appreciation
Lecce the name of a province and its capital city in the Puglia region, abbreviated LE
leccia this name covers at least four species of fish of which the two most important are SERIOLA OR RICCIOLA and *Lichia amia.* They are all firm-fleshed, flavorful fish comparable to tuna.
Lecco the name of a province and its capital city in the Lombardia region, abbreviated LC
leccone glutton, someone who licks the plate
leccornia some specially prized tidbit
legare, *p.p.* **legato** to bind, to thicken
leggerezza lightness
leggermente lightly, slightly
leggero *(adj.)* light
legno wood; firewood is called **legna**

legnoso *(adj.)* woody, can be used of wine or vegetables, in the latter case distinctly disparagingly

legumi legumes

lengua = SOGLIOLA (Liguria)

lentamente slowly

lente = DENTICE (Liguria)

lente lentil, straight from the Latin *lens*

lenticchia, *pl.* **lenticchie** lentil, lentils; **lenticchie di Castelluccio**, grown near a town near NORCIA, are a very small, tender variety

lentici = DENTICE (Sicilia)

lento *(adj.)* slow; low (as flame); done over a low flame or in a slow oven

lepre hare

leprotto leveret, a young hare

lepudrida vegetable soup with pork or beef

lesagnetes type of TAGLIATELLE sauced with cheese and butter, or with ground poppy seeds

lessare, *p.p.* **lessato** to boil

lesso *(adj.)* boiled; as a noun, boiled meat; **lesso misto**, = BOLLITO MISTO

letto bed, including figuratively

levacapsule bottle opener

levatorsoli corer

levigato *(adj.)* smooth; planed

levistico lovage, herb with a celery-like flavor; *Levisticum officinale* (*Ligusticum levisticum*)

libaggione libation

libro (1) book; (2) = OMASO. **Libro di cucina**, cookbook.

Licinio see LUCULLO

licurdia spicy vegetable soup of Calabria; spicy Calabrian pepper sauce

Liebig brand name of a popular meat extract

lièvero = LEPRE (Veneto)

lievitato *(adj.)* raised with yeast

lievito, *pl.* **lieviti** (1) yeast, leavening; **lievito acido**, **lievito**

chimico, baking powder; **lievito di birra**, brewer's yeast; **lievito naturale**, also called **crescente**; **lievito di pane**, or **lievito madre**, is "starter"; (2) pastry

lievo *(adj.)* light

ligure *(adj.)* Ligurian; **Mare ligure**, the Ligurian sea

Liguria long, narrow small region of the Italian Riviera on the Ligurian Sea, bordering France. Its unusual microclimate means it has more in common gasronomically with the southern regions than the others of the North. Genoa is the capital, but the Cinque Terre and the so-called Italian Riviera are probably its best-loved destinations, and PESTO ALLA GENOVESE its best-known food. The region's boomerang shape lends itself into traditional division between the western arm, called the Riviera del Ponente (of the setting sun) and the Riviera del Levante (the rising).

ligustico = LEVISTICO

lilla, *pl.* **lille** = ACCIUGA (Marche)

limonata lemon soda, lemonade, but see also ARANCIATA and SPREMUTA

limoncello lemon liqueur, once associated with seaside resorts and sun-kissed islands, now ubiquitous

limoncina = CEDRINA

limoncino lemon liqueur

limone lemon, lemon tree

limpidezza clarity

limpido *(adj.)* limpid, clear

linfa full body (of wine)

lingua, *p.p.* **lingue** (1) tongue; (2) sole-like fish; (3) potentially anything vaguely tongue-shaped; **lingua di bue** is a type of mushroom; **lingua delle suocere** (literally, "mother-in-law's tongues"), = CHIACCHIERE

linguata = PASSERA (Sicilia)

linguata impiriali = ROMBO CHIODATO (Sicilia)

linguate = SOGLIOLA (Sicilia)

linguattola fish of the Pleuronectidae family, like the PASSERA and the PLATESSA

lingue di gatto light delicate cookies, taken with tea (literally, "cat's tongues")

lingue di passero literally, "sparrows' tongues"; = LINGUINE

linguine thin, flat, spaghetti-like pasta strands (literally, "little tongues")

lino, semi di flax seeds

Linz Linzer tort

liofilizzato *(adj.)* freeze-dried

liquefare, *p.p.* **liquefatto** to liquefy

liquido *(n. and adj.)* liquid; see also PANNA

liquirizia licorice

liquore liqueur

liquoroso *(adj.)* viscous; **vino liquoroso**, fortified wine

lisca, *pl.* **lische** the backbone and other bones of a fish

liscio *(adj.)* (1) smooth, plain; (2) no bubbles; (3) no ice, neat. Also, figuratively, means smooth, without a hitch

liso *(adj.)* threadbare

lissa bastarda = RICCIOLA (Veneto, Venezia Giulia)

lista list, menu

listarella, *pl.* **listarelle** small strip

listino a little list (of prices)

litro liter

livornese, alla Livorno-style; TRIGLIE (mullet) *alla livornese* are sautéed with garlic and tomato and then sprinkled with parsley; BACCALÀ (salt cod) *alla livornese* is stewed with oil, onion, tomato, and a little sweet wine; CHECHE (eels) *alla livornese* are sautéed with garlic and sage

Livorno historic seaport, formerly known in English as Leghorn, a province and its capital city in the Toscana region, abbreviated LI

lo the

loasso = SPIGOLA (Liguria)

locanda inn

locca = CORVINA (Toscana)

Lodi the name of a province and its capital city in the Lombardia region, abbreviated LO

lodigiano *(adj.)* (1) of LODI; (2) a type of GRANA cheese, now becoming uncommon

lollo very curly, bright red or green LATTUGA, named in honor of "La Lollo," Gina Lollobrigida

Lombardia Lombardy, the region of which Milan is capital, looks north toward Austro-Hungarian Europe and south to the Po valley

lombardo a Parmesan-style cheese similar to LODIGIANO (and possibly the same cheese)

lombata loin; the meat (boned or boneless) along the lumbar vertebra; in beef, divided between the thoracic vertebra (COSTATE) and the six lumbar vertebra (the *lombate* proper); in American beef, the loin from the boneless rib to the boneless shell; veal or sheep loin and ribs

lombatina COSTOLETTA of veal or pork

lombo pork loin; sometimes the term refers to the boned meat, more usually referred to as LONZA

lombrichelli thick handmade spaghetti

longone = VONGOLA

lonza as *lonza di maiale*, this will almost always be boned pork loin. Elsewhere, *lonza* can be a synonym of LOMBO, or refer to a sausage (Lazio), pork neck or back (central Italy), and other variations; see CAPOCOLLO.

lonze *(pl.)* odd bits and parts of beef, used in a stew (Toscana)

loro they, their

loto persimmon

lovertis sprouted hops (Lombardia)

lucanica = LUGANEGA

Lucca the name of a province and its capital city in the Toscana region, abbreviated LU

lucchese, alla Lucca-style

luccio di acqua dolce *Esox lucius* and various other freshwater fish of the Esocidae family, all known in English as pike or pickerel

luccio marino sea pike, barracuda (*Sphyraena sphyraena*)

lucerna stargazer (fish) (*Uranoscopus scaber*)

lucioperca pike-perch (*Stizostedion lucioperca*)

Lucullo Lucius Licinius Lucullus (ca. 115–55 B.C.) was a wealthy ancient Roman senator and general who dedicated his retirement to the pursuit of luxury. His name is still invoked, in the adjective **lucullano** (Lucullan, in English), to describe the maximum in gourmet feasts. Unfortunately, Lucullus died insane.

luganega luganega sausage; mild pork sausage in various regional versions, variously spelled as well. It is long and narrow and appears in the shop coiled, where it is cut and sold by weight. The name comes from Lucania, the ancient name for (roughly) the Basilicata region.

luglio July

lumaca, *pl.* **lumache** snails, usually cooked in tomato sauce and quite small—not escargots. **Lumache di S. Giovanni** are traditionally those gathered from the vineyards and gardens of Rome on the feast of St. John, June 24, when they happen to be fat and full of flavor after the plentiful rains of early summer.

lumachella di mare "sea snail" (*Nassarius mutabilis*), various species of gasteropods with the classic twisted snail shell

lumachelle (1) small snails, of land or sea; (2) small curly pasta for broth

lumachina di mare = LUMACHELLA DI MARE

lumellu dried pork with hot peppers

lumia citrus fruit, a cross between a citron and a lemon

lunedì Monday

lunetta, *pl.* **lunette** (1) half-moon RAVIOLI; (2) potentially anything small and moon-shaped

lungo *(adj.)* long; **caffè lungo** is an ESPRESSO diluted with about double the usual amount of water; see AMERICANO

lupicante = ASTICE (*Homarus gammarus*)

lupino, *pl.* **lupini** lupin (*Lupinus albus*)

lupo di mare = ASTICE (*Homarus gammarus*)

lupo, pesce = NASELLO (Marche)

luppolo, *pl.* **luppoli** hops; the sprouts are used in RISOTTO and FRITTATA

lus = LUCCIO DI ACQUA DOLCE (Piemonte, Emilia-Romagna)

lusao de mar = LUCCIO MARINO (Liguria)

lusc = LUCCIO DI ACQUA DOLCE (Liguria)

luss = LUCCIO DI ACQUA DOLCE (Lombardia)
luss-persegh = LUCIOPERCA (Piemonte, Lombardia)
lustrare, *p.p.* **lustrato** to polish
lustrino = PAGELLO (Campania)
lustro shine, luster
luteo *(adj.)* yellow; saffron
lutto, in in mourning, i.e., dressed in black, literally or figuratively; usually indicates the presence of squid ink
luxenti = GRONGO (Sardegna)
lùxerna di schéuggio = CERNIA (Liguria)
luz = LUCCIO DI ACQUA DOLCE (Veneto, Friuli)
luzzetiello = CICERELLO (Campania)
luzzo = LUCCIO (Veneto, Puglia, Venezia Giulia, Friuli, Campania)

~ *M* ~

macafame = SMACAFAM
macarelo = SGOMBRO (Venezia Giulia)
macaroni (1) a non-Italian spelling of MACCHERONE; (2) in Veneto, can mean GNOCCHI
macc, al soup of rice and milk with chestnut cream (Piemonte, Val d'Aosta)
maccarello mackerel, syn. SGOMBRO
maccarone = GHIOZZO (Puglia)
macche *(pl.)* baked POLENTA slices with sausage or other toppings
maccherone, *pl.* **maccheroni** (1) PASTASCIUTTA in general; note that "macaroni" is not an Italian spelling; (2) macaroni (tubular pasta); **maccheroni dolci** are TAGLIATELLE made with chocolate and chopped nuts
macchiare, *p.p.* **macchiato** to spot, to stain; **caffè macchiato** is

coffee with a "spot" of milk—hot, cold or foamed; **latte macchiato** is hot milk with a shot of ESPRESSO

macchinetta da caffè generic term for stove-top coffee maker

maccioni = GHIOZZO (Sardegna)

macco di fave thick fava bean purée, dressed with olive oil (see 'NCAPRIATA) or used in soup; bean and fennel soup; POLENTA with beans and sausage

maccu = MACCO

macedonia fruit cocktail, a dessert

macellaio butcher

macellaro butcher

macelleria butcher shop, butchery; **macelleria equina**, butcher shop for horsemeat

macello slaughterhouse, abbattoir, shambles, literally and figuratively

macerare, *p.p.* **macerato** to steep, to marinate

Macerata the name of a province and its capital city in the Marche region, abbreviated MC

macerazione maceration

machetto paste of salt-preserved anchovies and sardines

machetusa = PISSADELLA

machitt dish of cabbage, boiled beans, and turnips with sautéed onions

macinacaffè coffee grinder

macinapepe pepper mill

macinare, *p.p.* **macinato** to grind, to mill; the noun is **macinazione**

macinato *(adj.)* ground, minced (used for both grains and meat)

macinatoio mill, press

macinino (small) grinder or mill; coffee mill; pepper grinder

macis mace

madera madeira wine

maderizzato *(adj.)* "maderized," used of wine that has begun to taste like Madeira

madia chest for making and storing bread; sideboard (furniture), buffet

madre mother, including that of vinegar
mafalde long fluted noodle
magasso = MORIGLIONE (Veneto)
magatello = GIRELLO POSTERIORE (Parma)
maggengo cheese (or other products) made from April to September, as opposed to QUARTIROLO OR TERZOLO
maggio May
maggiorana marjoram (*Origanum majorana* or *Majorana hortensis*)
maglia mesh, mail
magliola = ANGUILLA (Sicilia)
magna pègola = LAMPREDA (Venezia Giulia)
magna-peixe = LAMPREDA (Liguria)
magnusa = LUCCIO MARINO (Sicilia)
magro *(adj.)* thin, lean, meatless; any dish that conforms to Catholic fast-day requirements
magu = RANA PESCATRICE (Sicilia)
mai never
maiale pork
maialino da latte suckling pig; cf. PORCHETTA
maionese mayonnaise
maiorchino PECORINO cheese of Bronte in Sicilia
mairoùn d'ereva marinated or smoked goat meat
mais corn; sweet corn (maize); **fiocchi di mais**, cornflakes; **olio di mais**, corn oil
Maiyu, pizza di bread dough stuffed and baked with salami, cracklings, and cheese (Calabria)
maizena cornstarch
majocchino Sicilian INCANESTRATO cheese made with olive oil
makaria small, cylindrical GNOCCHI
Malaga a Spanish grape from which raisins are made; ice cream flavored with Malaga raisins
malfatti a type of vegetable gnocchi (Lombardia)
malfattini = MANFRIGUL
malgaragno = MELAGRANO
malico *(adj.)* malic
mallegato Tuscan blood pudding

mallo the fresh fruit of nuts or drupes, such as walnuts; see NOCINO
malloreddus typical small pasta of Sardegna, also known as *gnocchetti sardi*
malmaritati soup made with MALTAGLIATI (Bologna)
malolattica malo–lactic
maltaglià egg pasta, of irregular rhomboid shape, used in soup
maltagliati different pasta shapes mixed together or irregular triangles or diamonds, usually thrown in soup
maltese orange–flavored hollandaise sauce
malto malt
malva mallow
Malvasia perfumed grape variety primarily for white wines but also sweet and red, used throughout Italy
mamma Mama, mother—the final authority in the kitchen
mammunacchia = GRANCHIO (Campania)
manate handmade spaghetti
mancia tip
manciata handful
mandarancio cross between MANDARINO and orange; temple orange
mandarino mandarin, tangerine, satsuma (*Citrus nobilis*)
mandilli de saea literally, "silk handkerchiefs"; Ligurian lasagna noodles rolled to the thinness of silk
mandorla, *pl.* **mandorle** almond; **mandorla amara**, bitter almond
mandorlato almond cake, almond paste, nougat
mandovo an almond sweet (Marche)
mandurlicchi small POLPI
màneghi sweet gnocchi of Padova area
manfricoli, manfrigne = MANFRIGUL
manfrigne a pasta for broth (Romagna)
manfrigul chopped pasta for soup
mangiatutto anything that is eaten whole, e.g., tiny fish or snow peas
manicaio = CANNOLICCHIO

manicaretto some little tidbit, anything from hors d'oeuvres to pastries; crêpe filled with artichokes, tomatoes, and light cheese

maniche literally "sleeves"; a kind of pasta, more usually MEZZE-MANICHE; **maniche di frate**, "monk's sleeves"; large macaroni

manico handle

manico di coltello = CANNOLICCHIO (Lazio, Abruzzo)

maniera, alla, **di** in the style of

maniglia handle; **maniglia atermica**, heatproof handle

manna (1) sap of the manna-ash tree (*Fraxinus ornus*) used in sweets; (2) manna (from heaven)

mannaia cleaver

manovella crank handle

manteca butter or whey butter enclosed in a "bag" of plastic curd cheese, which may be lightly smoked

mantecato *(adj.)* (1) creamed; (2) as substantive, an ice cream; a cream dish; anything that has become creamy through cooking or mashing, such as RISOTTO OF BACCALÀ

mantecato, *pl.* **mantecati** ice cream; literally "whipped." This is the correct term for bulk ice creams scooped from a tub.

mantello mantle, cloak

Mantova city and province in the Lombardia region, abbreviated MN; Mantua in English and Latin, it was the birthplace of the poet Virgil ("Mantua me genuit . . .")

mantovano *(adj.)* Mantuan; **alla mantovana**, Mantova-style; AGNOLINI **alla mantovana** are stuffed with beef, sausage, and PANCETTA

manuelina type of FOCACCIA stuffed with fresh cheese

manzo beef; sometimes young ox (central Italy); sometimes CASTRATO (Basilicata)

mappa not only map, but a sort of table napkin (from the Latin *mappa*)

mappatelle unto e cacio thin crêpes (FRITTATINE) stuffed with MACCHERONE ALLA CHITARRA, boiled, topped with PECORINO, PANCETTA, and parsley, rolled up and baked. The name is taken from the meaning of MAPPA AS TOVAGLIE. (Abruzzo, Molise)

maracuja passion fruit

maranta arrowroot
marasca morello, marasca, a sour cherry
maraschino liqueur made from the marasca cherry
marbré marbled; layered terrine
marca = ANGUILLA (Sicilia)
marca, *pl.* **marche** (1) brand, brand name; (2) border territory
marcassin young boar
marcato *(adj.)* marked
Marche, le the central–north Marches region comprises rugged mountains and a long Adriatic coast. Gastronomically as well as geographically, it spans north and south and is best known for Verdicchio wine.
marchigiano *(adj.)* of the Marches
marchio brand, both as in brand name and as in a physical identifying mark burned into something. The right to use a particular food name is often subject to legal restriction; the *marchio* (e.g., on PARMIGIANO REGGIANO cheese or PROSCIUTTO DI PARMA) is a guarantee for the consumer of the product's origin.
marcino wine from overripe grapes
marcio *(adj.)* rotten
marcire, *p.p.* **marcito** to rot, to go bad
marciume rot; **marciume nobile,** = MUFFA NOBILE
mare sea
mare e monti see MONTI E MARI
marena morello cherry; marena cherry beverage
mareteca = ANGUILLA (Puglia)
margarina margarine
margherita, pasta a sponge cake made with potato flour
Margherita, pizza pizza with MOZZARELLA or FIOR DI LATTE, tomato and (ideally) basil. Pizzeria Brandi in Naples claims to have invented this red, white, and green tribute to Queen Margherita di Savoia in 1889.
margherite *(pl.)* literally, "daisies"; twisted, flat pasta for soup
mari, perchia di = CERNIA (Sicilia)
mariconda, minestra soup of egg, bread, milk, cheese, and stock
mariconde *(pl.)* little pasta dumplings for broth

marignano = MELANZANA (Rome)

marille twin-tubed RIGATONI

marinaio *(n. and adj.)* sailor, maritime

marinara, alla "sailor-style"; the name is given to any number of methods of preparation, though tomatoes, olive oil, garlic, olives, parsley, oregano, basil, and capers frequently figure. A *pizza alla marinara* is usually made with oil, tomato, oregano, and garlic.

marinato *(adj.)* marinated; = SCAVECCIO

mariola thinly sliced PECORINO-and-basil omelet in broth (Calabria)

maritozzo, *pl.* **maritozzi** BRIOCHE filled with whipped cream, eaten for breakfast or as a snack. Before cones became universal, they could be filled with ice cream as a street treat. They can still be found in Rome and Palermo.

marmellata properly, marmalade, but used loosely to indicate any type of CONFETTURA. Used figuratively, it means anything indistinct made of several parts, indistinguishable from one another.

marmitta pot, saucepan, kettle (also car muffler)

marmo marble

marmora syn. MORMORA

marmurà = TROTA MARMORATA

marò fresh beans, mint, cheese, and oil pounded in a mortar to accompany boiled meat (Liguria)

marro = GNUMMERIEDDI, with regional variations

marrochino very strong CAPPUCCINO

marrone, *pl.* **marroni** marron, a prized type of large chestnut; **marroni glassati**, *marrons glacés*

Marsala long degraded as a cooking wine, now being appreciated as the fine fortified wine it is; from Marsala, in the province of TRAPANI (Sicilia)

marsalato *(adj.)* "marsalized" (of wine)

martareddu = MUGGINE (Sicilia)

martedì Tuesday

martello hammer

martinsecco small, very tart pear

marubei = MARUBINI

marubino round AGNOLOTTO with serrated border, filled with beef marrow, egg, bread crumbs, and cheese; another version is filled with roast veal and pork, braised beef and boiled brains; both versions are served in a special broth made from beef, chicken, and a local SALAME (Lombardia)

maruzele small LUMACHE DI MARE (Veneto)

maruzza, *pl.* **maruzze** = LUMACA (Campania)

maruzzo = NASELLO (Sicilia)

marzaiola small wild duck, garganey

marzapane (1) a specialty of Sicily, almond paste with sugar and egg white, often molded and colored to imitate fruits or vegetables; baked almond-paste pastries of Genova, whose full name is **marzapane quaresimale** (Lenten); (2) a blood sausage of Piemonte (**marzapane novarese**)

Marzemino DOC red wine and grape variety from northern Italy

marzo March

marzolino Tuscan PECORINO, best eaten fresh, produced in March

marzotica aged RICOTTA (Puglia)

masaneta, mazaneta small, female GRANCHIO

mascarpone a rich fresh, very soft white cheese traditionally made in winter

mascherato *(adj.)* masked

mascherpa a skimmed-milk RICOTTA SALATA

mascherpone = MASCARPONE

masculinella = ACCIUGA

massaia, alla "housewife-style"; **salsa della massaia** is a thickened butter sauce

Massa-Carrara the cities of Massa and Carrara together form one of the ten provinces of the Toscana region, abbreviated MS

matarellu TRACINA (Sicilia)

mataroccu a Sicilian cross between PESTO and gazpacho, spooned over staled bread

Matera the name of a province and its capital city in the Basilicata region, abbreviated MA

matriciana, alla = AMATRICIANA

mattarello (1) = MUGGINE (Lazio); (2) rolling pin

matticella, alla on coals
mattonella literally, "brick"; Neapolitan layered ice cream, = STRACCHINO
matufi Friulian POLENTA layered with cheese, sausage, and mushrooms; maize GNOCCHI with RAGÙ or tomato and basil; soft POLENTA in various preparations
maturato *(adj.)* ripened
maturazione the ripening process, maturation
maturo *(adj.)* ripe, mature
mauro a type of edible seaweed
mazaro duck, specifically, the Royal German duck
mazzafegato (1) smoked sausage of pork, pork liver, and lungs (Marche); (2) sausage of pork liver, fat, sugar, raisins (UVA PASSA), and pine nuts (Umbria)
mazzancolla large Mediterranean shrimp, Penaeidae family
mazzarelle kid or lamb innards, sautéed with herbs and vegetables, rolled up and tied with strips of intestine
mazzo, *pl.* **mazzi** bunch; **mazzetto**, the diminutive, small bunch, as of herbs; **mazzetto guarnito**, bouquet garni
mazzone = GHIOZZO (Marche, Lazio, Campania)
mazzune = NASELLO (Puglia)
mazzuneddu = GHIOZZO (Sicilia)
mazzunu = GHIOZZO (Sicilia)
medaglione, *pl.* **medaglioni** medallions, small rounds. The term refers to the shape of the food and can be used for tender scallops of meat or for sandwiches on flattish round rolls.
mediamente on average
medicamentoso (vino) blending wine
medio *(adj.)* average, medium
medusa jellyfish named, of course, for the Gorgon with the wicked hair
meiroun 'd crava smoked or pickled goat, boiled (Piemonte)
mela, *pl.* **mele** apple
melacotogna *or* **mela cotogna** quince
melagrana pomegranate

melangolo = ARANCIA AMARA

melanzana, *pl.* **melanzane** eggplant, aubergine (usually in the plural)

melassa molasses

melato *(adj.)* honeyed, honey-flavored

mele (1) plural of MELA (apple); (2) honey (alternative spelling of MIELE)

meliaca kind of apricot

melica = MELIGA

melicotti Piedmontese cookies from cornmeal and eggs

meliga = GRANOTURCO

melissa the lemon-scented, slightly hairy leaves of *Melissa officinalis* are used in salads and as a flavoring

mellone melon, watermelon (South)

melmoso *(adj.)* turbid

melone melon

meluggine crab apple

melza = MILZA

meneghino *(adj.)* Milanese; the name of Milan's dialect

menestra = MINESTRA

menola picarel, smare, various species of the genus *Maenidae*

mensola shelf; **mensolina**, small shelf

menta mint, *Mentha* spp.; **menta peperina**, **piperita**, or **peperita** (or other variations), peppermint; **menta spicata** is common mint, spearmint. **Menta romana**, a type of *menta spicata*, is yet another species not to be confused with MENTUCCIA. Since everyone in Rome has trouble telling the mints apart, *menta romana* is invariably further specified as *quella della trippa*—the one used in TRIPPA ALLA ROMANA.

mentuccia pennyroyal (*Mentha pulegium*), a small-leafed, delicate, mint-like herb, used in Rome to flavor artichokes in the dish known as **carciofi alla romana**. Menus usually translate it wild mint on the not unreasonable grounds that few people know what pennyroyal tastes like.

menù menu; **menù degustazione**, tasting menu

menuei = BIGOLI

meo = CERNIA (Liguria)

mercato market

merce *(no pl.)* merchandise, goods, what you buy

mercoledì Wednesday

merello = FRAGOLA

merenda snack, usually used for the starch- and sugar-filled sweets given to children to hold them till it's time for the spaghetti. A grown-up's snack is likely to be called SPUNTINO. *Merenda* can also be a picnic.

meridionale southern, the adjective for the MEZZOGIORNO

meringa, *pl.* **meringhe** meringue

meringata frozen meringue and whipped cream dessert

merlan = NASELLO (Liguria)

merlo, *pl.* **merli** blackbird

merluzzo usually used to mean (fresh) cod. **Merluzzo bianco** refers to Atlantic and Pacific cod—*Gadus morrhua* or *G. macrocephalus*—usually preserved (as BACCALÀ or STOCCAFISSO); the name is also used to indicate a fresh fish from Italian waters, either NASELLO or the **merluzzo argentato** (*Merluccius merluccius*).

merluzzo imperiale = LUCCIO MARINO (Lazio)

merollo = MIDOLLO (Rome)

mescere, *p.p.* to pour (the wine), or less frequently, to mix; the word means literally, "to mix" (from Latin *miscere*), but usually it refers to pouring, with a slight ceremonial overtone, which the host or innkeeper does for the guests. The origin probably lies in the ancient practice of mixing wine and water, the proportions decided by a designated person, not by the drinker.

mescie mixed wheat and chestnut flour

mescita wine (as opposed to food) service

mesciua a Ligurian legume soup

mescolare to mix

mesoro = LUCERNA (Liguria, Toscana)

messicani literally, "Mexicans"; sautéed veal "olives" filled with chicken liver, sausage, and cheese (Milan); also synonym of INVOLTINI

Messina the name of a province and its capital city in the Sicilia region, abbreviated ME

messinese very large macaroni slit partway along their length for filling

mesticanza "mixed"; usually salad (see MISTICANZA); Molisan cabbage and potato purée with PANCETTA and peppers

mestolame set of kitchen utensils; cf. MESTOLO

mestolo ladle; **mestolino**, small ladle

mestolone a wild duck

metà half

metodo method. In the making of sparkling wine, **metodo classico** is what the *Méthode Champenoise* is called when used in Italy (also called **metodo tradizionale** or **metodo classico tradizionale**). See also METODO MARTINOTTI and SPUMANTE.

metodo Martinotti the *Charmat,* or *Cuve Close,* method of making sparking wines. Like Giuseppe Meucci, who invented the telephone, Martinotti invented—but did not patent—the method whereby the second fermentation needed to obtain effervescence (called *presa di spuma*) occurs in an autoclave rather than bottles.

metro meter; **al metro**, by the meter, among other things, a way of selling rectangular pizza

meu = CERNIA (Liguria)

meusa = MILZA

mezzaluna (1) mezzaluna, crescent-shaped chopping knife; (2) anything else crescent shaped, e.g., a particular CALZONE stuffed with sautéed greens

mezzaluna scolatutto semicircular drainer

mezzani long (like spaghetti), tubular pasta; **mezzanelli** are a thinner version, **mezzani tagliati** are a shorter version

mezzano *(adj.)* medium-sized

mezze maniche a short, tubular pasta similar to RIGATONI; literally, "short sleeves"

mezzena half, or side, of a carcass, as in a "side of beef"

mezzo *(n. and adj.)* half

mezzo, piatto di a course between the first and the main courses, such as a fish course served before the meat, though nowadays it often serves as a main course

mezzogiorno noon; south; capitalized, southern Italy
micca typical large bread loaf of Milan
michetta northern term for common bread rolls, sometimes rose-shaped
micon = PAGNOTTA (Piemonte)
midolla crustless bread, cheese, or anything similar; pulp
midollo bone marrow; pulp; **midollo spinale**, spinal cord; see SCHIENALE
miele honey; **miele amaro** is bitter acacia or CORBEZZOLO (arbutus) honey
mietitura harvest, crop
migliaccini crêpes
migliaccio black pudding, blood pudding, syn. SANGUINACCIO; chestnut cake, syn. CASTAGNACCIO; **migliaccio campano** is a kind of baked POLENTA with sausage, cracklings, and cheese
miglio millet (*Panicum miliaceum*)
mignana = TROTA FARIO
mignestre = MINESTRA
mignuicche home-style Pugliese GNOCCHETTI
milanese, alla of meats (especially pounded veal cutlets), breaded and sautéed in butter; of RISOTTO, made with butter, onion, beef marrow, and saffron; of RAVIOLI, stuffed with roast or stewed beef, prosciutto, AMARETTI, and cheese. A **salsa alla milanese** is chopped veal and ham sautéed with wine and vinegar, sieved, and thinned with stock. Otherwise, the name implies nothing precise except (frequently) the use of butter.
milangiane *(pl.)* = MELANZANE (Calabria)
Milano Milan, the second largest city of Italy; also the name of a province and its capital city in the Lombardia region, abbreviated MI
Milano soft, sweet cheese like BEL PAESE
mille, *pl.* **mila** thousand
millecosedde slow-cooked vegetable and bean soup of Calabria
millefiori *millefleurs*, literally, "one thousand flowers," a honey flavor
millefogli = OMASO

millefoglie millefeuille (like a napoleon pastry)
millerighe large, ribbed MACCHERONE
millesimo vintage (year of production)
milza spleen; milt
milzschnittensuppe meat broth served over CROSTINI spread with MILZA, egg, garlic, and marjoram (Alto Adige)
minerale, *pl.* **minerali** mineral; cf. OLIGOMINERALE
minestra (1) the PRIMO PIATTO of a meal, whether soup or pasta or rice; (2) soup; cf. ZUPPA
minestrina light or clear soup
minestrone hearty, mixed vegetable soup subject to enormous variation. Note that it is redundant to say "minestrone soup."
minghiarulo = GHIOZZO (Puglia)
minimo *(n. and adj.)* minimum, smallest
minni 'i virgini (mammelle di vergine) cassatina, a Sicilian sweet shaped supposedly like a virgin's breasts
minosa = LATTERINO (Sicilia)
minoscia = LATTERINO (Puglia)
minuscolo *(adj.)* tiny, minuscule
minuta = CORATELLA
minutaglia small fish for frying
minutina = ERBA STELLA
minutine = SCALOPPINE, usually of veal
minuto *(n. and adj.)* minute; tiny, minute
mio *(adj.)* my, mine
mirou = LUCERNA (Liguria)
mirride sweet cicely, myrrh (*Myrrhis odorata*)
mirruzzu = NASELLO (Calabria)
mirtillo bilberry, whortleberry (*Vaccinium myrtillus*), a relative of the American blueberry, which on its rare appearances in Italy is also called *mirtillo*
mirto (1) myrtle (*Myrtis communis*); a characteristic flavoring in Sardegna; (2) a Sardinian myrtle-flavored liqueur
miscela blend (usually of coffee)
miscelare, *p.p.* **miscelato** to blend
mischiarc, *p.p.* **mischiato** to mix

misoltino name used around Lake Como (Lombardia) for small AGONE

misoltitt Lombardian dialect for MISOLTINO, usually indicating an antipasto preparation in which the fish has been salted and dried, then skinned and sprinkled with lemon or oil and vinegar

misseau = PALOMBO (Liguria)

mistella a mixture of grape and grape alcohol used as a sweetening agent for MARSALA

misticanza the true *misticanza* is a salad of the superb bitter wild greens that grow around Rome. The word is not a synonym for INSALATA MISTA even if too many restaurants attempt to claim it is. Seed packets use it as an Italian equivalent of French *mesclun*, which is really more like INSALATA A TAGLIO.

misto *(adj.)* mixed

mistocchine, mistucchine oval pastries of chestnut flour

Mistrà anise-flavored liqueur

mistura mixing

misurare, *p.p.* **misurato** to measure; a very inexact science in Italian cooking since a good cook is supposed to know how much of anything to use without the benefit of measuring devices

misurino measure, measuring cup, measuring spoon (cf. MISURARE)

mitilo = COZZA

mitounnà, soupa soup made from broth spooned over stale bread slices and run under the broiler; may be sprinkled with cheese and/or wild herbs and enriched with egg yolk

mitunà see MITOUNNÀ

mlinci, mlinzi irregularly shaped pasta from Friuli, near Slovenia

mo = MARE (Liguria)

mocetta PROSCIUTTO made from chamois (or, goat in its absence)

moda, alla, di in the style of

Modena the name of a province and its capital city in the Emilia-Romagna region, abbreviated MO. It is home to a number of gastronomic specialties including ZAMPONE and ACETO BALSAMICO. Part of the province lies within the production zone of

PARMIGIANO REGGIANO cheese. (Modena is also known as the home of the Ferrari automobile.)

modenese *(adj.)* of Modena

modiola = COZZA PELOSA

moeca = MOLECA

moellin = GATTUCCIO (Liguria)

mohnnudeln sweet lasagne with butter, sugar, and poppy seeds

moka a common type of stove-top CAFFETIERA

moleca, *pl.* **moleche** Venetian name for the male soft-shell crab (variously spelled); not to be confused with Chesapeake Bay soft-shell crabs; for **moleche col pien**, the crabs are fed on egg and Parmesan before being fried. See also GRANCHIO.

Molise the Molise region; see note at ABRUZZO

molitano pliable southern Italian cheese usually from sheep milk

moliterno strong sheep cheese from Basilicata and Calabria

molla, *pl.* **molle** tongs, spring

mollane a salted cheese

molle *(adj.)* soft, weak

mollettone the pad placed under the tablecloth to protect the table

mollica crustless bread, soft bread crumbs

mollicato *(adj.)* with MOLLICA

mollo, mettere a to soak

mollusco mollusk

molto *(adj. and adv.)* very; much; many

monachino, *pl.* **monachini** bullfinch (*Pyrrhula pyrrhula*)

monaco, monaca monk, nun; the latter especially is frequently invoked in humorous food names

mòncoi POLENTA containing SPECK and cheese

mondare, *p.p.* **mondato** to trim, to clean (a vegetable)

mondeghili Milanese meatballs, breaded and fried in butter

monferrina of Monferrato (Piemonte)

mongana milk-fed veal

monocorde monotonous (of wine)

monovitigno single grape

montagna, prosciutto di see PROSCIUTTO

montare, *p.p.* **montato** to whip; **panna montata** is whipped cream

Montasio semi-firm to hard, sharp cow-milk cheese of Veneto or Friuli with DENOMINAZIONE D'ORIGINE

monte, *pl.* **monti** mountain; **monte e mare** (mountain and sea) is the Italian version of "surf 'n' turf" (seafood and meat) when referring to a second course. For pasta, it usually indicates seafood and mushrooms.

montebianco Montblanc

Montepulciano d'Abruzzo red wine grape used in blends and in a DOC wine of the same name from the PESCARA area

Montepulciano, Vino Nobile di celebrated Sangiovese Tuscan DOCG wine

montone mutton (sheepskin coats are also called *montoni*)

monzese, risotto alla RISOTTO with sausage

mora, *pl.* **more** blackberry (*mora di rovo*)

morai = BORRAGINE

moraiolo black olive or cherry, potentially anything small and dark (MORO)

morbidelle AGNOLOTTI made from gnocchi dough

morbido *(adj.)* soft, tender

morchella, *pl.* **morchelle** morel mushroom, syn. SPUGNOLA

morchia, *pl.* **morchie** dregs, residue, especially of cooked butter or what collects in the bottom of the olive oil bottle

moreccio = PORCINO

morellini *(pl.)* purple artichokes, potentially anything small and dark

morello morel mushroom

morena = MURENA (Veneto)

moretta (1) various species of duck; (2) a mushroom (*Tricholoma terreum*)

moriglione type of duck, the pochard

Morlacco firm cow-milk cheese of the Friuli-Veneto area, similar to Montasio

mormora bream (*Pagellus mormyrus*), a member of the Sparidae family; = PAGELLO (Toscana)

moro *(adj.)* dark; as substantive, Moor

morseddu = MURSEDDU

mortadella this is the genuine bologna sausage from Bologna. It is approximately the size of a torpedo (it can weigh up to 200 kg) and bears a superficial resemblance to American bologna, but is so superior that the nomenclature must be kept separate. It is made of finely ground cooked pork with pieces of white lard and pistachios.

mortadelline di Campotosto Abruzzese pork sausage, sometimes called **mortadella abruzzese**

mortaio mortar; cf. PESTO

morte *(n.f.)* death; **la morte sua**—"its own death"—is the absolutely best way to cook a given food

morto *(adj.)* dead; see ARROSTO

morzeddu = MURSEDDU

mosa POLENTA made with milk and butter, sometimes also sugar and cinnamon (Veneto)

moscardino octopus, various members of the genera *Eledone* and *Ozaena*. Though *moscardini* are typically very small, some are larger than some POLPI; the *moscardino* has only a single row of suckers where the POLPO has two.

moscardino bianco = POLPO BIANCO

moscato muscat, fragrant grape used in a variety of sweet wines ranging from the delightful light Moscato d'ASTI to the deep golden Moscato di Pantelleria—but also in dry wines as well

moscato, noce nutmeg

mosciame dried dolphin meat, but nowadays, the dried meat of tuna and other large fish

mosciolina = COZZA (Puglia)

mosso *(adj.)* literally, "in movement"; for the sea, it means a bit rough, for wine, it means slightly sparkling

mostaccini spice cookies from around Crema (Lombardia)

mostaccioli *(pl.)* (1) a pasta similar to PENNE; (2) various hard cookies (BISCOTTI) such as a Sicilian version made with honey, almonds, and orange peel; an Emilian ring-shaped version; a Lazio recipe that includes pepper; a Campanian version spread with apricot marmalade; and others

mostarda (1) mustard in the broadest sense; (2) any of a variety of chutney-like fruit-based condiments ranging from the spicy candied fruits of the north used to accompany boiled meats (most famously that of Cremona) to a sweet Sicilian fruit concoction; cf. SENAPE and COGNA

mostella = MUSDEA

mosto grape must, which is the not-yet-fermenting juice of grapes pressed for wine; **mosto fiore**, first pressing; **mosto cotto**, cooked must—in other words, must which has been cooked down to a concentrate; it is kept in the kitchen and used in cooking, notably in sweet and sour dishes

moulard male duck

mozzarella soft, fresh white cheese, properly from water buffalo milk, but often from cow milk, as labor-intensive buffalo-herding declines each year. Premium-priced buffalo mozzarella (*la vera mozzarella di bufala* or simply *la vera bufala*) is often not 100 percent buffalo milk. **Mozzarella milanese** is not mozzarella, but BEL PAESE cheese breaded and fried. Italians find it strange when Americans talk about "mozzarella cheese"; certainly, in Italian one does not say "FORMAGGIO mozzarella." The best mozzarella comes from southern Lazio and northern Campania.

mozzicare to bite, to cut off; a **mozzicone** is a cigarette butt

mucca milk cow; cf. VACCA

mucische salted, dried, smoked sheep or goat meat sliced thin and served with oil and hot pepper (Molise)

muddica = MOLLICA; **pasta cc'a muddica** is spaghetti with anchovies, sardines, wild fennel, and dry bread crumbs (Sicilia)

muffa mold, i.e., what grows in the refrigerator. The mold that gives a shape to a pudding is STAMPO. **Muffa nobile** is noble rot (*Botrytis cinerea*), a desirable mold which permits production of highly prized dessert wines.

muggine gray mullet (*Mugil cephalus*) and other members of the Mugilidae family; syn. CEFALO

mugnaia, alla literally, "miller's style," exactly the French *meunière*, which is to say breaded and sautéed with butter; with butter, lemon, and parsley

muletta a cured meat from Molise
mulincianu = MELANZANE (Sicilia)
Müller Thurgau (1) light, aromatic white wine of Alto Adige; (2) the grape variety
murazzano fresh sheep-milk cheese of the ROBIOLA family (Piemonte)
murena moray; serpentine fish (*Muraena helena*); often served grilled or in fish soup; its skin is used for bookbinding
murice spinoso murex (*Murex brandaris*), a varied species of gastropods with helical shell
murseddu various meats (such as tripe, veal, pork livers, or innards) sautéed in lard with tomato, red wine, and herbs (Calabria)
mursiello = MURSEDDU
muscari = LAMPASCIONI
muschiata, anatra Barbary duck
muschio musk
musciame = MOSCIAME
musciona = LATTERINO (Sardegna)
muscolo (1) muscle; (2) shank (boneless), either hind (*posteriore*) or fore (*anteriore*); when cut in pieces across the bone, this is the source of veal for OSSOBUCCO; the meat alone is often used for BOLLITO; various cuts of meat (varying from region to region) from the upper leg; (3) = COZZA
musdea hake (*Phycis phycis*)
musetto a pork sausage typical of Friuli-Venezia Giulia and northern Veneto, similar to COTECHINO but more finely ground and with the inclusion of meat from the pig's face (MUSO)
musillo the thickest part of the BACCALÀ
musino = BONDELLA
muso, musetto face, muzzle; usually of veal or pork
musso Veneto dialect for ASINO
mussola, mussolina muslin
mussolo = ARCA DI NOÈ
mussula = PALOMBO (Sardegna)
mustazzoli Sicilian MOSTACCIOLI

mustica tiny salted anchovies in peppery oil
muta, anatra = MUSCHIATA

≈ N ≈

naccarijello = SGOMBRO (Puglia)
nacchera = PINNA (Liguria)
nana duck
napoletana (1) a stove-top coffee maker with two parts to be inverted during the coffee making; (2) **alla napoletana**, Neapolitan-style; usually implies the presence of rich tomato sauce. See also PIZZA. **Ragù alla napoletana** is the sauce from an elaborate, stuffed pork or beef pot roast.
Napoli Naples is the third largest city in Italy and the capital of the Campania region; it is the home of pizza, but its gastronomic traditions also owe much to the French influence of the Bourbon kings
nappare to nap; to cover with a sauce
nasello the name refers most properly to the Atlantic Gadidae family, but also to several members of the Mediterranean Merlucciidae family, notably *Merluccius merluccius*. As *Gadus morrhua*, et al., it is sold fresh or else preserved as STOCCAFISSO and BACCALÀ; the Merlucciidae are generally translated as hake, sometimes as whiting or sea pike (see LUCCIO MARINO).
nastrini di monaca literally, "nun's ribbons," = CENCI
nastro ribbon, band; **Nastro Azzurro** (blue ribbon) is a domestic beer
nasturzio watercress
Natale Christmas

natalizio *(adj.)* of Christmas

natante *(pres. part.)* literally, "swimming"; equivalent to the French *à la nage*; served in the cooking broth

naturale (1) plain, unsweetened, uncarbonated; (2) natural

navone, *pl.* **navoni** nape, rutabaga, parsnip; sometimes called *cavolo navone* based on its similarity to CAVOLO RAPA

nazionale *(adj.)* domestic; Italian

'ncaciata see INCACIATI

'ncantrata salt-preserved pork, cooked with tomato or vegetables

'ncapriata fava beans cooked to a creamy purée, dressed with olive oil and served with boiled wild chicory or other greens

'ncasciata pasta pie with varying ingredients

'ndocca 'ndocca spicy Abruzzese soup of pork rind (and often tail, tongue, and snout) sometimes served chilled in gelatin

nebbiolo important red grape of Piemonte and Lombardia

neccio, *pl.* **necci** crêpes or waffles from chestnut flour, often cheese-stuffed or to accompany ricotta; chestnut cakes; sausages in the shape of such cakes. The word is thought to be a corruption of CASTAGNACCIO; around Pistoia it is used to mean the CASTAGNA itself.

negli in the

negroamaro literally, "black bitter"; red grape variety of Puglia

nei in the

nel in the

nella in the

nello in the

neonato *(adj.)* newborn

nepitella calamint (*Satureia calamintha*), sometimes called basil-thyme. This herb is sometimes called MENTUCCIA, but is not what is called *mentuccia* in Rome. To add to the confusion, there exists the variant spelling *nepetella*, which is also attributed to *Satureia nepeta* and *Calamintha nepetoides*. Just remember it is not what Romans put on their artichokes.

nepitelle sweet Calabrian RAVIOLI filled with grapes, chocolate, and nuts

neretese, capra alla kid rinsed, poached with herbs, rinsed again, browned with onion and garlic, and then cooked with white wine, tomato, hot peppers, and cloves (Abruzzo)

nero *(adj.)* black, dark. As a noun it means squid or cuttlefish ink. The emperor Nero is called Nerone in Italian. **Nero di seppia** is cuttlefish ink.

nervetti (insalata di) (salad of) boiled calf's shank and knee cartilage, cut in strips and usually dressed with oil, onions, and capers (Lombardia)

nervitt = NERVETTI

nespola medlar fruit (*Mespilus germanica*); loquat (*Eriobotyra japonica*). The loquat is sometimes called Chinese or Japanese medlar, but the true medlar is the **nespola comune** (*nespolo* for the tree) and the loquat is more properly **nespola del Giappone**.

netino *(adj.)* of Noto, in Sicilia

nettare nectar, both what the gods drank and the brand-name of a drink of fruit juice, sugar, and water

nettarina nectarine, also called **pesca noce**

nettezza urbana city garbage collection

netto *(adj.)* clean, sharp

neunata = NUNNATA

neutro *(adj.)* neutral

neve snow; **in neve compatta**, stiff (for egg whites)

ngernia = CERNIA (Puglia, Sardegna)

nicchio, *pl.* **nicchi** the shell of certain mollusks; **nicchiole** *(pl.)*, its diminutive, is a short pasta

nida = LATICELLO

nido, *pl.* **nidi** nest, literally and figuratively; long egg pastas (such as FETTUCCINE) are often packaged in little bunches called *nidi*

nini = ACCIUGA (Veneto)

Nizza Nice (the French city)

nizzarda, alla niçois(e)

nnuglia Calabrian sausage

nocca knuckle

nocca neigra = GATTUCCIO (Liguria)

noccheredde *(pl.)* Calabrian bow-tie pasta

nocchette bow-tie pasta

nocchia = NOCCIOLA in Lazio (where they grow in abundance)

nocciola hazelnut; nut-shaped (French *noisette*); nut colored

noccioline americane peanuts, groundnuts

nocciolo (1) hazelnut tree; (2) stone of some fruits (e.g., plums)

noce, *pl.* **noci** (1) nut, black walnut; **noce di cocco** is coconut; **noce moscato** is nutmeg. *Noce* can also be used as a unit of approximate measurement: **un noce di** BURRO is a walnut-sized piece of butter. (2) Part of the veal hindquarter, the area running along the front of the femur, bounded by the SCAMONE, SOTTOFESA, and the side of the FESA, roughly synonymous with ROSETTA; the term may also apply to the same cut of beef; the meat is lean and is used for SCALOPPE, roasts, and for BISTECCA.

nochette ring-shaped pasta (Abruzzo)

nocillo = NOCINO

nocino AMARO-like liqueur made from green walnuts and spices

nocken GNOCCHI; GNOCCHETTI; dumplings

nockerln noodles; small GNOCCHI; *Salzburger nockerln* is a vanilla-flavored soufflé

nodino (di vitello) (veal) loin chop, *noisette*

noisettes *(pl.)* French term for the boneless COSTOLETTE

nonna (1) grandmother; **alla nonna** means "grandma-style"; **torta della nonna** is a plain yellow cake with some CREMA PASTICCERA inside and pine nuts on top; (2) = MENOLA (Liguria)

norcina, alla see NORCINERIA

norcineria pork butchery; pork products in general. The name is from Norcia, a town in Umbria, whose pork butchers were already famous in the Middle Ages; they practiced a sort of seasonal migration as itinerant specialists not only in killing and butchering swine but also in curing both the animals' illnesses and their meat. When these experts went into Rome or Toscana they were called *norcini*, "citizens of Norcia." The geographical association with the job became so strong that the word *norcino* entered the Italian language, with a lowercase "n," and the rest of the people of Norcia took the designation *nursini*, after the ancient name of the town (Nursia). Even today, *norcino* also means a clumsy surgeon. In the names of prepared dishes, **alla norcina** refers to pork, specifically a sauce for pasta of sausage and cream; **alla nursina,** which refers to the town, indicates the presence of black truffles, for which Norcia is also famous.

norcino see NORCINERIA

nord north

Norma, pasta alla the Sicilian pasta par excellence, named for the opera *Norma* by the Catanian Vincenzo Bellini, with fried eggplant, rich tomato sauce, RICOTTA SALATA, and basil

nostrale = NOSTRANO

nostrano hard cheese of Trentino, similar to ASIAGO; also a Piedmontese cheese

nostrano *(adj.)* homegrown, domestic, regional; the basic meaning is "ours" as opposed to some unspecified "theirs"

Novara the name of a province and its capital city in the Piemonte region, abbreviated NO

novarese, alla from Novara, in Piemonte; INSALATA DI RISO *alla novarese* is layered rice and white truffles with an oil, lemon, and anchovy dressing

novellame *(n.m.), pl.* **novellami** newborn ACCIUGA (Liguria, Sicilia, Marche, Abruzzo)

novello new; VINO *novello* is fresh-bottled red wine released annually on November 4 and best drunk within six months. After a slow start, it has become extremely popular.

novembre November

novità freshness, newness; also something new, like a new item at the supermarket where banners proclaim "una novità assoluta"

nuci = NOCI

nudini = BIANCHETTI

nudinni *(pl.)* young ACCIUGA (Marche)

nunnata = BIANCHETTI

nuocere, *p.p.* **nociuto, nuociuto** to harm. The battle cry *Almeno non nuoce* means "at least it can't hurt"

Nuoro the name of a province and its capital city in the Sardegna region, abbreviated NU

nursina, alla see NORCINERIA

Nutella® proprietary name of an inordinately popular hazelnut and chocolate spread, vaguely reminiscent of peanut butter

o or (**od** before a vowel)

oca goose; **oca alla piemontese** is preserved in fat

occhiata *Oblada melanura*, a member of the Sparidae family of fish

occhio, *pl.* **occhi** eye, or anything that looks like an eye; FAGIOLI *all'occhio* are black-eyed peas or cowpeas (*Vigna unguiculata*); **occhio di bue**, bull's eye, potentially anything that looks remotely like a large eye, including a round, flat cookie with a jam center; = ALIÒTIDE; *al occhio di bue* indicates fried eggs sunny side up; **occhi di lupo**, short pasta tubes, especially used in PASTA E FAGIOLI; **occhi di Santa Lucia**, cookies for Saint Lucy's day (patron saint of eyes). *Occhi* are also the holes formed in cheese.

occiouni = LATTERINO (Liguria)

occorre verb meaning "is needed"; **l'occorrente** (present participle used as noun) means "what is needed," i.e., the ingredients for a recipe

ocio gander

odorare (di) to smell, to have the scent (of) (trans. and intrans.)

odori herbs

offella, *pl.* **offelle** (1) Lombardian, ovoidal cookies from PASTAFROLLA or PASTA SFOGLIA dough, particularly those from Parona (Pavia); (2) RAVIOLI with various meat and vegetable fillings (Friuli)

officinale, erba medicinal herb

ogio = OLIO (Veneto)
oidio oidium (mildew)
ojo = OLIO
ojosa wild green
olandese *(adj.)* Hollandaise, or simply Dutch
oleata, carta grease-proof paper, oil-paper
olfatto olfactory, sense of smell
olfazione (act of) smelling
oliera oil pourer, oil cruet
oligominerale, acqua bottled (i.e., spring) water with a low concentration of minerals
olio oil; if the kind is not specified in recipes, it means olive
oliva, *pl.* **olive** olive
olive all'ascolana *(pl.)* the terms **olive ascolane** and *olive all'ascolana* are not synonymous, though they are often treated as such on menus. The former term refers to a specific variety of green olive grown in the hills around ASCOLI PICENO, in the MARCHE, the latter to a specific preparation, preferably of these same olives. The olives are cured, pitted, cut in a spiral, filled with a meat stuffing, put back together again, and breaded and fried. Poor imitations are staples on the pizzeria menu.
olivette *(pl.)* name for various olive-shaped creations
olivo olive tree
Oltrepò "beyond the Po," i.e., the land lying north of the river Po
Oltrepò pavese a number of DOC wines from the province of Pavia (Lombardia) covering the spectrum from red to SPUMANTE
omaso pocket tripe
ombra literally, "shadow"; small glass of wine; **andar all'ombra** is a Veneto expression meaning "to go out for a glass of wine" or, more broadly, to go on a kind of a pub crawl for wine and small plates of food
ombretta diminutive of OMBRA
ombria = CORVINA (Veneto, Friuli)
ombrina corb, croaker (*Umbrina cirrhosa*)—so named for the sound they make when pulled from the water; related to the CORVINA and BOCCADORO, which may also be marketed as *ombrina*

ombrina stella = LAMPUGA (Lazio)

omento caul

omogeneizzare, *p.p.* **omogeneizzato** to homogenize

onto, in preserved under fat, e.g., goose or duck

opa = BOGA (Calabria, Sicilia, Puglia)

oparelli = BOGA (Sicilia)

oppa = BOGA (Sicilia)

ora, *pl.* **ore** hour; in singular, also means "now"

orario schedule, timetable, hours,

orata gilt-head bream (*Sparus auratus*), a fish of the Sparidae family known in France as *daurade*; its flesh is white and firm, with a delicate flavor

orcio crock, jar; the diminutive, **orciolo**

ordinazione, su by (prior) request

orecchia see ORECCHIO; **orecchie di elefante**, "elephant ears," a fanciful name for a COSTOLETTA MILANESE or anything big and flat

orecchiette *(pl.)* literally, "little ears"; a handmade pasta typical of Puglia made of disks of dough poked with the thumb to form the characteristic shell—or, with a stretch of the imagination, ear-shape

orecchio, *pl.* **orecchie** ear; **orecchia**, the feminine form, is used when the sense is figurative (not hearing organs but things that look like ears or stick out); **orecchio di mare**, = ALIOTIDE

orecchioni literally, "large ears"; ricotta-stuffed TORTELLI; = CAPPELLETTI in some areas of Romagna. The same word also means mumps.

organello = NASELLO (Veneto)

organico organic, but organic food or farming is more likely to be called BIOLOGICO

organolettico *(adj.)* organoleptic; **caratteristiche organolettiche**—taste or sensory characteristics—a favorite multisyllabic expression in contemporary Italian gastronomic discourse

origano oregano (*Origanum vulgare*); the Italian diaspora has successfully sold this herb to the world as the preeminent Italian flavoring agent, but in fact it is used mostly in the southern regions

origine origin; **vino/formaggio di origine** is wine/cheese with "appellation of origin." Many foods are grown or produced only in legally designated areas of origin (**zone di origine**).

orion Piedmontese dialect for the pig's ear (ORECCHIO), also a stew made with it

Oristano the name of a province and its capital city in the Sardegna region, abbreviated OR

ortaggi vegetables, greens; literally, "what comes from the kitchen garden" (ORTO)

ortica nettles (*Urtica dioica, U. urens*); **ortica di mare**, an alga, eaten stewed

orto (kitchen) garden (from the Latin *hortus*), as opposed to a flower or decorative garden, which would be *giardino*

ortolano *(adj.)* "from the garden" or "from the market"—generally indicates the presence of vegetables

ortolano *(n.m.)* (1) gardener, greengrocer; (2) small bird (*Emberiza hortulana*)

Orvieto mostly white DOC wine from upper Lazio and southern Umbria, the area around the famous cathedral town of Orvieto

orzata a drink made of water, malted barley or almonds, and orange water

orzo barley; name for a small pasta used in soup

osei *(pl.)* small game birds (generic)

ossibuchi plural of OSSOBUCO

ossidazione oxidation

osso buco = OSSOBUCO

osso, *pl.* **ossa** bone (of animal); stone (of fruit). Note that a fish bone is called SPINA OR LISCA.

ossobuco braised shin or knuckle of veal, prepared in many regional variations. The connoisseur's delight is the marrow (MIDOLLO), best attacked with a special, elongated spoon or scoop (called an **esattore**, meaning tax collector).

ossolana, all' GNOCCHI *all'Ossolana* are small boiled potatoes cooked in butter and garlic, with a meat sauce and cheese

oste publican, host, innkeeper

osteria inn, tavern; traditionally, a place for a glass of wine and simple food. Most *osterie* today are indistinguishable from

TRATTORIE and RISTORANTI; one of Italy's finest, most expensive restaurants calls itself an *osteria*.

ostia very thin flour-and-water wafer; Communion host

ostrega = OSTRICA (Liguria)

ostrica, *pl.* **ostriche** (1) oyster, any of several species in the Ostreidae family; (2) anything oyster-sized and squishy, such as a chunk of mozzarella used as a stuffing for meat

ota = JOTA

ott. abbreviation of October

ottobre October

ottone brass

ousores sour cherries

ovest west

ovini the whole category of sheep and goat meat

ovino *(adj.)* pertaining to sheep

ovo = UOVO

ovolina small MOZZARELLA ball

ovolo *Amanita caesarea,* a highly prized mushroom of delicate flavor whose orange caps have an ovoid shape. Nowadays it is usually sliced thin and eaten raw, considered too expensive to waste by cooking. At one time, however, *ovoli* were so plentiful that people used to throw them in the FRITTATA.

ovuli *(pl.)* small MOZZARELLA balls

ozzirina = SMERIGLIO (Puglia)

paccheri large RIGATONI used in the Naples area

Pachino, pomodoro di fragrant, sweet winter tomatoes from a limited area in the province of Trapani (Sicilia) that range in size from cherry to medium and enjoy enormous popularity

padano *(adj.)* pertaining to the Po or the Po valley; see GRANA PADANO

padella frying pan, skillet

Padova the name of a province and its capital city in the Veneto region, abbreviated PD

padovano *(adj.)* of Padova (Padua); POLLO *alla padovana* is a chicken FRICASSEA

paesana, alla (1) country-style (generic); (2) translation of the French *paysanne,* meaning containing slices or dices of carrots, turnips, potatoes, and cabbage; RISOTTO and FRITTATA are two dishes that can be served *alla paesana*

paese country, village, region

paeta = TACCHINO

paganeo = GHIOZZO (Veneto)

pagello red sea bream, any of several species of the genus *Pagellus*

pageo = PAGELLO (Liguria)

paglia e fieno literally, "hay and straw"; mixed green and yellow pasta strands

pagliata see PAJATA

paglierino *(adj.)* light straw-colored

pagnotta loaf of bread; crust made of bread dough for baking *en croûte*

pagnottella literally, "little loaf"; a kind of BRIOCHE

pagro sea bream, braize, including *Pagrus auriga* and *Pagro mediterraneo* (*Sparus pagrus*)

pala da forno pizza peel

paiata = PAJATA

paillard steak, pounded thin and grilled; the restaurant name for what is called FETTINA at home

paiolo copper pot, most classically an unlined one with a round bottom for making POLENTA; a **paiolo elettrico** does the tedious stirring by means of a motor-driven blade attached to a cage that holds the bowl over a flame

pajata the duodenum (small intestine) of the milk-fed calf, with its milky contents. Prepared in various ways, it is a classic ingredient of Roman cooking. It is most frequently cooked in tomato sauce and served over RIGATONI. The important thing is that the animal has not yet eaten grass or anything else besides its mother's milk. The same name is also given to cooked veal, beef, goat, or lamb intestine.

palacinche Italianized spelling of PALATSCHINKEN

palaia = SOGLIOLA (Campania, Puglia, Calabria, Sardegna)

palamita syn. TONNETTO

palato palate

palatschinken pancakes

Palermo regional capital of Sicilia as well as the name of a province and its capital city, abbreviated PA

paletta spatula, turner, paddle; **paletta forata**, slotted spatula; **paletta rigaburro**, butter-ball paddle

paletta, coltello a broad knife held vertically for cutting large cheeses

palla, *pl.* **palle** ball; **le palle del nonno** (literally, "grandfather's balls") are a dessert of fried RICOTTA balls

pallette maize GNOCCHI with RAGÙ or tomato-basil sauce; see MATUFFI

pallido *(adj.)* pale (color)

pallino small ball

palma, olio di palm oil (rare)

palmipede *(adj.)* web-footed

palombaccio, *pl.* **palombacci** wood-pigeons

palombo (1) ring-dove; (2) various members of the genus *Mustelus*; dogfish, smooth dog fish, smooth hound

palummeddu = GATTUCCIO (Sicilia)

pampano, pesce = LAMPUGA (Campania)

pampavia dry biscuit similar to Pavesini (as in *pane* + Pavia)

pan de mej sweet cornmeal cake, traditional in Milano for the Festival of San Giorgio (April); the name records that they were originally made from millet (MIGLIO)

pan di miglio = PAN DE MEJ

pan di ramerino a Tuscan cake flavored with rosemary

pan di Spagna sponge cake, used as the basis of countless confections

pan dolce Ligurian bread for Christmas, filled with raisins, candied fruit, and pine nuts

pan meino = PAN DE MEJ

pan molle see PANZANELLA

pan sotto alternate layers of bread and spaghetti baked with a sauce of PANCETTA and sausage

pan speziale = CERTOSINO (1)

panato *(adj.)* breaded

panca, *pl.* **panche** bench

pancarrè, pancarré sliced bread; actually packaged bread used for canapés and sandwiches where the need for regularity of shape takes precedence over flavor and texture; sliced sandwich bread; = PANE IN CASSETTA

pancetta salt-cured, fatty pork belly, the same cut used in the U.S. for bacon; the analogous cut of veal breast can be stuffed and rolled for a classic recipe of Lombardia; **pancetta arrotolata**, the same in rolled form, usually sliced thin in the slicing machine; **pancetta coppata** is wrapped around a piece of COPPA; **pancetta tesa** is in a slab, another name for common pork PANCETTA

pancia belly; in beef and veal, the rear part of the plate, starting about the eighth rib, mostly used for ground meat; most of the belly section in sheep

panciuti = PANSOUTI

pancotto bread soup, literally "cooked bread"; at its simplest it is not much besides bread, olive oil, and cheese, although the possibilities for variation are considerable. It may contain tomato broth, egg, garlic, and herbs; it may also be bread cooked with broth, then layered with vegetables to make a PASTICCIO.

pancrocino see BRUSCHETTA

pandispagna = PAN DI SPAGNA

pandoro type of pound cake. Industrial *pandoro* is widely sold at Christmastime, along with PANETTONE.

pane, pan bread, loaf, but also any number of cakes as well, notably spicy fruitcakes in many local variations, such as the celebrated **panforte** of Siena

pane cotto = PANCOTTO

pane in cassetta = PAN CARRÉ

pane integrale whole-wheat bread

panedda = CASIGIOLU

panella chickpea FOCACCIA of Sicilia

panelle, *pl.* **panelli** fried chickpea pancakes

panerino pudding dessert, a cross between PANNA COTTA and CREMA CARAMELA

panetteria bakery for bread (as opposed to pastry)

panetto loaf, stick; = FOCACCIA

panettone sort of an Italian coffee cake, almost always made commercially and traditionally served at Christmas

panforte (di Siena) (Sienese) cake with almonds and dried fruit

pangrattatto dry bread crumbs

paniccia chickpea FOCACCIA of Liguria

panico foxtail millet, Italian millet (*Setaria italica*)

panificazione bread-making

panificio bakery; but not including sweets, except some biscuits to dunk in the morning coffee

panigacci a type of FOCACCIA; simple batter of flour and water, usually cooked between heated terra-cotta plates, used then as a crêpe or cut up for TESTAROLI; there are local variations in thickness and cooking method (Liguria)

panigazi, panigazzi = PANIGACCI

panino bread roll; properly speaking, for the *panino* to be a sandwich it should be called **imbottito** (filled) or otherwise modified, though few people are so careful. The *panino* is certainly not a special kind of sandwich; the term could not be more generic; cf. TRAMEZZINO.

paninoteca neologism for a place that sells PANINI

paniscia (1) rice cooked with broth, red beans, and SALAME; (2) POLENTA variant made with chickpea flour; (3) a typical dish from around Novara, a type of RISOTTO with beans

panissa = PANICCIA

panna cream; this is dairy cream for cooking (also called **crema di latte**) that can be whipped (MONTATA) or pourable (LIQUIDA) or spoonable (*da* CUCINA); **panna acida** is sour cream; **panna cotta** is a gelatin-thickened, molded cream dessert

pannarone semisoft cheese of Lombardy, GORGONZOLA BIANCO

pannocchia (1) ear of corn (maize), corn-on-the-cob; (2) mantis shrimp, squill; syn. CANOCCHIA

panpepato gingerbread

pansoti a Ligurian pasta stuffed with PREBOGGION

pansouti triangular Ligurian RAVIOLI, usually stuffed with ricotta and PREBOGGION, in thick sauce of oil, walnuts, bread, pine nuts, and curdled milk (SALSA OR SUGO DI NOCI)

pantesco of the island of Pantelleria

panunta = FETTUNTA

panuntella slice of bread to absorb grilling juices; see COSTARELLE

panunto = PANUNTA, BRUSCHETTA

panura dry bread crumbs (Calabria)

panzanella salad made of moistened dry bread, tomato, onion, and other ingredients; in western Toscana can sometimes mean fried strips of dough

panzarotto, *pl.* **panzarotti** something stuffed; turnover, a kind of RAVIOLI

panzerotto = PANZAROTTO

panzetta stuffed veal breast

panzuta = ALBORELLA (Marche)

papacelle sharp peppers shaped like little pumpkins

papalina sprat (*Spratus spratus*); **alla papalina**, see FETTUCCINE

papardele = PAPPARDELLE

paparele = PAPPARDELLE; homemade TAGLIERINE, cooked in broth, possibly with the addition of sautéed chicken giblets; **paparele e bisi** are thin noodles with pea sauce or in broth with peas (Veneto)

paparot spinach soup (Friuli–Venezia Giulia)

paparuccia = CASSAGAI

papassinos, papassinas Sardinian dry sweets
papavero, semi di poppy seeds
papazoi bean soup with barley and corn
papero, papera goose; Paperino, however, is Donald Duck
pappa mush; babyfood; soup thickened with bread
pappa col pomodoro potage of fresh tomatoes and stale bread, usually associated with Toscana but also found in other parts of central Italy
pappagallo = LAMPUGA (Liguria, Abruzzo)
pappardelle broad, flat noodles; like TAGLIATELLE but much wider
pappare, *p.p.* **pappato** to eat with pleasure, devour
pappici = TAGLIOLINI
paprica paprika, rare in Italian cooking
paranza fishing boat, often evoked on menus to emphasize the randomness or freshness of the fish offerings
paranzoli *(pl.)* = ACCIUGA (Marche)
parasàula TRACINA
paraspruzzi, paraschizzi "splatter platter"
Parma the name of a province and its capital city in the Emilia-Romagna region, abbreviated PR. Parma lies at the center of the production zone of some of Italy's most important and most respected traditional food products. It is also a major center in modern food production, processing, and the processing-equipment industry as well as the home of a number of major corporations and site of major food trade fairs.
Parma, prosciutto di a prized type of very sweet PROSCIUTTO CRUDO, aged for at least a year and produced under controlled conditions in a limited geographical area in Emilia-Romagna. The English expression "Parma ham" tends (improperly) to refer to any *prosciutto crudo,* while the specificity of the Italian expression is backed up by law.
parmigiana, alla Parma-style, but not necessarily with Parmesan cheese; what Americans call, for instance, eggplant Parmesan is, in Italian, *una parmigiana di melanzane* or *melanzane alla parmigiana* and does, in fact, have some cheese in the recipe. But *stracotto alla parmigiana* is a kind of pot roast with nary a crumb of

cheese. Grammatically, something made with the cheese should be called *al parmigiano*.

parmigiano *(adj.)* of Parma; see PARMIGIANO REGGIANO

Parmigiano Reggiano as Henry Ford took off his hat every time he saw an Alfa Romeo pass, so we doff ours before a FORMA of this giant among cheeses, made the same way in the same zone of Emilia-Romagna, spanning the provinces of Parma, Reggio, and Modena, for seven hundred years. It is a hard GRANA-type cheese, aged two years, used throughout the world for grating and eating. The word PARMIGIANO is sometimes used loosely to indicate *grana*, but the full name is applied only to (and branded on) the inspected product from the legal production zone.

parpadelle = PAPPARDELLE

parpagliui butterfly-shaped, whole wheat pasta of Liguria

parrozzo breadlike, chocolate-covered almond-paste cake (Abruzzo)

parte, a apart, on the side

partenopeo *(adj.)* Neapolitan

parzemolo = PREZZEMOLO (Veneto)

Pasqua Easter

Pasqua, pizza di see PIZZA AL FORMAGGIO

pasquale *(adj.)* Easter

pasqualina, torta flaky pie filled with greens, cheese, and boiled eggs. The name derives from Pasqua (Easter).

passapatate potato ricer

passare, *p.p.* **passato** to strain, to sieve, to force through a sieve or food mill

passata (di pomodoro) tomato purée (usually sold or conserved in bottles and rather liquid in consistency)

passatelli homemade soup noodles from an extruded mixture of bread crumbs and egg; *alla Romagnola* indicates beef marrow in the pasta

passato *(adj.)* sifted, strained, puréed

passato *(n.)* purée

passaverdure food mill

pa̲ssera flounder, fluke (*Plastichthys flesus*); plaice (*Pleuronectes* *platessa).* The Italian name is also applied to the *Plastichthys flesus* and other members of the family Pleuronectidae.

passero sparrow; **lingue di passero** are a LINGUINE-like pasta

passino strainer, sieve

passira pitrusa = ROMBO CHIODATO (Sicilia)

passito a type of dessert wine, usually sweet or semi-sweet, made with **uva passa**, partially dried grapes usually of aromatic varieties such as MOSCATO and MALVASIA. The hot climate of Sicily and the smaller islands of the Sicilia region (famously Pantelleria) are suitable for outdoor drying of the grapes; indoor *passito* wines of the chillier regions include VIN SANTO, VINO SANTO, AMARONE, and RECIOTO.

passo *(adj.)* = APPASSITO; see UVA

passolone a type of seasoned Sicilian olive

passona = PASSERA (Liguria)

pasta (1) generically dough, pastry, paste (as in anchovy paste), equivalent to the French *pâte* (see individual entries); (2) for cheese, curds, for potatoes, flesh; in other words the body or stuff of a food, especially with an adjective (see, for example, FORMAGGIO A PASTA DURA); (3) short for **pasta alimentare**, the Italian staff of life

pasta asciutta = PASTASCIUTTA

pasta di . . . paste of (something); **pasta d'acciughe**, anchovy paste; **pasta di mandorle**, almond paste or marzipan

pasta e . . . pasta and (something); usually means the pasta and the other ingredient are used together in a very thick soup in approximately equal amounts; **pasta e** FAGIOLI, LENTICCHIE, CECI, or PATATE are common; **pasta e broccoli con brodo di arzilla**, skate broth with broken spaghetti and broccoflower

pasta filata literally "spun paste," from *filare*, to spin (in the sense of wool or thread on a spinning wheel). *Pasta filata* is the category of cheeses that melt and stretch when heated, including MOZZARELLA and PROVOLONE. During manufacture, the curds are heated, then stretched or kneaded, and finally molded into the desired shape. The Italian term is found in English, but the USDA uses the term "plastic curd."

pasta secca dry pasta as opposed to fresh

pastafrolla short pastry dough, pie crust

pastarasa egg, bread crumb, and cheese mixture for grating into soup

pastasciutta "dry" pasta; *pasta asciutta* is properly not "dried" pasta (as opposed to fresh), but pasta that is drained after being boiled (as opposed to being served in broth); not to be confused with PASTA SECCA (Italians themselves sometimes commit this error)

pastella batter; the classic flour and water batter for deep frying

pastetta = PASTELLA

pasticcere = PASTICCIERE

pasticceria (1) pastry, collectively as a food group; (2) pastry shop. **Piccola pasticceria** means an assortment of small cakes and cookies (*petits fours*).

pasticciata *alla pesarese*—braised beef with wine and spices; *pasta pasticciata*—a kind of LASAGNE; see POLENTA PASTICCIATA

pasticciato *(adj.)* with RAGÙ, cheese, and butter

pasticciere (1) as noun, pastry cook; (2) as adjective, pertaining to pastry

pasticcio LASAGNE-like pie of layered pasta; other layered mixtures or pasta casseroles; potentially any mixture of ingredients; *un bel pasticcio* is how Italians say "a fine mess"

pastiera (napoletana) characteristic (Neapolitan) cheesecake with slow-cooked, whole kernels of wheat, orange water, candied fruit, and ricotta in a pastry crust. It is traditional for Easter.

pastificio pasta-making plant

pastina small pasta for soup, as in **pastina in brodo**

pastinaca parsnip

pastissada = PASTIZZADA

pastizzada horse, donkey, or beef marinated in red wine and braised slowly; **pastizzada alla feltrina** is made with beef and calls for vinegar, cinnamon, and cloves (Veneto)

pasto meal; **vino da pasto** is table wine. Many people will claim they do not drink wine **fuori pasto**, meaning they drink only with meals.

pastora, alla shepherd-style; **maccaruni alla pastora** is sauced with either melted lard and fresh ricotta or a mix of fresh and smoked RICOTTA and a pork RAGÙ (Calabria)

pastore sini sharp, semi-hard sheep-milk cheese

pastorizzare to pasteurize; **pastorizzazione**, pasteurization

pastoso *(adj.)* soft, doughy; of wine: very slightly sweet, mellow

patanabò Jerusalem artichoke

pataraccia = LINGUATTOLA

patata, *pl.* **patate** potato; **patata americana** or **dolce** is sweet potato

patatina, *pl.* **patatine** potato chip, but as always diminutives have a life of their own, and *patatine* can also be used for small potatoes or potatoes cut into small pieces.

patella reale = ALIOTIDE

paternostri literally, "Our Fathers"; small pasta for soup; cf. AVEMARIE

pattona a kind of POLENTA; = CASTAGNACCIO (Toscana)

pattumiera kitchen-sized garbage can

patugoli POLENTA made with milk and topped with grated cheese or RICOTTA (Friuli–Venezia Giulia)

patuvanu = BAVOSA (FISH)

pàuru = DENTICE (Sicilia)

pauscatta = LATTERINO (Liguria)

pavese, zuppa alla broth with bread, egg, and cheese (like French onion soup with egg instead of onion); the name suggests its origin in Pavia, but it belongs to the classic repertory

Pavia the name of a province and its capital city in the Lombardia region, abbreviated PV

pavoncella lapwing, plover; peewit

pavone peacock

pazlache = AGNOLOTTI

pazzo *(adj.)* "crazy"; see ACQUA PAZZA

peagallo = GRONGO (Liguria)

pearà, salsa sauce of bread crumbs with butter, cheese, beef marrow, and broth, to go with boiled meats (Veneto)

peccato, *pl.* **peccati** sin; *peccato di gola* is gluttony, one of the Seven Deadly Sins; *che peccato!* means "what a pity"

pecora, *pl.* **pecore** sheep, ewe

pecorara, agnello alla lamb cooked with a little butter and onions, sealed in a special airtight copper pot (Abruzzo)

pecorino sheep-milk cheese (the name comes from *pecora,* sheep); the family is large and varied, but most often its members are on the hard and sharp side. **Pecorino romano** is a hard, sharp cheese and one of the major *pecorino* cheeses; it is produced in a geographically limited zone that includes Lazio and Sardegna, but also parts of Toscana ("romano" as used here is a style and not a geographic designation). It can be grated (and is essential in pasta ALL'AMATRICIANA, *alla* CARBONARA and *alla* GRICIA) or eaten (in Rome, with raw FAVA beans in spring). **Pecorino sardo** is a semisoft, uncooked eating cheese from Sardegna.

pedocchio = COZZA (Veneto, Venezia Giulia)

pei san peire = *pesce* SAN PIETRO (Liguria)

pei spa = *pesce* SPADA (Liguria)

pelapatate vegetable peeler, potato peeler

pelare, *p.p.* **pelato** to peel; the participle can mean peeled, plucked, stripped, or, jokingly, bald

pelati, pomodori peeled, canned tomatoes

pelle skin

pellegrina = CAPASANTA (Venezia Giulia, Toscana, Sicilia)

pellegrini, conchiglia dei = CAPASANTA

pellicano, piè di see PIÈ DI PELLICANO

pellicina, *pl.* **pellicine** thin skin, film, membrane

pellicola film, plastic wrap

pelo, *pl.* **peli** hair, but hair of the head is called CAPELLO

peloso *(adj.)* hairy

penchi thick TAGLIATELLE cut in short pieces

penini = PIEDINI

penna, *pl.* **penne** (1) feather; SELVAGINA *di penna* are game birds; (2) in plural, pasta "quills"; slim, tubular pasta cut on a slant; short, hollow pasta, thinner than rigatoni

penne all'arrabbiata PENNE with tomato, garlic, and PEPERONCINO

pennellare, *p.p.* **pennellato** to paint, to apply with a brush

pennello brush of the kind used for applying, e.g., oil to the skin of a fish to be grilled

pennuli Sicilian cherry tomatoes

pentola (cooking) pot; **pentola a pressione**, pressure cooker; **pentola (per) asparagi**, asparagus cooker

pentolame pots and pans, collectively

pentolone large pot

peocio, *pl.* **peoci** = COZZA (Veneto, Venezia Giulia)

pepaiola a jar or wooden box for keeping ground pepper

pepare, *p.p.* **pepato** to season with pepper

peparola pepper

pepatelle, *pl.* **pepatelli** peppered BISCOTTO of bran, honey, and almonds (Abruzzo)

pepato *(n. and adj.)* "peppered" or "spiced"; Romano-style cheese with peppers; *pan pepato* is gingerbread

pepe black pepper

pepe verde green peppercorns

pepentò chili pepper

peperini small pasta for soup

peperonata stew of sweet peppers, onion, and tomato; the Italian answer to ratatouille

peperoncino hot red pepper

peperone, *pl.* **peperoni** sweet pepper, bell pepper; **peperoni arrostiti** are sweet bell peppers, roasted and skinned. The word has nothing to do with the American pizza sausage called pepperoni.

pepolino = TIMO SERPILLO

peposo slow-cooked beef or veal stew from northern Toscana

pera pear; **pera cotogna** is quince (but so is MELACOTOGNA); **pera di vacca**, = CASIGIOLU

peragallo = GRONGO (Liguria)

perca = *pesce* PERSICO (Piemonte)

perchia = *pesce* PERSICO (Campania); syn. SCIARRANO; **perchia di mari**, = CERNIA (Sicilia)

perciatelli BUCATINI with a slightly larger hole

perdere, *p.p.* **perso** to lose, to leak

perlato *(adj.)* pearled; ORZO *perlato* is pearled barley
pernice partridge
persa Roman dialect for MAGGIORANA
persego = *pesce* PERSICO (Veneto, Friuli–Venezia Giulia)
persichina = CEDRINA
persico trota black bass, large-mouthed bass (*Micropterus salmoides*); the American species introduced into Italian lakes
persico, pesce perch (*Perca fluviatilis*)
persicu, pisci = *pesce* PERSICO (Sardegna)
persuto = PROSCIUTTO
Perugia capital of the Umbria region and the name of a province and its capital city, abbreviated PG
perugina, alla "Perugia-style"; veal scallops with anchovy, chicken liver, prosciutto, and lemon peel; a MINESTRA of strong broth with leek, carrot, celery, and chopped beef
pes zentil = ALBORELLA (Veneto)
pesante *(adj.)* heavy; **pesantezza** is heaviness or the feeling of heaviness
pesantune = SARDINA (Campania)
Pesaro e Urbino the cities of Pesaro and Urbino together form one of the four provinces of the Marche region, abbreviated PS
pesbianc = ALBORELLA (Piemonte)
pesca noce nectarine
pesca, *pl.* **pesche** (1) peach; (2) singular only (*la pesca*), fishing
Pescara the name of a province and its capital in the Abruzzo region, abbreviated PE
pescatore fisherman
pescatrice see RANA PESCATRICE; also the feminine of PESCATORE
pesce, *pl.* **pesci** fish; many names compounded with *pesce* will be found under their second part, e.g., *pesce persico* will be under PERSICO
pesce limone syn. *pesce* SERRA
pesce serra bluefish, mackerel (*Pomatomus saltatrix*)
pesce spada alla pizzaiola swordfish baked with a slice of mozzarella, tomato, and oregano
pescecane shark. There are large sharks in the Mediterranean, and several small species are eaten.

pesche peaches (plural of PESCA)
pescheria (1) fish market; (2) mix of very small fish for frying
pesciolini *(pl.)* small fish, usually fried
peso weight; *peso lordo*, gross weight; *peso netto*, net weight
pessina = ALBORELLA (Lombardia)
pestare, *p.p.* **pestato** to crush in a mortar with a pestle
pestariei pasta from grated bread, used in broth or milk
pestazzuole = ORECCHIETTE
pestello pestle, used with a MORTAIO
pesto anything that has been *pestato*, that is, pounded in a mortar. The word usually, however, refers to **pesto alla genovese**, the Ligurian sauce for pasta of basil and nuts (usually pine nuts, but occasionally walnuts or whatever else is available) with the addition of Parmesan and/or other sharper cheese. **Pesto alla siciliana** (or **trapanese**) adds tomato. In Parma, the word *pesto* used alone means horseburger.
pestun di fave = MARÒ
petramennula *or* **petrafennula** candy-like concoction of boiled honey with orange peel and chopped almonds (Sicilia)
pettine = CANESTRELLO
pettirossi robins (literally, "red-breasts")
petto breast, chest; in beef, the area fore and aft of the front legs, a source of brisket; in swine it is a source of both LARDO and spareribs (SPUNTATURE); in fowl, it is the breast
pettola eggless TAGLIATELLE
peveraccio type of mushroom (*Lactarius piperatus*)
peverada rice baked with chicken livers, anchovies, and pepper
peverel poppy plants
peverone = DATTERO DI MARE (Veneto)
pexe = PESCE (Veneto)
pezza (1) rag, piece of cloth; (2) part of the upper beef sirloin and rump (Rome); part of the rump (Perugia)
pezzagna fish of Vico Equense area that recalls something of the DENTICE or the ORATA; = OMBRINA BOCCADORO
pezzenta spicy sausage of Basilicata
pezzettino little piece

pezzetto, *pl.* **pezzetti** small piece

pezzo, *pl.* **pezzi** piece; *pezzo duro* is a kind of ice cream in Naples

Piacenza the name of a province and its capital in the Emilia-Romagna region, abbreviated PC

piacere, a literally, "at pleasure," meaning any way you like it or as much as you like

piada, piadina, piè flat, unleavened bread and/or the sandwich made with it, typical of Romagna

piano *(adj.)* flat (also soft, as in pianoforte)

pianuzza = PASSERA (Sicilia)

piastra, *pl.* **piastre** the basic meaing of *piastra* is plate or slab. In the kitchen the term applied to practically any hot, flat surface where food is cooked. It can be an oven pan, a stove-top burner, a hotplate, a griddle, or a cast-iron grill pan. **Alla piastra** means cooked on the (steel) griddle; a **piastra di terracotta refrattaria** is a terra-cotta pizza stone.

piattino saucer, small plate

piatto plate, dish, course; eggs *al piatto* are fried; **piatto fondo**, soup plate, also used for pasta in informal service; **piatto piano**, dinner plate; **piatto unico**, one-dish meal—but don't take that too literally. The only one-dish meal in Italy is, just possibly, PIZZA. Otherwise if it's one dish, it's not really a meal.

picaja, picaia = PUNTA DI VITELLO (Emilia-Romagna)

picara pitrosa = RAZZA CHIODATA (Sicilia)

piccagge Ligurian FETTUCCINE; historically, but not always these days, made from chestnut flour, often sauced with PESTO or artichokes; **piccagge matte** are made in part with chestnut flour

piccante *(adj.)* (1) piquant; spicy; (2) *moustillant* (for wine); (3) as substantive, sauce with pickle and vinegar

piccata slices of boneless veal, sautéed—e.g., in butter with parsley and lemon (*al limone*)—or with MARSALA wine, or done in many other versions

picchi pacchiu tomato, basil, and onion sauce for spaghetti or MACCHERONE (Sicilia)

picchiante veal or beef lungs and spleen with herbs and tomatoes.

The ingredients are first pounded (*picchiato*), hence the name. (Toscana)

picchiapò NERVETTI with beans (Lazio)

piccione (1) pigeon; (2) = CAMPANELLO (Rome)

piccola pasticceria *petite patisserie, petits fours*

piccolo *(adj.)* little, small

picecui berries of ROSA CANINA (Friuli)

pici handmade pasta similar to spaghetti (Toscana)

Picolit a dessert wine of Friuli

picula, picula 'd caval chopped horsemeat braised with tomato (Emilia-Romagna)

piè d'asino literally, "donkey's foot"; dog cockle, comb shell (*Pectunculus glycimeris*)

piè di pellicano literally, "pelican's foot"; = MURICE SPINOSO (Veneto)

piede *or* **piè di papavero** poppy greens

piedestallo pedestal, elevated foot, e.g., of a cake plate

piedino, *pl.* **piedini** trotter, foot; veal, pork, sheep, and goat trotters are all eaten, if the latter two only rarely; see ZAMPONE

Piemonte region of northwest Italy (Piedmont in English) whose capital is Torino. In Rome the name evokes the style of mid-nineteenth-century architecture brought by the Savoia monarchs; elsewhere the association is truffles and important red wines.

piemontese *(adj.)* of PIEMONTE, Piedmontese; sometimes indicates the presence of truffles (TARTUFI)

pieno *(adj.)* full

pietanza meat or main dish, second course

pigara petrosa = RAZZA CHIODATA (Puglia)

pigiare, *p.p.* **pigiato** (1) to crush (grapes); (2) to press, to push

pignata in Puglia, octopus cooked in an earthenware jug (PIGNATA). The *pignata* or *pignatta* might also be a copper pot and filled with different items.

pignatiello an earthenware pot and the fish stew cooked therein

pignato grasso = MINESTRA MARITATA

pigneti, la lamb baked with PECORINO, sausage, and potatoes

pignoccata a Sicilian sweet of fried balls of dough mounded in the shape of a pine cone (*pigna*), something like STRUFFOLI

pignolata fried or baked balls of dough, coated half-and-half with chocolate or sugar glaze (Sicilia)

pignoli see PINOLI

pilafi *or* **pilau** Sardinian dish of stewed goat or lamb (like BRODETTATO) served with rice

pilau pilaf

pillottare, *p.p.* **pillottato** to baste

pillotto type of spouted ladle for basting a roast

pilota, risotto alla RISOTTO with sausage and cheese

pimento della Giamaica allspice

pimpinella pimpernel, salad burnet (*Poterium sanguisorba*), an ingredient of the Roman MISTICANZA

pinci = PICI (Siena)

pincinelle homemade VERMICELLI

pinna fan shell, fan mussel (*Pinna nobilis*)

pinna, *pl.* **pinne** fin

pinoccata pine-nut sweet from Perugia

pinocchiata pie or tart with pine nuts

pinolo, *pl.* **pindo** pine nut(s). *Pignolo* is an alternative but unusual spelling except as an adjective to mean super-fussy.

pinoso *(adj.)* piny

Pinot Bianco white grape used in many wines of northeast Italy

Pinot Grigio a dry white wine from northeast Italy

Pinot nero red grape and DOC wine of northeast Italy

pinza, *pl.* **pinze** (1) several kinds of sweets from bread or flour mixtures, dried and candied fruits, and the like (Emilia-Romagna, Trentino, Veneto); (2) tweezer, tongs

pinzimonio seasoned olive oil used for dipping crudités. The name is often used for the entire spread, but correctly it is the condiment only.

pinzin fried strips of pasta from flour, yeast, and broth (Veneto)

piopparello, pioppino small, wild mushroom (*Agrocybe agerita*)

pipistrello literally, "bat"; = ALI

pirofila correctly speaking, this is the proprietary name of a type of flameproof porcelain, but the word can mean any flameproof or ovenproof dish

Pisa the name of a province and its capital city in the Toscana region, abbreviated PS

pisarei tiny GNOCCHI, usually made from flour and bread crumbs, and often sauced with tomato and BORLOTTI beans (FASO), from around Piacenza (Emilia-Romagna)

piscatrice RANA PESCATRICE (Puglia, Calabria, Campania)

pisci dialectal form of PESCE

pisci-cani = PALOMBO (Sicilia)

pisciadela, piscialandrea, pisciarà = PISSADELLA

pisciarada Ligurian potato pie

piscicoltura fish culture, fish farming

piscistoccu = STOCCAFISSO

pisello, *pl.* **piselli** peas; **piselli alla fiorentina**, peas cooked with onion and PROSCIUTTO CRUDO

pissadella type of FOCACCIA or PIZZA from Liguria, topped with tomato, olive, onion, and anchovy or stockfish; a variation of the *pissaladière* of Provence

pistacchio pistachio

pistillo, *pl.* **pistilli** pistil; **pistilli di zafferano** are saffron threads

Pistoia the name of a province and its capital city in the Toscana region, abbreviated PT

pistum sweet and sour gnocchi in pork broth (Friuli)

pitò turkey; **pitò al fieno maggengo** is cloth-wrapped turkey boiled along with spring hay (Piemonte)

pitocca, alla RISOTTO with chicken meat and livers (Lombardia)

pitta = PIZZA or FOCACCIA in Calabria, often ring-shaped; can be filled with MURSEDDU; **pitta maniata** or **serritana** is a stuffed version with egg, cheeses, salami, and spicy peppers; **pitta chicculiata** is with oil, garlic, parsley, and spicy peppers, often other ingredients such as tomato, anchovy, or capers; **alla reggina** is with sheep RICOTTA, parsley, boiled egg, and salami; **calabrese** is with tomato, anchovy, tuna, and capers

pittule, pettole risen fritters served with honey or VIN COTTO, something like Salentine pancakes (Puglia)

piuma, *pl.* **piume** feather

piunca = GATTUCCIO (Venezia Giulia)

piviere plover

pizza the word can be applied to virtually any bread or pie. What the world knows as "pizza" is **pizza napoletana**, even when interpreted elsewhere, such as Rome (where the crust is thin). In the Marche it is a kind of bread-dough pie with egg, cheese, and saffron; *alla pizza*, when referring to pasta, means that it is baked with tomato sauce, MOZZARELLA, and herbs; **pizza ripiena** is an Abruzzese dessert with cream and raspberry jam. Some classic pizzas are **Margherita** (tomato and mozzarella), **quattro stagioni** ("four seasons," with quadrants devoted to various ingredients, including mushrooms, artichokes, anchovies, olives, and PROSCIUTTO) and **napoletana** (mozzarella, tomato, basil, and possibly anchovies and oregano). **Pizza alla Campofranco** is made from a butter- and egg-enriched dough, filled with meat, cheese, and tomato; **pizza rustica** or **salata** is a short pastry dough or bread-dough pie with varied meat and cheese fillings; **pizza al formaggio**, a type of cheese bread; **pizza dolce** can cover many types of sweet pies. A pizza with tomatoes, mozzarella, and anchovies is called *napoletana* in Rome and *romana* in Naples.

pizza al taglio ready-made rectangular pizza cut in slices and sold by weight

pizza al testo FOCACCIA cooked over coals on a TESTO

pizza all'Andrea = PISSADELLA

pizza bianca in Rome, where it is worshiped, an undressed PIZZA AL TAGLIO cooked on both sides, from which portion-sized slices are cut. These may, if desired, be split horizontally and filled, usually with prosciutto and mozzarella, or mortadella or ricotta. In early summer, *pizza bianca con* PROSCIUTTO *e* FICHI is considered the delicacy to end all delicacies.

pizza fritta = FRAPPE

pizzaiola, alla in tomato and olive oil sauce with oregano, usually used for a slice of beef

pizzaiolo pizza cook

pizzelle alla napoletana pieces of fried dough, usually filled with meats, cheese, and anchovies or vegetables, something like a CALZONE

pizzetta, *pl.* **pizzette** tiny pizza used as canapés or bar snack food

pizzicagnolo (*or* **pizzicaiolo**) = SALUMIERE

pizzicare, *p.p.* **pizzicato** to pinch (or, for a violin, to pluck)

pizzicata = PIZZICO

pizzichi tiny, square egg pasta

pizzico pinch

pizzo (1) point, tip; (2) lace

pizzoccheri buckwheat noodles, traditionally served with potato, cabbage, and cheese; a specialty of VALTELLINA in Lombardia

pizzutello a sweet green grape of characteristic pointed shape

placca del forno oven pan, more usually called TEGLIA

plant = GHIOZZO (Venezia Giulia)

platessa see PASSERA (*Pleuronectes platessa*)

plin, dal strictly speaking, the *plin* is an instrument that pinches AGNOLOTTI closed. Practically, the name usually indicates a traditional Piedmontese way of serving *agnolotti*, wrapped in a white linen napkin and without sauce, the better to appreciate the pasta and filling. Today, a simple sauce of butter and sage, or even juice from a roast, may moisten the *agnolotti*.

Plombières fancy dessert named for the city where Cavour met Napoleon III

Po the great river that runs across northern Italy from near Torino to the Adriatic. Its adjective form is **padano**.

pocc any of a number of sauces for POLENTA (Friuli)

pociacche = ORECCHIETTE

pocio, bigoli col BIGOLI with a hearty meat sauce (Veneto)

poco (di) not much; a little; few

podere farm

poenta = POLENTA

polastro = POLLASTRO

polenta porridge, gruel, best known as a thick cornmeal preparation, something like grits, though other grains (and even potatoes) can be used. As a pasta substitute, especially but not exclusively in the northern regions, polenta is infinitely variable. It can be served fresh or left to cool and then sliced and toasted or sautéed. **Polenta grassa** may have sausage; **polenta grigia** or **nera** (gray or black) has buckwheat flour mixed in; **polenta impastoiata** has beans cooked in tomato sauce; **polenta alla lodigiana** is a breaded and fried sandwich of cheese between polenta disks; **polenta in lutto** (mourning) consists of slices of toasted polenta with cuttlefish and a sauce from its black ink; **polenta mòncoi** is made with water, milk, and bits of SPECK and cheese; **polenta taragna** is usually made with a mixture of corn and buckwheat flours and enriched with butter and cheese; **polenta concia**, **cunscia**, or **consa** is often like the **taragna**, but with garlic and (sometimes) TOMA or FONTINA cheese; **polenta rustida** is sliced and fried with butter and onions, after which cheese and milk are added; **polenta pasticciata** is baked with meat RAGÙ, butter, and cheese (and other variations); **polenta de siouri** is sliced and heated with meat sauce, cheese, and truffles; **polenta smalzada** is a Trentino dish of buckwheat (GRANO SARACENO) with white wine, anchovy, and grated cheese. **Polenta con le spuntature** puts spare ribs (and possibly sausage) on top in parts of Lazio and Abruzzo. Bergamo makes a sweetened polenta cake with spices called **polenta dolce**. The **polenta d'Ivrea** is also a dessert, with butter, sugar, and vanilla.

polenta bianca made with white maize

polentina soft, baked polenta with cheese

polietilene polyethylene

polipo = POLPO

pollame poultry

pollanca young turkey

pollastra = POLLO

pollastrello young chicken

pollastro pullet

pollin turkey; **pollin cont el pien** is a Milanese preparation of turkey stuffed with sausage, liver, and chestnuts

pollo chicken

pollo a busto roasting chicken, cleaned, sans head, sans neck, sans feet, sans everything (cf. *As You Like It*, II, ii, 139)

pollo sfilato whole chicken with head and feet still attached, and only the intestinal cavity cleaned

polmoncino diminutive of POLMONE

polmone lung; **polmoncino**, the lung of something small

polpa (1) lean, boneless veal, beef, or pork; (2) pulp, or flesh of a fruit; (3) potentially anything else that can be loosely considered a pulp. **Polpa di granchio** is crabmeat; **polpa di pomodoro** is peeled, seeded tomatoes

polpa di spalla part of the beef biceps and chest muscle used mostly for pot roast and braising

polpett Milanese dialect for INVOLTINI

polpetta, *pl.* **polpette** meatball(s); also meatless "meatballs" of other ingredients

polpettina the diminutive of POLPETTA

polpettone meatloaf, often cooked in a pot rather than baked

polpo *Octopus vulgaris* and other members of the genus *Octopus*, sometimes called **polpo verace** (the true octopus), identifiable by a double row of suckers on its eight legs; see MOSCARDINO

polpo bianco curled octopus (*Ozaena* or *Eledone cirrhosa*)

polposità pulpyness

polposo *(adj.)* pulpy

polsonetto little copper saucepan for ZABAIONE or egg-based sauces

poltiglia paste, pulp, mush; **poltiglia bordolese**, Bordeaux mixture

polvere powder, dust

pomidoro variant spelling of POMODORO, sometimes construed as a plural

pommarola a tomato sauce of Naples

pomodori secchi see POMODORO

pomodorino, *pl.* **pomodorini** the diminutive of POMODORO; any small tomato; sun-dried tomato

pomodoro, *p.p.* **pomodori** tomato. For eating raw, fairly immature tomatoes are generally preferred, while for sauces, the riper the better. **Pomodori pelati** are red, pear-shaped tomatoes (plum tomatoes) preserved in cans or jars; the best variety is considered the SAN MARZANO. Note that tomato varieties are carefully matched to the dishes they are used in (though opinions vary on which varieties to use). **Pomodoro col riso**, tomato with rice; a large tomato filled with rice and baked, with potatoes on the side, and usually eaten, in summer as a PRIMO PIATTO. **Pomodori**, or **pomodoretti, secchi**, sun-dried tomatoes, not nearly as widespread in Italy as abroad.

pompelmo grapefruit

pompilo = TONNO COMUNE (Venezia Giulia)

ponce punch

pontina, alla in the style of the Pontina, or Pontine (Pomptine) Marsh, reclaimed land in southern Lazio

popone = MELONE

porcacchia, porcaccia = PORTULACA

porceddu Sardinian spit-roasted PORCHETTO

porcellana (1) porcelain; (2) = PORTULACA

porcellino suckling pig, diminutive of PORCELLO

porcello young hog

porcetto = PORCHETTO

porchetta the whole hog, roasted, and not to be confused with any of the many words that mean suckling pig. The hog is boned, flavored inside with salt, garlic, and wild fennel and stuffed with its liver, heart, and lungs, cut into pieces, then sewn and roasted whole. It is usually eaten sliced and cold, in sandwiches sold at special stands. *Porchetta di* Ariccia, a town south of Rome, is considered the best, though the preparation actually originated in Umbria. Pork chops and other items are sometimes prepared **porchettata** or **in porchetta** (i.e., *porchetta*-style).

porchetto roast suckling pig, diminutive of PORCO

porcinello a mushroom (*Leccinum*)

porcino, *pl.* **porcini** a wild fungus, boletus, for which most of Italy goes mad annually. Depending upon weather, the season for fresh *porcini* begins as early as spring, extending into late fall. Frozen or dried *porcini* are used in the off season. There are four basic types:

porcino comune (*Boletus edulis*); **porcino nero** (*B. aereus*); **porcino reticolato** (*B. reticulatus*); **dal gambo rossaceo** (*B. pinicola*).

porco pig; used more to describe the man than the animal, which is more usually MAIALE

Pordenone the name of a province and its capital city in the Friuli–Venezia Giulia region, abbreviated PD, in Friuli

porpo = POLPO

porraccio literally, "nasty leek"; = AGLIO D'ORIENTE

porrata leek pie

porre, *p.p.* **posto** to put, to place (irregular verb)

porro, *pl.* **porri** leek(s); in other contexts, "warts"—so be careful when you ask if someone has any *porri*

portafogli "wallets"; pockets cut in meat (e.g., chicken breasts) to be stuffed

portainnesto rootstock

portaposate cutlery holder

portare a cottura finish cooking

portasapone soapdish

portata course (of a meal); (a tray, a spoon) **da portata** is anything meant for serving

portauovo egg cup

porto port (wine); seaport

portoghese *(adj.)* Portuguese; **latte alla portoghese** is a kind of crème caramel

portulaca purslane (*Portulaca oleracea*) is a leaf used in salads as a potherb and as a vegetable

porzione serving; portion

posate *(pl.)* flatware

posilippo, alla with seafood and tomato sauce

posteriore (adj.) posterior

potabile potable, drinkable

potacchio, in braised with garlic, hot pepper, white wine, and rosemary, sometimes also tomato

potaggio = POTACCHIO

potenza power

Potenza regional capital of Basilicata and the name of a province and its capital city, abbreviated PZ

poutina young SARDINA (Liguria)
povero *(adj.)* poor; **la cucina povera** is poor folk's food, often using stale bread and less-valuable animal parts
pralina praline, filled candy
pranzo lunch, dinner. From the Latin *prandium,* for purists it refers to the evening meal but is more commonly used for lunch. An official meal is always called *pranzo* regardless of the time of day.
prataiolo, *pl.* **prataioli** field mushrooms, CHAMPIGNONS (*Agaricus campestris, A. macrosporus*)
prato meadow
Prato the name of a province and its capital city in the Toscana region, abbreviated PO
pratolino, pratella = PRATAIOLO
preboggion mix of wild herbs typical of Liguria and used in FRITTATE and soups
precchia di sciumi = *pesce* PERSICO (Sicilia)
precotto *(adj.)* precooked
pregiato *(adj.)* valuable, costly
pregio, di valuable, worthy, excellent
prelibatezza delicacy
premere, *p.p.* **premuto** to press
prendere, *p.p.* **preso** to take
prenotare, *p.p.* **prenotato** to reserve
prenotazione reservation; **fare una prenotazione**, to make a reservation
preparare, *p.p.* **preparato** to prepare, prepared
preparato *(n.)* preparation
presame = CAGLIO
prescinsoea Ligurian fresh curd
presina pot holder
pressa (vino di) press (wine of)
pressione pressure; **pentola a pressione**, pressure cooker
prete priest; **budino di prete**, = ROSADA
prete, pesce = NASELLO (Veneto); stargazer, *Uranoscopus scaber* (the fish)
prezzemolo flat-leafed parsley, usually *Petroselinum crispum*
prezzo price

prima (*adv.*) before
primavera spring (season); springtime-style
primaverile (*adj.*) of spring
primi see PRIMO
primitivo red grape variety of southern Italy
primizie (*n. pl.*) first fruits or vegetables of the season
primo (*adj.*) first, early; **primo piatto**, the first course of the meal (not counting the antipasto), the one consisting of pasta, rice, or soup (often shortened to **primo**)
primosale lightly salted, fresh sheep cheese
probusti garlic-flavored veal and pork sausage of Rovereto (Trentino)
prodotto (*n.m.*) product
produrre, *p.p.* **prodotto** to produce; produced; **prodotto e imbottigliato**—"produced and bottled"—on a bottle of olive oil, for example, signifies that the olives were grown where the oil was bottled
produttore (*n.m.*), **produttrice** (*n.f.*) producer
produzione production; **produzione propria**, literally, "own production," i.e., homemade, but sometimes in the same way a paint-by-numbers kit produces a piece of original art
profiterole profiterole
profumare, *p.p.* **profumato** to flavor, aromatize; literally, "to perfume." For wine, the participle means aromatic.
profumo (*n.*) fragrance, aroma, scent, flavor, smell, bouquet (of wine); also perfume
pronto (*adj.*) ready, ready-made
propellente propellent
proposta bill of fare; suggestions
proprio (*adj.*) (one's) own
prosciutto ham, any ham, meaning, literally, "dried out." **Prosciutto crudo**, "raw ham," is what is called prosciutto in the U.S. and PARMA ham in Britain, which is air- and salt-cured, occasionally smoked (see SAURIS, SPECK); see also SAN DANIELE. **Prosciutto cotto** (cooked ham) is usually boiled but can be **al forno**, baked. Note that the English term "Parma ham" is thrown around rather loosely and does not assure that the ham

comes from the legal *prosciutto di Parma* zone. The prosciutto method can be used to make similar products from other animals, e.g., CINGHIALE, LEPRE, OCA.

prosciutto bianco = LARDO, a modern euphemism

prosciutto di montagna general term for nonspecific artisanal prosciutto, which tends to be saltier than Parma, San Daniele, and other prized hams, and is often sliced by hand. It is delicious on the saltless breads of central Italy.

Prosecco white wine grape and the DOC wine made from it, which is famously, but not always, sparkling

proteine protein

protetto *(adj.)* protected (a person so designated is a protégé)

provare, *p.p.* **provato** to try, to test

provatura a soft, fresh white cheese from cow or buffalo milk, similar to MOZZARELLA; little MOZZARELLA balls

provincia (1) second-largest political division (after REGIONE) of modern Italy; (2) the sticks; (3) with capital "P," Provence. **In provincia di** means "in the province of," referring to a specific place, while **in provincia** alone means something like in the sticks or in the countryside. Cf. REGIONE.

provinciale, alla *provençal;* usually indicates a FRICASSEA

provola fresh buffalo-milk cheese similar to SCAMORZA

provolone smooth, mellow, light-colored cheese in many versions

prugna plum (= SUSINA) or prune

pruppusiccia = SEPPIA

puddica type of (usually) stuffed pizza (Puglia)

puddicineddu = *pesce* SPADA (Sicilia)

puddighinos roasted stuffed young birds (Sardegna)

Puglia the modern region of Puglia, extending from the spur to the heel of the boot. Although Apulia is sometimes seen in English, the usage is archaic, as is the term le Puglie.

pugliese *(adj.)* Pugliese

pugno handful, fistful

puina RICOTTA (Toscana); smoked RICOTTA (Veneto); ROBIOLA-type cheese of goat and sheep milk

pulcino young chicken

puledro, puledra colt, filly
puleggio = MENTUCCIA, but not in Rome
pulire, *p.p.* **pulito** to clean, to trim
pulito clean, pure
pulizia cleanliness, purity
pullastrella young ANGUILLA (Campania)
puloti alla vercellese small birds barded with PANCETTA and done AL TEGAME (Piemonte)
pumaroru tomato
pumate tomatoes; sun-dried tomatoes
pungitopo a wild asparagus
Punt e Mes proprietary name of an aperitif
punta, *pl.* **punte** point, tip; tine (of a fork); **punta di vitello**, veal breast (see CIMA); cf. PUNTO
punta di mezzo breast of veal, most likely for braising or stew
punta di petto the fore part of beef or veal breast
puntarelle *(pl.)* the Roman name for CICORIA CATALOGNA, an agreeably bitter crunchy green vegetable available only in the cooler months. In Rome, its central buds are cut painstakingly into strips, which are soaked in cold water to curl them, and served raw *con la salsa*, with a sauce of anchovy and garlic mashed together in a mortar with olive oil, and sometimes vinegar. The slicing of *puntarelle* in just the right way is a dying art, as increasingly they are cut mechanically.
puntell pork chop; **risotto col puntel** is the Mantovan version of RISOTTO ALLA PILOTA served with grilled pork chop
puntine *(pl.)* small pasta for soup
pupidde *(pl.)* small MENOLA in Puglia; **pupidde alla gallipolina** are fried, then boiled in a solution of vinegar with mint, garlic, and saffron and left to cool in the marinade
purciddata = BUCCELLATO (Sicilia)
purè, purea puréed, mashed; used by itself it is nearly always shorthand for PURÈ DI PATATE or "mashed potatoes"
purea see PURÈ
purgatorio, in/al literally, "purgatory"; POLPI or POLIPI (octopus) prepared with oil, tomato, garlic, parsley, and peppers

purpetti = POLPETTI; see CRESPEDDI

purpo = POLPO

purtuisa, coniglio a rabbit fried with a great many ingredients: celery, onions, eggplant, potato, herbs, vinegar, and sugar, with mint, basil, and garlic added at the end (Sicilia)

puttanesca, spaghetti alla literally, "whore's style"; the quick-cooked tomato sauce contains black olives, capers, anchovies, and red peppers

puzza nasty smell; **puzzare**, to stink

puzzone "big stinker"; cheese of Trentino with an oily crust, slightly fermented; it is used for FONDUTA and as a filling in RAVIOLI

p.v. *prezzi vari*, varying prices, or *pezzi vari*, different sized pieces

≈ Q ≈

q.b. (quanto basta) as needed, to taste; used in recipes. Literally "as much as is enough," as in "add enough salt" (then cook it till it's done).

quadaro fish soup of Crotone (Calabria)

quadaruni = MURENA (Sicilia)

quadrettare to turn food on a grill so that the grid imprints its line on the food in little squares (QUADRETTI)

quadretti small, square egg pasta usually used in broth

quadrucci = QUADRETTI

quadruplicare to quadruple

quagghia = QUAGLIA (Sicilia)

quagghiariedde the odds of running across this Pugliese dish are slim to none, but its name (and composition) was too good to leave out. It is a mixture of mutton innards, SCAMORZA cheese, eggs, rucola, and salami, enclosed in the peritoneal sac of a pig and then in a boned breast of mutton and then baked. See CAZZMAR.

quaglia, *pl.* **quaglie** (1) quail (*Coturnix coturnix*); (2) Sicilian snack of fried eggplant in a bun; (3) potentially any food the approximate size and shape of a very small quail. **Quaglie di vitello** are veal birds. The diminutive is **quaglietta**.

quaglio = CAGLIO; **quaglio dolce** is sweetened curdled milk with lemon (Sardegna)

quaietta veal cutlet stuffed with chopped, roasted meat

qualità, *(sing. and pl.)* quality; but also "type" ("tre qualità di broccoli" implies variety, in the case, not value judgment)

quaquà just what it sounds like—wild duck—from the Venetian lagoon, often used in pasta sauce or oven roasted with sage and herbs

Quaresima Lent, in the liturgical calendar, the forty days before Easter, a period of penitence and meatless meals

quaresimale *(adj.)* (1) Lenten; (2) as substantive, = MARITOZZO; (3) potentially anything else eaten in Lent

quartino quarter-liter carafe

quartiretto roast, vegetable-stuffed kid

quartirolo cheese similar to Taleggio, made in autumn

quarto quarter. For wine, frequently used to mean a quarter-liter (also called by the dimunitive, QUARTINO). For meat, the **quinto quarto**, or "fifth quarter," means the innards, tail, and other less-valued parts left over after the animal has been quartered.

quasi almost

quattro four

quattro stagioni, pizza alle "four seasons"; pizza topped in each of four sectors with a different ingredient (ham and artichoke figure frequently, but there is no categorical list)

quinto fifth; for *quinto quarto,* see QUARTO

R

rabarbaro rhubarb
raccogliere, *p.p.* **raccolto** to gather, to harvest
raccolta *(n.)* harvest, picking
raddoppiare, *p.p.* **raddoppiato** to double
radicchio any of several species of chicory (genus *Cichorium*). Some are red, some green, so further specification is needed, though red (*Cichorium endivia*) is expected. Some, such as the Chioggia and Verona varieties, are eaten raw, while the varieties of RADICCHIO DI TREVISO are usually cooked.
radicchio di Treviso family of prized red chicories (*Cichorium intybus*) from the province of TREVISO. Three types have IGP certification: **Rosso Precoce** (early red), a long-leafed loose head of red leaves with white ribs; **Rosso Tardivo** (late red), with feathery inward-curling red leaves with white ribs and a woody root; **Castelfranco Variegato** (also called **Castellano**), a beautiful white head with red variegations.
radice, *pl.* **radici** root; sometimes also radish
radichetta, *pl.* **radichette** rootlet
rafano horseradish (*Raphanus raphanistrum*); cf. CREN
raffermo *(adj.)* stale, day-old (of bread)
raffioli = RAVIOLI
raffiuoli *or* **raffioli a cassata** disks of pasta MARGHERITA enclosing a filling of sweetened ricotta and candied citron (Campania)
raffreddare, *p.p.* **raffreddato** to chill, to cool (*raffreddarsi*, however, is to catch a cold)
raggiungere, *p.p.* **raggiunto** to reach, to arrive, to meet

ragnetti *(pl.)* a bread of Ferrara (Emilia-Romagna)

ragno literally, "spider"; (1) = SPIGOLA (Toscana); TRACINA (Veneto); (2) a type of wire ladle used for deep frying

ragù meat sauce for pasta or polenta; the southern regions tend to cook the meat in one piece, the northern, led by Emilia-Romagna, use finely chopped meat and less tomato. The use of the term is often extended to other hearty sauces, but this is not quite correct.

Ragusa the name of a province and its capital city in the Sicilia region, abbreviated RG

ragusano, quattro facce cheese from Ragusa, Sicilia, named for its brick-like shape ("four faces"). It is made from the milk of the Sicilian *modicana* breed of cow and seasoned from four to twelve months.

raja = RAZZA; **raja pitrusa**, = RAZZA CHIODATA (Calabria)

ramaiolo ladle

Ramandolo Friulian dessert wine

rambasicci stuffed cabbage rolls of Trieste

rame copper

ramerino = ROSMARINO

ramolaccio horseradish

rana pescatrice angler, anglerfish, monkfish, frog-fish (*Lophius piscatorius*); generally only the tail is eaten on its own (CODA DI ROSPO), though the rest of the fish may find its way into a ZUPPA DI PESCE. There is no connection to frogs.

rana, *pl.* **rane** frog

rancetto, spaghetti col an Umbrian variation on the classic AMATRICIANA using marjoram

rancio = SCAMPO (Abruzzo)

rancitiello = GRANCHIO (Puglia, Campania)

ranetta = RENETTA

rangosta = ARAGOSTA (Toscana)

ranocchio the green frog

rapa turnip; also used as an epithet for someone who seems to have a turnip for a brain

rapanello = RAVANELLO

rapata soup with onion, RAPA, and parsley (Lombardia)
rape amare = CIME DI RAPA
raperonzolo rampion, small wild turnip-like root (*Campanula rapunculus*)
rapini = CIME DI RAPA
raponzolo = RAPERONZOLO
rapprendersi to "take," stiffen, cook, become firm, as of eggs in CARBONARA
rasagnole TAGLIOLINI-style egg pasta, called after a Marchigiano name for a rolling pin
rascatelli = RASCATIEDDI
rascatieddi CAVATELLI made partly with potato (Calabria)
raschera cylindrical cow-milk table cheese, with small amount of sheep or goat milk, from around Cuneo in Piemonte
raso *(adj.)* level (as in tablespoonful)
rasojas marinas = CANNOLICCHIO
raspadura GRANA cheese from Lodi
raspo grape stalks still in a bunch
rassa = RAZZA; **rassa spinusa**, = RAZZA CHIODATA (Liguria)
rastrello scolaspaghetti "rake" for draining spaghetti
rastremato *(adj.)* tapering
ratafià black cherry liqueur
ratatuia ratatouille, though not necessarily prepared according to Provençal tradition
rattin, ratto = CICERELLO (Liguria)
ravanello radish
raveggiolo a goat- or sheep- (or sometimes cow-) milk cheese of central Italy, also known as GIUNCATA
Ravenna famous for its Late Antique mosaics, a province and its capital city in the Emilia-Romagna region, abbreviated RA. On the Adriatic, it is in the Romagna part of the region.
raviole sweet baked RAVIOLI
raviolo, *p.p.* **ravioli** the basic small stuffed pasta—savory or sweet—that comes in innumerable variations, but the most traditional filling is ricotta, with or without greens; cf. AGNOLOTTI
ravizzone, olio di rapeseed oil

ravosta = ARAGOSTA (Puglia, Campania)
ravuschella = BAVOSA
razza chiodata ray, skate, thornback ray, roker, maiden ray (*Raja clavata*)
razze (*f. sing.*) = ANATRA (Friuli)
reale (*adj.*) "royal," often with cream or custard; **pasta reale**, = MARZAPANE; **consomme reale** is broth with pastry puffs or light dumplings
reale (*n.*) beef shoulder blade chops and part of the chuck short ribs, also called TAGLIO REALE; typically used for BOLLITO, braising and stewing; in veal, this cut is part of the upper shoulder
reblec a fresh cheese
reblochon cylindrical cow-milk cheese of Piemonte and Valle d'Aosta, something like FONTINA
recchie, recchietelle = ORECCHIETTE
Recioto a dessert wine from the Veneto
refe thread
Refosco red wine and grape from Friuli
refrigerare, *p.p.* **refrigerato** to refrigerate
reggenza brown sauce from demi-glace base
reggina, alici alla same as ALICI ALLA FUSCALDESE but with green olives, capers, garlic, parsley, and black pepper (Calabria)
Reggio di Calabria ancient Rhegium, regional capital of Calabria and the name of a province and its capital city
Reggio nell'Emilia the name of a province and its capital city in the Emilia-Romagna region, abbreviated RE
regina literally "queen"; type of grape and plum (Regina Claudia); REGINA IN PORCHETTA is spit-roasted carp stuffed with herbs
regina scura = CARPA (Toscana, Umbria)
reginelle (*pl.*) pasta strips with curly edges
regionale (*adj.*) regional, from the region
regione, *pl.* **regioni** region, usually indicating the specific political regions of Italy, not usually used generically. The twenty regions are usually listed in a canonical geographical order,

roughly from north to south and east to west rather than in alphabetical order: PIEMONTE, VALLE D'AOSTA, LIGURIA, LOMBARDIA, TRENTINO–ALTO ADIGE, VENETO, FRIULI–VENEZIA GIULIA, EMILIA-ROMAGNA, TOSCANA, UMBRIA, MARCHE, LAZIO, ABRUZZO, MOLISE, CAMPANIA, PUGLIA, BASILICATA, CALABRIA, SICILIA, SARDEGNA.

rehaminà, indivia a curly-endive soup (a Roman-Jewish dish)

reina = CARPA (Toscana, Umbria, Veneto)

renetta rennet apple

renga = ARINGA (Veneto)

rentice = DENTICE (Campania)

rentrocele, lu wonderfully elaborate, celebratory *ragù* and pasta dish of Abruzzo. With a day or two's notice, some restaurants will make it for you. The *rentrocelle* is a toothed wheel for cutting the pasta into square strands.

resinoso *(adj.)* resinous

restare, *p.p.* **restato** to remain

resto remainder, change (for money)

restringere, *p.p.* **ristretto** literally, "to restrict"; to reduce, to concentrate

rete *(n. sing.)* caul, net, mesh; **rete di maiale**, pork caul fat, is used with pork liver. Butchers will often wrap boneless roasts in an elasticized mesh they call *la rete*.

reticolo honeycomb tripe

retina (per la spesa) mesh (shopping) bag

retrogusto aftertaste

rhum rum

rianata type of pizza made with PECORINO and oregano, from Trapani (Sicilia)

ribes red or black currants (*Ribes rubrum*)

ribollita bread-thickened cabbage soup Toscana

ricavare, *p.p.* **ricavato** recipes use the word to mean obtain or make, as in, "*ricavare* fifty little cookies from that one heap of dough"

riccetta = INDIVIA SELVATICA

ricchielle = ORECCHIETTE

ricciarelli Sienese almond cookies, usually covered with powdered sugar

riccio *(adj.)* curly; **cavolo riccio** is kale

riccio, *pl.* **ricci** literally, "curl" or "curls"; **ricci di mare** are sea urchins (which are eaten raw or lightly cooked with oil, garlic, and white wine and then tossed with pasta)

ricciola amberjack, yellowtail (*Seriola dumerili*); also called SERIOLA

ricciolina = INDIVIA RICCIA

ricciolino "curly" tripe from the first part of the cow or veal intestine, used in Rome for PAJATA and in Milano for BUSECCA

ricciolo, *pl.* **riccioli** curl, roll

ricercato *(adj.)* special, unusual, hard to find, *recherché*

ricetta, *pl.* **ricette** (1) recipe; (2) batch: in the sense of baking two *ricette* of cookies. The whole Italian approach to recipes is different from the so-called Anglo-Saxon, in that it is implied that too much instruction suggests lack of faith in the cook. Quantities and temperatures seem maddeningly vague—until you throw yourself into the spirit of the thing and start to get the hang of it. Even so, it is annoying to buy a box of rice or frozen food and read only "use your usual recipe" in place of manufacturer's instructions. The tendency, however, is toward more detail as fewer and fewer people have expert grandmothers to teach them.

richiesta *(adv.)* (by) request

ricolmo *(adj.)* full to overflowing, full to the brim

ricoprire, *p.p.* **ricoperto** to cover, covered

ricotta a soft, very fresh cow or sheep LATTICINO obtained from the whey as a byproduct of cheesemaking; the basic stuff is subjected to various types of handling—including aging—and is both eaten and used as an ingredient in every sort of dish from pasta sauces to sweets. **Ricotta romana** is properly made of sheep milk and very soft, while in Calabria it is made from milk rather than whey and can be baked (**infornata**), salted (**salata**), or smoked (**affumicata**).

ricotta salata ricotta that has hardened and can be grated

ricotta schianta *or* **'scante** extremely strong, sharp fermented RICOTTA

ridurre, *p.p.* **ridotto** to reduce
riduzione reduction
riebl whole-wheat fritters (Trentino-Alto Adige)
riempire, *p.p.* **riempito** to fill
Rieti the name of a province and its capital city in the Lazio region, abbreviated RI, located in the Sabine country northwest of Rome
rifare, *p.p.* **rifatto** redone, remade; name given to a dish that might, e.g., use meat that is fried and then braised
riflesso, *pl.* **riflessi** reflection, highlight
rifreddo a meat terrine (Emilia-Romagna)
riga, *pl.* **righe** line, row
rigaglie *(pl.)* giblets. These include the liver, heart, crest, stomach, gizzard (called *ventriglio* or *durello*), and testicles or unlaid eggs, as the case may be
riganella = ORIGANO
rìganu = ORIGANO
rigatino lean PANCETTA of Toscana
rigato *(adj.)* with ridges, grooves; often applied to pasta (e.g., *penne rigate*)
rigatoni short, hollow pasta with a large hole in the middle. The name comes from the ridges around the sides.
rigirato *(adj.)* reheated
rimbulu = ROMBO CHIODATO (Sardegna)
rimescolare, *p.p.* **rimescolato** to mix or stir well; to mix again
rimestare, *pp.* **rimestato** to stir, stir up, stir again, toss, shake, or put back in the pan; see STRASCINARE, RIPASSARE
rimettere, *p.p.* **rimesso** to put back
Rimini ancient Ariminum is the hometown of Federico Fellini, and a province and its capital city in the Emilia-Romagna region, abbreviated RN. At the terminus of the ancient Via Aemilia, it is today famous as a beach resort.
rinforzo, insalata di salad of cauliflower, olives, pickled vegetables, anchovy, and other ingredients; the name means "reinforcement" (South)
rinfusa, alla "confused"; *sedani alla rinfusa* are stewed celery
rintici = DENTICE (Sicilia)

rintrocilo type of fluted, square TAGLIOLINI; see RENTROCELE

rinvenire, *p.p.* **rinvenuto** literally, "to recover" or "come to"; used of wilted salad which has got a second wind, or for plumping raisins in water

ripassare (in padella) to sauté (in a skillet) after cooking; in the case of green vegetables it means to sauté, after boiling, in olive oil, garlic, and PEPERONCINO. It is also standard treatment for leftover pasta with its sauce.

ripassiellu = MAIALINO (Calabria)

ripieno *(adj.)* stuffed, filled; as a noun, stuffing, filling

riportare, *p.p.* **riportato** to carry back, to report

riposare, *p.p.* **risposato** to rest; **far(e) riposare**, to let rest, leave to rest

riposo rest; a restaurant's weekly closing day is the *giorno di riposo*

riprendere, *p.p.* **ripreso** to resume, to take up (again)

riquagghiu spaghetti or macaroni with egg, parsley, and cheese

ris e riondele rice cooked with mallow leaves and milk (Piemonte)

risaia, *pl.* **risaie** rice field, rice paddy

riscaldare, *p.p.* **riscaldato** to heat; heated up

riserva reserve; indicates that a wine has been aged longer than usual; *riserva speciale* means longer yet

riservare, *p.p.* **riservato** to reserve

risetto POLPETTE of newborn ALICI OR SARDE (Marche)

risi e bisi rice and peas in thick soup (Veneto)

riso (1) rice, the grain (*Oryza sativa*); Italian rice comes in four classifications based on grain length, in decreasing order: **superfino** (which includes **Arborio** and **Canaroli**), **fino**, **semifino**, and **comune**, or **originario**. (2) Cooked rice with any number of condiments, not synonymous with RISOTTO, which is a very specific preparation; **riso arrosto** is a Milanese dish of rice with veal, Parmesan cheese, and peas or artichokes, finished in the oven.

riso indiano = RISO SELVATICO

riso selvatico wild rice, a grain, not a rice; also called **riso degli indiani**

riso, insalata di rice salad, a summer buffet standby. It usually contains small pickled vegetables as well as small pieces of meat or fish. **Insalata di riso alla novarese** is baked rice layered with white truffle in sauce of oil, lemon, anchovies, parsley, and garlic.

risolata RISOTTO with Romaine lettuce

risone unhulled, unpolished rice

risoni tiny rice-shaped pasta for use in soups

risotto rice, usually but not always ARBORIO, slow-cooked in broth to a creamy consistency and usually enriched with meat, vegetables, cheese, and other flavorings. *Superfino* rice (which includes *Arborio* and *Canaroli*) is often the first choice for making *risotto*, based on the longer cooking time required for it to become *al* DENTE. In some areas and recipes, however, a *semifino* such as *Vialone nano* is preferred. See RISO. **Risotto alla milanese** is cooked with butter, Parmesan, onion, beef marrow, and saffron; **alla pilota** with sausage and cheese; **al salto** uses half-cooked *risotto alla milanese* and sautés it in a little butter until crisp.

ristorante restaurant. A distinction is usually made between the more casual TRATTORIA and the *ristorante*, but the differences can be subtle. A true *trattoria* (as opposed to a de facto *ristorante* that is simply using the original name of *trattoria* the premises have always had) is usually family-run and has a limited menu of local specialities. The "family" today may be a group of friends who thought it would be amusing to open a restaurant. In any case, it should serve traditional dishes of its locality or the owner's hometown, but (*O tempora! O mores!*) may well offer *penne al salmone* and antipasti purchased ready-made at wholesale markets. The wise diner will simply ignore such aberrations. The *ristorante* as a category has no upper limit (though an amusing affectation at the very top is to take the title of OSTERIA); at its lowest rung it is much like a *trattoria*. If you want to say an eating place is not fancy but neither is it a hole-in-the-wall, you can shrug and say that it's a *ristorante*.

ristoratore restaurateur

ristretto *(adj.)* concentrated; consommé; **caffe ristretto** is made with less water than usual

ritagliare, *p.p.* **ritagliato** to cut, cut again, to cut out

ritaglio, *pl.* **ritagli** scraps, odd bits, trimmings

ritocchino a retouch, a little snack

ritto *(adj.)* "upright"; **carciofi ritti** are Tuscan artichokes with parsley, garlic, and PANCETTA braised in water and oil

riuscire, *p.p.* **riuscito** to succeed, to manage (to do something), to come out all right (as in the case of soufflés)

rivoltare, *p.p.* **rivoltato** to turn over, to flip. *Rivoltare la fritella* (to flip the pancake) means to turn an argument on its head.

rizza lacy fat covering kid or lamb intestines, used like RETE DI MAIALE (Abruzzo, Molise)

robatà *(n. and adj.)* (1) rolled out; (2) type of Torinese GRISSINO; (3) elongated bread

robiglio a wild pea (*Pisum arvense*) cultivated now mostly for forage, but eaten by the ancient Romans and still used in modern Umbria to make a flour

robiola creamy, rich cheese of the Lombardia region

robiolino any of a number of small, cylindrical cheeses, fresh or aged, often from a mix of cow and goat milk (Piemonte)

rocambola a kind of garlic

rocchi sausages

rocciata di Assisi mixed-fruit roll with nuts

rodoleti = ROTOLINI, little rolls; **rodoleti di persuto** are ham-wrapped pickles

roefioej = STRANGOLAPRETI (Trentino–Alto Adige)

rognone kidney, when destined to be cooked (in anatomy the word is *rene*); when the animal is small, the diminutive, **rognoncino**, is used

rolata di vitello veal breast stuffed with prosciutto, mushrooms, vegetables, and herbs (Piemonte)

rollè roll, rolled roast

romagnolo *(adj.)* of Romagna

romana, alla Rome-style, which means nothing by itself; see individual dishes and cf. ROMANESCO

romanello very hard skim-milk cheese for grating
romanesco *(adj.)* Roman; the adjective for anything Rome-grown, from the fresh vegetables to the accent
rombo brill, turbot, various members of the Scophthalmidae family, flat fish with both eyes on the left side; **rombo liscio** (*Scophthalmus rhombus*) is brill; **rombo maggiore** or **rombo chiodato** (*Rhomobus maximus*) is turbot
rompere, *p.p.* **rotto** to break, broken
rompifiamma heat diffuser, also called SPARGIFIAMMA, DIFFUSORE
rosa rose, pink; *rosa canina* is rose hip or sweetbriar; anything vaguely rose-shaped, including certain heads of lettuce and cabbage; **rosa di verza** is cabbage stuffed with meat, mushrooms, and olives
rosa, salsa literally, "pink sauce"; at its worst a ketchup-and-mayonnaise concoction used to dress things like shrimp cocktail or hard-boiled eggs, but also a tomato-and-cream sauce for pasta popular in the 1970s, now dated
rosada dessert pudding from pulverized nuts, milk, and sugar
rosade a custard pudding flavored with vanilla and lemon (Friuli-Venezia Giulia)
rosamarina BIANCHETTI preserved in oil with hot pepper and used as a sauce (Calabria)
rosato *(adj.)* pink; as noun, rosé (wine)
Rosato del Salento dry rosé wine from the heel of Italy
rosbif roast beef
roscano = BARBA DI FRATE
rosetta, *pl.* **rosette** (1) bread roll; a hollow roll in the form of a rosette; (2) veal sirloin, roughly corresponding to the NOCE in beef; (3) closed, stuffed pasta tubes; (4) anything rose- or rosette-shaped (cf. ROSA)
rosmarino rosemary (*Rosmarinus officinalis*)
rosolaccio a kind of poppy (*Papver rhoeas*)
rosolare, *p.p.* **rosolato** to brown
rosolio a rose-petal liqueur, used in confectionery; also any flavored liqueur containing, in addition to the flavoring agent (e.g., mint, fruit), equal amounts of alcohol, sugar, and water

rospo RANA PESCATRICE (Veneto, Marche, Abruzzo); **coda di rospo**, its tail

Rossese di Dolceacqua grape and red DOC wine from Liguria

rossetto, *pl.* **rossetti** tiny fish (*Aphia minuta*), a member of Gobidi family. It also means lipstick.

Rossini beef tournedos sautéed with truffle, goose liver, and Madeira, supposedly a dish often enjoyed by the composer and still served around Pesaro, his hometown. There is also a version of UOVA *in* CAMICIA with his name attached, again indicating the addition of *foie gras* and truffles.

rosso *(adj.)* red; **rosso d'uovo**, egg yolk; **rosso siena**, is a mild cheese from blended sheep and cow milk

rossumata = ROSUMADA

rosti a fried potato cake

rosticceria storefront eating place purveying, among other ready to eat foods, roasted meats, often only spit-roasted chicken; usually indistinguishable from a TAVOLA CALDA

rosticciana grilled pork chops (Toscana); = ROSTISCIADA

rosticciata = ROSTISCIADA

rosticciere roast chef

rosticini skewered lamb pieces roasted over charcoal (Abruzzo)

rostida = RUSTIDA

rostiera, rosticciera roasting pan

rostin negàa pan-roasted veal or pork loin with PANCETTA, rosemary, sage, and white wine; the Milanese dialect is saying ARROSTINO ANNEGATO (Milan)

rostisciada slices of pork meats and sausage simmered with onions—often with white wine and tomato—served with POLENTA in Lombardia or Piemonte

rostisciana = ROSTISCIADA

rosumada Milanese eggnog made traditionally with red wine, for which water or milk is sometimes substituted

rotella, *pl.* **rotelle** pastry wheel; in the plural, wheel-shaped pasta; **rotella dentellata**, pastry jagger; **rotella tagliapasta**, wheel pasta cutter

rotellina, *pl.* **rotelline** small disks or rounds, potentially of anything

rotini wheel-shaped pasta

rotolo roll (of anything, from paper towels to elaborate pasta dishes made like a jelly roll)

rotondo *(adj.)* round

rottami broken bits, broken pieces

roveia = ROBIGLIO (Umbria)

rovente *(adj.)* red hot (in temperature, not pepper content)

roventino typical Tuscan blood sausage

rovere oak

rovesciare, *p.p.* **rovesciato** to turn upside-down, to reverse; **crema rovesciata al caramello** is crème caramel

Rovigo the name of a province and its capital city in the Veneto region, abbreviated RO

rovinare, *p.p.* **rovinato** to ruin, wreck, make the soufflé fall

rovinassi, rovinazzi = VITALBA

rovinazzi chicken livers, combs, and other parts, served with BIGOLI or in RISOTTO

rovo blackberry (MORA) bush

rraù = *ragù alla* NAPOLETANA

rubiglio syn. ROBIGLIO

rubinetto water tap; **acqua del rubinetto** is tap water

rubino *(adj.)* ruby

ruccul white pizza with garlic, oil, oregano, and peppers

ruchetta (coltivata) rocket, arugula; varieties of *Eruca vesicaria*

ruchetta (selvatica) roquette, rocket; varieties of *Diplotaxis tenuifolia, D. muralis*

rucola variation of RUCHETTA

rucola palustre type of CRESCIONE

ruenche = GRONGO (Puglia)

rufioi potato GNOCCHI rolled into cylindrical pieces

rughetta Roman for RUCHETTA

rumbo = ROMBO CHIODATO (Lazio)

rumine flat or smooth tripe

rungu = GRONGO (Calabria, Sicilia)

ruonco = GRONGO (Abruzzo, Campania)
ruongo = GRONGO (Campania)
ruota, *pl.* **ruote** wheel, in plural, wheel-shaped pasta
ruspante *(adj.)* free range
russo *(adj.)* Russian; **insalata russa** is a salad of cooked vegetables bound with mayonnaise and sometimes encased in gelatin
russola a wild mushroom (*Russula aurata*)
russulidda young CICERELLO (Sicilia)
rustico *(adj.)* rustic, country-style; see also TORTA RUSTICA
rustico *(n.)* (1) a number of savory snack foods, such as small pizzas; (2) semi-soft cheese from sheep milk with either red pepper flakes or black peppercorns
rustida braised pork organ meats (Piemonte, Lombardia)
rustin see ROSTIN
rustisciada = ROSTISCIADA
ruta rue, a bitter plant (*Ruta graveolens*)

saba, sapa white syrup from grape must (Sardegna, Emilia-Romagna); = vino cotto (Puglia)
sabadoni sweet ravioli, filled with chestnut cream and fruit, in a sauce of boiled must (Emilia-Romagna)
sabato Saturday
sabbia, alla "sandy," e.g., made with toasted bread crumbs
saccarina saccharine
saccarosio saccharose
sacchetto (small) bag, sack
sacco, *pl.* **sacchi** bag, sack; in plural, filled pasta "pouches"

saccoccia stuffed veal breast (Piemonte)
saccottini crêpes closed like little bags
sacripantina name used for various sweets of the northwest regions
sagao neigro = SARAGO (Liguria)
saggiatorte cake tester
saggina sorghum (*Sorghum vulgare*)
sagne *(pl.)* stubby strips of pasta made from chickpea or spelt flour; LASAGNE; **sagne chine** are handmade lasagne stuffed with meat, cheeses, egg, and vegetables
sagra festival
sagù sago, a starch from palms, used as a thickening agent
salagione curing, pickling, or salting
salagnun RICOTTA of Valle d'Aosta
salama da sugo a special sausage, typical of Ferrara, containing red wine and encased in a pig's bladder; also called *salamina*
salame, *pl.* **salami** salami; also used figuratively for anything formed into the shape of a salami; also used as a derogatory term for a person who just stands there with his jaw hanging open
salamella various types of sausage (Naples, Lombardia)
salamina (ferrarese) = SALAMA DA SUGO
salamino small SALAME
salamm d'la duja preserved sausage of Piemonte
salamme = GATTUCCIO (Puglia)
salamoia brine, pickle
salàmoreci Sicilian salad of tomato with oil, garlic, and basil over staled bread squares
salare, *p.p.* **salato** to salt; see also SALATO
salatini salted crackers
salato *(adj.)* salted; savory (as opposed to sweet). One of the major food divisions, like that between meat and fish, is between the DOLCE and the *salato.*
salatura salting, as for making salt beef or salt cod
salcrautte = CRAUTI
sale salt; **sale fino**, "fine" salt, i.e., ordinary table salt; **sale grosso**, coarse salt, used for salting the pasta water, among other things

Salerno the name of the southernmost province and its capital city in the Campania region, abbreviated SA

Salice Salentino red and rosé DOC wines from the Salentina Peninsula, the heel of Italy (Puglia)

salicornia saltwort (*Salicornia herbacea*); bay leaves have been suggested as a substitute

saliera salt cellar, salt shaker

salignon ricotta flavored with salt, pepper, and vinegar (Valle d'Aosta)

salixi = GRONGO (Sardegna)

salmerino salmon trout, char (*Salvelinus malma*)

salmerino di fontana brook trout, speckled trout, salmon trout (*Salvelinus fontinalis*)

salmì game marinade; stew; **in salmì**, marinated in wine

salmistrato *(adj.)* pickled

salmo trota = TROTA DI MARE

salmonata, trota salmon trout

salmone salmon. None of the various species are found in Italian waters, but the fish, both fresh and smoked, is certainly popular on Italian menus.

salmoriglio oil, lemon, and oregano sauce for fish (Sicilia)

salpa goldline (*Sarpa salpa*)

salsa generically sauce, condiment, also dip; **acqua salsa** is salt water; **salsa madre**, any of the four basic sauces from which others derive, namely: BESCIAMELLA, VELLUTATA, SPAGNOLA, and *salsa di* POMODORO

salsa rossa cooked red sauce for BOLLITO of tomatoes, carrots, celery, onions, rosemary, garlic, and basil (Piemonte)

salsa verde green sauce for BOLLITO of minced herbs, anchovies, and capers in a mild vinaigrette, thickened with bread and potato (Piemonte)

salsacoltello literally, "sauce knife"; tasting spoon, the French *cuiller de dégustation*, a piece of silverware resembling a flattened spoon, often used in restaurants in place of a knife or spoon with dishes containing a particularly interesting sauce

salsamenteria store where cured meats and cheeses are sold
salsefica = SCORZOBIANCA
salsiccia, *pl.* **salsicce** sausage, usually fresh
salsiera sauceboat
salsina an uncomplicated quick sauce or dressing
saltaleone = RICCIOLA (Toscana)
saltare, *p.p.* **saltato** literally, "to jump" or "skip"; *saltare in* PADELLA means to sauté
saltiere sauté pan, Italian back-formation from the French *sautoir*
saltimbocca alla romana literally, "jump in the mouth"; SCALOPPINE with PROSCIUTTO and a sage leaf attached with a toothpick
salto, al sautéed, shallow-fried; **riso**—or **risotto—al salto** is a partially cooked RISOTTO ALLA MILANESE finished in the frying pan so it forms a nice crust; it is a traditional after-theater treat following opera at La Scala
salumeria shop where SALUMI are sold
salumi *(pl.)* the entire category of cured, ready-to-eat pork products including PROSCIUTTO, SALAME, and many others
salumiere vendor of SALUMI
salvastrella salad burnet (*Sanguisorba minor*), = PIMPINELLA
salvavino wine-bottle pump
salvia sage (*Salvia officinalis*)
salviade airy, sage-scented fritter (Friuli-Venezia Giulia)
salviata sage custard
salvo except
sambuca anise-flavor liqueur customarily served **con le mosche** ("with flies," meaning with three coffee beans floating in it)
sambuco elderberry (*Sambucus nigra*), an aromatic herb whose fresh flowers are also used in some recipes
sambudello sausage from pig innards, herbs, and pepper
sampiero = *pesce* SAN PIETRO (Veneto)
sampietro, pesce = *pesce* SAN PIETRO (Marche)
San Bernardo gouda-like cheese
San Bernardo, salsa sweet and sour sauce of Sicily

San Daniele, prosciutto di sweet, highly prized prosciutto from around the town of San Daniele del Friuli. The whole ham is easily recognized by its squared off shape (the result of pressing) and by the pig's foot still attached to the leg

San Jacopo, conchiglia di = CAPASANTA

San Marzano plum tomato named for the town of San Marzano, near Naples; elsewhere called *perini* or *botticini*

san petru, pisci = *pesce* SAN PIETRO (Calabria)

San Pietro, pesce John Dory, St. Peter's Fish (*Zeus faber*)

sanaculus = GATTUCCIO (Sardegna)

sanato, vitello prized white veal of Piemonte, formerly raised on milk and egg yolks; nowadays a term used for any milk-fed veal of the area

sancele, sanceli, sancucauru, *or* **sancunazzu** boiled pork sausage made with the animal's blood, plus nuts, grapes, RICOTTA, PECORINO, cloves, and other flavorings (Sicilia)

sancrau = CRAUTI

sandra syn. LUCIOPERCA

Sangiovese principal red grape of Italy, especially of Tuscany, but also Umbria, the Marche, and Romagna

sangue blood; **al sangue** means rare. In Piemonte, **lasagne al sangue** is made with pork blood, sweetbreads, marrow, and sausage.

sanguetta dè mare = LAMPREDA DI MARE (Puglia)

sanguetto sauté of poultry innards with coagulated blood, herbs, and tomatoes (Umbria)

sanguinaccio blood pudding, black pudding, blood sausage; sweet pudding of pig's blood with chocolate

sanguinello blood orange

sano *(adj.)* (1) healthy; *sano come un pesce*, "fit as a fiddle"; (2) whole

sanpiero = *pesce* SAN PIETRO (Veneto)

sansa, olio di husk oil, usually of olives; the oil extracted with chemical solvents from the solids that remain after all possible oil has been extracted mechanically

Santa Maddalena, Santa Magdelener red wine from around Bolzano

santo, olio extra-virgin oil in which hot pepper has been left to macerate, used as a condiment for meat, fish, vegetables, and salads

santoreggia summer savory (*Satureia hortensis*); wild herb reminiscent, some say, of rosemary or of mint and thyme

saor sweet vinegar and onion marinade for fish, SARDE **in saor** (Venice)

saorina VINO COTTO sauce for BOLLITO or desserts (Mantova)

sapa reduced grape must (Marche)

sapere (1) to know; (2) **sapere di (qualcosa)**, to taste like (something), to have the flavor of; cf. TAPPO

sapido *(adj.)* tasty, flavorful, savory

sapiotto = LAMPREDA (Veneto)

sapone soap

saponoso *(adj.)* soapy

sapore taste, flavor

saraca = SARDINA (Campania, Sicilia)

saracca = ARINGA

saraceno *(adj.)* "Saracen"; GRANO *saraceno* is properly buckwheat, though some sources translate it as whole wheat

sarachein = ALBORELLA (Emilia-Romagna)

saraghina = PAPALINA (Veneto, Friuli)

sarago white bream (*Diplodus sargus*); **sarago sparaglione**, syn. SPARAGLIONE

sarda = SARDINA

sarda, alla of Sardegna

sarde, pasta con le the Sicilian pasta par excellence: BUCATINI or PERCIATELLI with fresh sardines, fresh wild fennel greens, ZIBBIBO raisins, and pine nuts

Sardegna the region which lies across the Tyrrhenian Sea on the west coast of Italy and comprises the main island (Sardinia in English) and its offshore islets; it is characterized by its magnificent coastline, with many resorts, and mountainous, pastoral interior

sardel = AGONE (Lombardia)

sardela = ACCIUGA (Veneto, Marche)

sardella = SARDINA

sardena = ALACCIA (Calabria)

sardenaira = PISSALADIÈRE; FOCACCIA OF PIZZA from the Liguria region topped with tomatoes, olives, and anchovies or stockfish

sardenèa Ligurian pasta pie with sardines, garlic, oregano, thyme, and other herbs

sardi, pasta cch'i see SARDE

sardina comune sardine, pilchard (*Clupea pilchardus*)

sardina dorata = ALACCIA

sardinella = ALACCIA, PAPALINA

sardo = SARAGO (Veneto, Toscana)

sardôn = ACCIUGA (Veneto)

sardon = SARDINA (Venezia Giulia)

sardone = ALACCIA (Sardegna)

sargo white bream (*Diplodus sargus*)

saricu monicu = SARAGO

sartù a Neapolitan BOMBA *di riso* is a rice timbale filled with sautéed meats, mozzarella, Parmesan, peas, and mushrooms; it is one of the only truly southern rice dishes

sarzegna duck, teal

sarset = VALERIANELLA

sarzenta = TORTA BONISSIMA

sasizza di tonno tuna sausage in pork casing, cooked in tomatoes, onions, and white wine (Sicilia)

sasizzeddi stuffed veal rolls, e.g., with egg, onion, salami, and cheese (Sicilia)

Sassari the name of a province and its capital city in the Sardegna region, abbreviated SS

sassolino anise liqueur of Sassuolo, as well as the local name for ZAMPONE (Emilia-Romagna)

saticulano very sharp, aged pecorino (Campania)

sauersuppe gruel with tripe and vinegar

Sauris, prosciutto di PROSCIUTTO CRUDO smoked with spruce, juniper wood, and aromatic herbs (Friuli)

sauro = SURO (Puglia, Sicilia)

sauté, sautè used as a noun, clams or mussels cooked over high heat with a little tomato and served with their broth

Savoia a cheese similar to BEL PAESE

savoiardi ladyfingers
Savona the name of a province and its capital city in the Liguria region, abbreviated SV
savor, sapore a type of fruit MOSTARDA
sbattere, *p.p.* **sbattuto** to beat
sbattitore small electric mixer
sbianchire, *p.p.* **sbianchito** to blanch
sbira tripe (possibly also meat or bone marrow) stewed in broth with CROSTONI, cheese, and meat TÖCCO (Genova)
sbirraglia, risi in a rice soup with chicken RIGAGLIE (Veneto)
sbirro = MENOLA (Puglia); = SCIARRANO (Toscana)
sboccatura in winemaking, *dégorgement*
sbollentare, *p.p.* **sbollentato** to parboil
sbramato *(adj.)* unpolished, unhulled (of rice)
sbriciolare, *p.p.* **sbriciolato** to crumble (from BRICIOLA)
sbriciolona a crumbly Tuscan sausage (from BRICIOLA)
sbrinare, *p.p.* **sbrinato** to defrost (the freezer)
sbrisolana an almond TORTA
sbrisolona an apple crumble (Lombardia)
sbrofadej thin egg-and-cheese noodles made by extrusion and cooked in broth (Lombardia)
sbroscia a lake-fish soup (Lazio)
sbucciare, *p.p.* **sbucciato** to peel
sbufù = ALBORELLA (Lombardia)
sburrita = CACCIUCCO
scabeccio, in like SAOR OR CARPIONE; fish are fried and then placed in vinaigrette with onions, garlic, bay leaf, sage, and rosemary
scaccia pasta pie baked with tomato and broccoli
scacciata Sicilian stuffed pizza with onion, tomato, anchovy, and cheese; sweet version with fresh ricotta and coffee; other variations
scachi tiny "crackers" for soup
scafa peas, artichokes, fava beans, and potatoes stewed with a little white wine
scafata spring vegetable STUFATO with fresh beans, chard, GUANCIALE, and tomatoes (Umbria)
scaffettune = SCHIAFFETTONI in Calabria

scaglia, *pl.* **scaglie** scale, flake; *scaglie di* PARMIGIANO, made with quick short strokes of the cheese slicer, are modish (but good) on various salads and pastas

scalatielli fresh egg pasta of Campania, thicker and shorter than TAGLIATELLE

scalcare, *p.p.* **scalcato** to carve

scalco steward, carver

scaldapasta a settori large pot with four suspended colanders to permit the cooking of different shapes of pasta at the same time

scaldapiatti plate warmer

scaldare, *p.p.* **scaldato** to heat

scaldatelli fennel bread shaped in a ring

scaldavivande food warmer, hot tray

scalfo upper rear section of the beef PANCIA (Milano)

scaligera, zuppa a SOPA COADA enriched with turkey, chicken, and cheese

scalmarita an Umbrian cured meat similar to CAPOCOLLO

scalogna = SCALOGNO

scalogno, *pl.* **scalogni** shallot (*Allium ascalonicum*); scallion is CIPOLLINA VERDE, CIPOLOTTO

scaloppa a slice of meat or fish; see SCALOPPINE

scaloppina, *pl.* **scaloppine** thin-sliced, pounded veal scallops; scallops of other meats, such as turkey or pork

scambirru = SGOMBRO (Sicilia)

scamerita di maiale upper thigh of the hog

scammarita = CAPOCOLLO (Lazio)

scamone part of the rump; boneless cut of beef or veal, beginning at the base of the LOMBATA and extending toward the hip joint, formed principally by the gluteus muscle. Most of it is quite tender and used for pan-frying, for stewing, and for boiled beef.

scamorza a pear-shaped white cheese that can be melted on the grill and served as a main course; mild, plastic-curd, cow-milk cheese

scampirru = TONNO COMUNE (Sardegna)

scampo, *pl.* **scampi** Dublin Bay prawn, langoustine, Norway lobster (*Nephrops norvegicus*). Note that in Italy *scampi* is the name of the animal, not the prepared dish, and that *scampi* are not shrimp.

scampolo = SCAMPO (Venezia Giulia)

scanalato *(adj.)* fluted, grooved

scanata large PAGNOTTA of Foggia in Puglia

scannello cut of pork or veal that runs from the base of the lumbar vertebrae toward the tail and hip joint (roughly equivalent to the SCAMONE in beef) used for grilling and for FETTINE

scannese, agnello alla from Scanno in the province of L'Aquila, lamb cooked in terra-cotta with oil, garlic, rosemary, and white wine

scanno Abruzzese sheep cheese dipped in mixture of iron oxide and sulfuric acid. This process turns the outside black while leaving the inside yellow and imparts a burned taste. Usually eaten with fruit.

scapare, *p.p.* **scapato** to remove the head (CAPO) of an anchovy (or potentially anything)

scapece, a zucchini prepared in this fashion are sautéed in olive oil and then sprinkled with vinegar and mint leaves; similar preparation with sardines; pickled eggplant or mixed vegetables, similar to Sicilian CAPONATA

scarafuogli = FRISULI

scarcedda sweet Pugliese bread decorated with whole eggs for Easter

scardlina = ALBORELLA (Emilia-Romagna)

scarola escarole; **scarola 'mbuttunata**; **pizza di scarola**, a Neapolitan specialty consisting of a dough crust filled with cooked *scarola* and flavored with olives, raisins, and pine nuts

scarpariello, allo in a sauce with tomatoes, spicy peppers, and basil

scarpazza mixed vegetable pie (Milan)

scarpazzit vegetable fritter (Milan)

scarpazzone = ERBAZZONE

scarpena = SCORFANO (Venezia Giulia)

scarpetta, fare la to wipe the plate with a piece of bread to get the last drop of sauce. The practice is not considered polite at the best tables, but there are situations where omission of the *scarpetta* will offend the cook, especially if she is somebody's mother.

scatola box, can, tin; **in scatola**, canned

scatolame canned goods

scattiata Pugliese PEPERONATA

scaveccio eel, fried and steeped in boiled vinegar with red pepper and rosemary, served cold

scavino any of several small utensils, such as the melon-baller, used to dig (*scavare*) foods

scazzatielli = ORECCHIETTE

scazzone chub; Miller's thumb; bull-head (*Cotus gobio*)

scegliere, *p.p.* **scelto** to choose; choice

scellòne = ALALUNGA (Puglia)

scelta choice; **a scelta** means as you choose or however you like; **di prima scelta**, as a modifier, means first choice

scelto see SCEGLIERE

scheggia, *pl.* **scheggie** chip, flake

schermo = LUCCIO MARINO (Abruzzo)

schéuggio, lùxerna di = CERNIA (Liguria)

schiacciare, *p.p.* **schiacciato** to crush, to flatten. The name of various kitchen and table gadgets derive from this word: **schiaccia aglio**, garlic press; **schiaccianoci**, nutcracker; **schiaccia-patate**, potato ricer. **Schiacciata** is a Tuscan flat bread, and **schiacciato** is a pressed salami.

schiaffettoni filled pasta "purses" (Calabria)

schiaffoni large handmade *maccheroni*, often with lamb *ragù* (Campania)

schianta see RICOTTA

schiavone, pane fruit and nut MOSTARDA (Calabria)

schidionata spitted birds for roasting

schidione archaic name for SPIEDO

schidoni skewers of mixed meats or of cheese (Sardegna)

schie *(pl.)* tiny shrimp of the Venetian lagoon

schiena back (anatomy)

schienale, *pl.* **schienali** on the menu, spinal marrow, though the word can have various meanings having to do with backs

schile = SCHIE
schinco = STINCO (Friuli)
schirifizu = PANNOCCHIA (Sicilia)
schissoeula kind of Lombard FOCACCIA
schiuma foam; mousse; **schiuma di mare** are very small anchovies
schiumare, *p.p.* **schiumato** to skim
schiumarola skimmer
schmarrn omelet of Trentino–Alto Adige, usually sweet with fruit, but savory versions exist as well
schnitte essentially Friulian French toast
schopsernes lamb, potato, and cabbage stew (Trentino)
sciabbacheddu frittu a Sicilian dish of tiny fish, floured and fried in oil with garlic
Sciacchetrà dessert wine of Cinqueterre
sciakisciuka spicy Sicilian vegetable stew
sciancà literally, "torn"; homemade Ligurian pasta served with mixed vegetables and garlic
sciapo without salt; used both pejoratively and merely descriptively; **pane sciapo**, bread made without salt in the dough, common in parts of Lazio and Tuscany
sciaragno gigante = CERNIA (Venezia Giulia)
sciarrano comber, gaper (*Serranus cabrilla*)
sciatt fried whole-wheat or buckwheat pasta batter enclosing a bit of cheese (Lombardia); whole-wheat or buckwheat fritter, with cheese in the batter, served as a snack (Valtellina); see CHISCIOI
scienide sea trout
scifa small, handmade board with slight indentation for serving polenta (Lazio)
scifuloti large handmade egg MACCHERONI formed by rolling pasta squares around a rod (Emilia-Romagna)
scimud skim-milk cheese of VALTELLINA
sciocco *(adj.)* literally, "silly," but in the kitchen = SCIAPO
sciogliere, *p.p.* **sciolto** to dissolve, to melt
scirenga = CERNIA (Sardegna, Sicilia)
sciroppato *(adj.)* (of fruit) in syrup

sciroppo syrup
scirubetta type of SORBETTO or GRANITA with fruit syrup, once upon a time made with fresh snow (Calabria)
sciué-sciué supposedly indicates a dish improvised at the whim of the chef from ingredients at hand
sciumetta = LATTA ALLA GROTTA
sciuscieddu thick broth or thin gruel with bread crumbs, cheese, egg, parsley, and garlic; another version adds fresh ricotta and meatballs (Sicilia)
scivateddi large handmade spaghetti with pork RAGÙ and smoked, salted ricotta (Calabria)
sclupit, sclopit selene (the herb *Silene vulgaris*) (Friuli)
scocchiariello = SGOMBRO (Puglia)
scodella a small bowl
scodellare, *p.p.* **scodellato** to ladle (the soup), to dish up, to serve
scogliera reef, rocks, cliff, usually suggesting seafood therefrom
scoglio, *pl.* **scogli** shoal. Fish designated *di scoglio* are usually more prized than those from sandy areas.
scognariente = TELLINA (Liguria)
scolapasta colander
scolapiatti dish drainer
scolare, *p.p.* **scolato** to drain
scombro = SGOMBRO
scomparto compartment (as in the refrigerator)
sconciglio = MURICE (Campania)
scondito *(adj.)* undressed (as a salad)
scongelare, *p.p.* **scongelato** to defrost, to thaw
scontrino cash-register slip, cash-register receipt; under the complicated Italian fiscal laws, this is to be distinguished from a **ricevuta**, or proper receipt you can deduct from your taxes
scopa broom
scopeton (1) = ARINGA; (2) herring filets in oil with herbs, sometimes served over POLENTA (Veneto)
scoprire, *p.p.* **scoperto** to uncover, to discover; uncovered
scorfano Mediterranean scorpion fish (*Scorpaena scrofa*); the French

call it *rascasse*; the Latin name translates as "scorpion sow"—not a pretty fish even if prettily colored, but very good eating

scorpena = SCORFANO

scorrevole, porta sliding door

scorza rind; **scorzetta**, rind of something small (like a lemon), or small piece of rind

scorza a filetto sirloin half of the LOMBATA (Napoli)

scorzobianca salsify

scorzone a black truffle (*Tuber aestivum*) that grows all year long except spring

scorzonera black salsify

scottadito, abbacchio a plain grilled lamb chops, usually pounded before cooking, which "scorch the finger"

scottare, *p.p.* **scottato** to burn, to singe; parboil; **scottarsi**, to burn oneself

scottato *(adj.)* seared, blanched; not to be confused with SCOTTO

scottiglia Tuscan dish calling for a wide variety of chopped meats (six to eight different kinds) stewed with wine, tomato, and herbs, sometimes referred to as a meat CACCIUCCO

scotto = CERNIA (Puglia)

scotto (*p.p.* of SCUOCERE) overcooked, the worst thing you can say about pasta

Scozia Scotland

scozzese *(adj.)* Scottish, Scotch; plaid, tartan. Note that the word "scotch" is used in Italian for cellophane tape.

scrappani = SCORFANO (Sardegna)

scremato *(adj.)* skimmed (literally, "uncreamed"); **parzialmente scremato**, part skim

screziato *(adj.)* variegated, speckled, flecked

scripelle Abruzzese CRESPELLE OR FREGNACCE, thin pasta crêpes. When **'mbusse**, they are in broth as a first course. They also are used as the pasta for a TIMBALLO.

scritta perdosa = RAZZA CHIODATA (Sardegna)

scroccafusi crunchy balls of fried or baked sweetened dough for Carnevale (Marche)

scrocchiarello *(adj.)* crispy-crunchy; as a noun, a type of crisp pizza

scrofa sow; the ancient Romans enjoyed parts of the sow's gynecology as a delicacy and even today connoisseurs of variety meats confirm the opinion. The *scrofa* also enjoys a place in the Roman gastronomy of this century, having given her name to a street (thanks to her representation in relief on a Roman monument) and hence a restaurant (Alfredo alla Scrofa) where one of the best-loved Italian dishes—abroad at any rate—of all time was invented. See FETTUCCINE.

scuffion = TINCA (Marche, Umbria, Lazio)

sculettata, alla pasta dough worked by the buttocks—not likely to be found in contemporary restaurants, but an interesting concept to conjure

scuma = CAPELLI D'ANGELO

scuma di patati potato soufflé with egg, cheese, and sausage (Calabria)

scumuni ice cream enclosing a kind of ZABAGLIONE center (Sicilia)

scungilli whelks

scuocere, *p.p.* **scotto** to overcook

seadas = SEBADAS

sebadas large cheese-filled dessert RAVIOLI of Sardegna, fried in oil (or occasionally grilled) and drenched with bitter honey (MIELE AMARO)

secca, frutta dried fruit

seccare, *p.p.* **seccato** to dry, to dehydrate; cf. ASCIUGARE

seccetella = SEPPIA (Campania); **seccetella 'e fango**, in Naples, a kind of SEPPIA (*Sepia elegans*)

secchiello see SECCHIO

secchio bucket; **secchiello**, the diminutive, means ice bucket or wine cooler

seccia = SEPPIA (Puglia)

secco *(adj.)* "dry," used for wine, the air, the desert, or dehydrated foods; it can also mean thin (for a person); cf. ASCIUTTO

secoe = SECOLE

secole bits of meat from beef backbone used in a classic Venetian RISOTTO

Secondigliano type of SALAME

secondo (1) second *(adj.)*, often used alone, short for **secondo piatto**, which means the second, or main, course; (2) as a preposition, "according to" or "by"; **secondo mercato** means "depending on what is available in the market"

sedanini short, tubular pasta

sedano celery (*Apium graveolens*); **sedani** are ridged MACCHERONI; **sedano di montagna**, = LEVISTICO; **sedano di Verona**, celeriac; **sedano rapa**, celeriac

sedersi, *p.p.* **seduto** to sit down, to be seated (reflexive)

sedia, *pl.* **sedie** chair

sedimentare, *p.p.* **sedimentato** to deposit

sedimento deposit

seduto *p.p.* of SEDERSI

segale rye

segato *(adj.)* finely chopped and mixed with cheese

seggiolone highchair for the *bambino*

seghettato *(adj.)* serrated; **coltello a lama seghettata**, knife with serrated blade

segretu = LATTERINO (Sardegna)

seirass = RICOTTA (Piemonte, Valle d'Aosta)

seladas = SEBADAS

selezionato *(adj.)* selected; from selected grapes

selezionato e imbottigliato selected and bottled; on olive oil bottles, this means the oil was not grown in the same place it was bottled and was probably not even grown in Italy

selinka = ŠELINKA

sella saddle of lamb, veal, venison, rabbit, or potentially anything with hind legs; a seat on a horse

sellero = SEDANO (Rome)

seltz soda water

selvaggina any game animal

selvaggio *(adj.)* wild

selvatico *(adj.)* undomesticated, wild (plant or animal)

sembrare, *p.p.* **sembrato** to seem, to look like

seme, *pl.* **semi** seed, seeds; **olio di semi** or **semi vari**, generic term for non-olive vegetable oil

sementine *(pl.)* sprinkles, jimmies (literally, "little seeds")

semicotto *(adj.)* half-cooked. **Formaggio semicotto**, half-cooked cheese, describes hard cheese heated during manufacture to temperatures between 35°C and 48°C (95°F and 118°F).

semifreddo literally, "half cold"; generic term for ice-cream-based desserts; type of soft ice cream made with meringue and whipped cream

semigrasso *(adj.)* "half-fat," used for cheese containing between 20 and 42 percent dry substance; more than that is GRASSO, less MAGRO

semilavorato *(adj.)* half-worked

semini small pasta for soup; literally, "little seeds," hence potentially anything resembling same

semisecco *demisec*

semola ground durum wheat flour

semolina soup from SEMOLINO

semolino ground durum wheat flour, called "semolina" in English

senape mustard; cf. MOSTARDA

senapiera mustard pot

senese *(adj.)* of Siena

senso direction, sense

sentire, *p.p.* **sentito** to feel, to hear, to perceive

senza without

sepa = SEPPIA (Veneto, Venezia Giulia)

separare, *p.p.* **separato** to separate

seppia cuttlefish, members of the large Sepiidae family; see CALAMARO

seppiolina = SEPPIA

seriola amberjack, yellowtail (*Seriola dumerili*); also called RICCIOLA

serpe *(n.f.)* serpent, any of several sweets made in the form of a snake

serpentone see SERPE

serpillo see TIMO

serra greenhouse (the greenhouse effect is *l'effetto serra*); **pesce serra** is bluefish

serrana = SCIARRANO (Sardegna)
serrania = CORVINA (Sicilia)
servire, *p.p.* **servito** to serve, to be of use, to be necessary
servizio service, service charge
sesamo sesame (*Sesamum indicum*); sesame seeds are **semi di sesamo**
setacciare, *p.p.* **setacciato** to sift, to sieve
setaccio sieve, sifter
setoso *(adj.)* silky
settembre September
settembrino late-summer fig
settentrionale northern
seupa de gri barley soup with pork, PANCETTA, and vegetables (Valle d'Aosta)
seupa valtellinese soup of broth, VERZA DI MONTAGNA, fontina, and stale bread (Lombardia)
sfarrata FARRO soup
sfaticata, alla "for the lazy," e.g., already peeled
sfazo = ROMBO LISCIO
sfiandrine large, grayish mushrooms
sfiatatoio porcelain bird for pie
sfigghiata = ACCIUGA (Sicilia)
sfilacciato *(adj.)* in threads; as a feminine noun can mean dried, shredded meat
sfilatini type of long, thin bread
sfilettare, *p.p.* **sfilettato** to bone, to fillet
sfincione = SFINCIUNI
sfinciuni *(pl.)* (1) type of thick, soft Sicilian FOCACCIA covered with various ingredients; double-crust FOCACCIA stuffed with cheese, olive oil, and lemon juice or perhaps with ricotta, pork, sausage, and bread crumbs; (2) small sweetened rice timbales, fried and dusted with sugar
sfinge "doughnuts"; = ZEPPOLE
sfizi little hors d'oeuvres, accompaniments, or snacks
sfiziosità *(pl. invar.)* anything that catches the fancy, hence a toothsome goody or something tasty and possibly recherché, usually savory rather than sweet

sfogio = SOGLIOLA (Veneto, Venezia Giulia)
sfoglia (1) rolled sheet pasta; (2) millefeuille, phyllo pastry; (3) = SOGLIOLA (Venezia Giulia, Toscana, Marche, Abruzzo, Puglia)
sfogliatella fan-shaped pastry made of overlapping SFOGLIE and filled with RICOTTA and candied fruits, a specialty of Campania
sfogliatine *(pl.)* Venetian puff pastry sandwich cookies
sformato flan or savory pudding made in a mold (FORMA) and turned out
sfornare, *p.p.* **sfornato** literally, "to remove from the oven" (FORNO); also used to mean simply to bake
sfornato *(adj. and n.)* anything baked in the oven
sforzare, *p.p.* **sforzato** to force
sfranto *(adj.)* mashed, crushed
sfrappole *(pl.)* = FRAPPE
sfregare, *p.p.* **sfregato** to rub, as garlic on bread for BRUSCHETTA; to scrape, scratch
sfriccioli = FRICCIOLI
sfriggere, *p.p.* **sfritto** = SFRIGOLARE
sfrigolare, *p.p.* **sfrigolato** to sizzle, frizzle, sputter
sfrizzoli pork cracklings
sfuso *(adj.)* (in) bulk, i.e., not packaged; **vino sfuso** is bulk wine
s.g. (secondo grandezza) that is, by size
sgabello stool, small chair
sgaloppine = SCALOPPINE
sgassare, *p.p.* **sgassato** to make flat, remove the gas
sgattula = GATTUCCIO (Campania)
sgocciolare, *p.p.* **sgocciolato** to drip, to drain (from GOCCIA, drop); **sgocciolatoio**, drainboard
sgombro mackerel (*Scomber scombrus*)
sgonfioni rum- or cognac-flavored cookies with jam
sgonfiotti pastry puffs, fritters
sgranato *(adj.)* husked, shelled
sgranocchiare, *p.p.* **sgranocchiato** to crunch or munch, especially a cracker
sgroppino liquidy sorbet (Veneto)

sguazzarotti TORTELLI stuffed with bean purée and sauced with boiled grape must

sguazzetto alla bechera stewed innards (Veneto)

sgurmino = SGOMBRO (Sicilia)

sgusciare, *p.p.* **sgusciato** to shell, to husk

shaker cocktail shaker

shakerato shaken, as in a cocktail shaker—and yes, there exists the infinitive, *shakerare*

Sicilia the region of Sicily includes the main island, the football of Italy's boot, as well as several small islands and groups, including the Aeolians (Eolie or Lipari), the Egadi, Lampedusa, and Pantelleria, famous for its sweet wines.

siciliana, alla Sicily-style; **costoletta alla siciliana** is a veal or beef chop wiped with vinegar, coated with cheese and bread crumbs, dipped in egg, floured, and fried in oil

sidro cider

Siena the name of a province and its capital city in the Toscana region, abbreviated SI

siero whey, the liquid in which fresh cheeses, especially mozzarella, float. The same word also means serum.

sigaro, *pl.* **sigari** cigar, or anything cigar-shaped

sigillare, *p.p.* **sigillato** to seal

silano fresh SCAMORZA-type cheese of Calabria

siliqua di vaniglia vanilla bean

sinfonia symphony, in other words, a harmonious and imaginative blending of different elements

sinistra left

siouri (de) sliced polenta baked with meat sauce, cheese, and TARTUFO

Siracusa ancient Syracuse, the name of a province and its capital city in the Sicilia region, abbreviated SR

siracusana, spaghetti alla Syracuse-style: spaghetti with black olives, anchovy, SOFFRITTO, and spicy peppers

siringa decorating syringe

siringato *(adj.)* filled, stuffed (with a syringe)

sistemare, *p.p.* **sistemato** to arrange

sivé = CIVET
slegare, *p.p.* **slegato** to untie, release
smacafam *schiacciafame* or hunger smasher; type of buckwheat FOCACCIA with sausage or raisins; also exists in a sweet version (Trentino)
smalto enamel
smeriglio mackerel shark, porbeagle (*Lamna nasus*)
sminuzzare, *p.p.* **sminuzzato** to mince
smoccolatoio candle-snuffer
snocciolare, *p.p.* **snocciolato** to pit, to stone
soaso = ROMBO LISCIO
Soave popular white DOC wine from the Veneto that can be much better than many people believe
sobbollire to simmer
sobrich = FRITELLE
socca = FARINATA
sodo *(adj.)* firm; **uovo sodo**, hard-cooked egg
soffiato *(adj.)* puffed; **pasta soffiata** is puff or choux pastry; **riso soffiato** is puffed rice or Rice Crispies®
soffice *(adj.)* soft, soft and light
soffriggere, *p.p.* **soffritto** to sauté
soffritto see BATTUTO; ZUPPA *di soffritto* consists of pork innards stewed in tomato sauce
sofisticazione adulteration
sogliola sole (*Solea solea*)
soia soy, soya
solaio attic
soma d'aj toasted bread with oil and garlic
somaro donkey, sometimes in the diminutive, **somarino**
soncino lamb's lettuce or corn salad, = VALERIANELLA
Sondrio the name of a province and its capital city in the Lombardia region, abbreviated SO
sópa coada pigeon meat and broth over bread, slowly baked, a Veneto classic
sope di croz frog soup or stew
soppressata in Molise, large sausage with strips of lard that form a design (usually a star or a cross) when sliced; other sausages

soprassata cured ham; pork sausage
sopressa Veneto sausage
sorazzu an aged mozzarella
sorbetto sherbet, sorbet
sorbevole *(adj.)* drinkable
sorello = SURO
sorgente spring, source (of mineral water)
sorgiva, acqua spring water
sorpresa surprise
sorpresine *(pl.)* small pasta for soup
sorrentina, alla "Sorrento-style"; pasta with cooked tomato-basil sauce and SCAMORZA or MOZZARELLA
sorzo = MUSDEA (Veneto, Friuli)
sospiri di monaca literally, "nun's sighs"; cookies of chocolate-covered almond or hazelnut paste from Sicilia and Sardegna
sostanza substance
sostegno support, base
sotè a phonetic spelling of sauté; most often refers particularly to a Campanian preparation of sautéed oysters or mussels
sott'olio *(adv.)* (conserved) in oil
sottaceto, *pl.* **sottaceti** preserved in vinegar; hence pickled vegetables; used as a noun in the plural
sottile *(adj.)* thin
sottiletto thin slice, as of processed supermarket cheese
sotto under; in; also used as prefix; **sotto sale**, salt-packed; **sotto spirito**, conserved in liquor
sottobicchiere coaster (literally, "under glass")
sottobosco is used to describe products of the forest floor or undergrowth, most often meaning "wild berries." In other contexts it can refer to mushrooms, truffles, or even asparagus.
sottobottiglia wine coaster
sottofesa part of the beef round; in a beef and veal hindquarter, the exterior part of the side and rear area of the COSCIA
sottofiletto cut of beef or veal from under the filet mignon
sottolio = SOTT'OLIO
sottopentola trivet (literally, "under pot")
sottopiatto service plate; i.e., the decorative large dinner plate you

find already at your place at table. In Italy they are not removed; the dinner plates are placed on top.

sottospalla part of the beef shoulder chuck; in beef and veal, meat from just behind the shoulder used typically for BOLLITO

sottovuoto vacuum-packed

souté = SAUTÉ

sovace = PASSERA (Toscana)

sovra- over- (prefix)

spaccaossa meat cleaver (literally, "bone breaker")

spaccare, *p.p.* **spaccato** to split, cut in half

spaccatelli very large macaroni slit along their length

spada, pesce swordfish (*Xiphias gladius*)

spadon = *pesce* SPADA (Veneto, Venezia Giulia)

spaghetti the classic long, thin pasta of hard-wheat flour and water, usually made industrially by extrusion. The name means "little strings" (diminutive of *spago*, meaning string or twine), and it can be disconcerting the first time you hear the word used in its original sense. See individual entries for the sauces.

Spagna, di literally, "from Spain" or "Spanish"; **fagioli di Spagna** are large, white beans, or runner beans

spagnola, salsa *sauce espagnole*

spagnolin = PEPERONCINO ROSSO (Piemonte)

spagnolo *(adj.)* Spanish

spago string, twine; see also SPAGHETTI

spalla shoulder, clod; **spalla di San Secondo** is not the saint's shoulder but cured pork shoulder from the town of San Secondo near Parma; it can be raw but is more usually presented cooked

spalmare, *p.p.* **spalmato** to spread; **spalmabile** is spreadable

spalmino spreading knife

spannocchio = GAMBERO (Veneto, Toscana, Lazio)

sparacalaci = TRIGLIA (Sicilia)

sparaceddi dark green Sicilian BROCOLETTI

sparacelli Sicilian BROCOLETTI

sparaglione *Diplodus annularis*, a close relative of the SARAGO

sparasi = ASPARAGI

sparecchiare (la tavola) to clear (the table)
spargere, *p.p.* **sparso** to scatter, to sprinkle
spargifarina a molla spring-action flour sifter
spargifiamma flame diffuser
spargizucchero sugar dredger
spargi . . . prefix meaning "sprinkler"
sparnocchia = PANNOCCHIA (Campania)
spars = ASPARAGI
spatieddo = *pesce* SPADA (Sicilia)
spato pulcinella = young *pesce* SPADA (Sicilia)
spatola spatula, turner; **spatola da pasticciere**, icing spatula
spazzatura trash, garbage
spazzola brush
speciale *(adj.)* special
specialità specialty
specie kind, sort, species
speck a type of smoked prosciutto; **speck in pasta di pane**, a Trieste specialty consisting of a whole ham encased in bread dough and baked
spegettu = MUGGINE (Liguria)
spegnere, *p.p.* **spento** to turn off
spellare, *p.p.* **spellato** to peel, to skin
spelta spelt (see FARRO)
spelucchino paring knife
spennare, *p.p.* **spennato** to pluck
spennellare, *p.p.* **spennellato** to paint, hence to brush, as with egg white
spento *(adj.)* dull, not bright (of color)
spernocchia = PANNOCCHIA (Campania)
speronare, *pl.* **speronari** large ACCIUGA (Puglia)
spesa, fare la shop, do the shopping
spess a fresh cheese
spesso *(adj.)* thick
spesso *(adv.)* often
spezia, *pl.* **spezie** spice, spices (not to be confused with herbs)
speziare, *p.p.* **speziato** to spice

spezzare, *p.p.* **spezzato** to cut up, break up
spezzatino stew, but not very liquid; the word is a diminutive of the participle of a word meaning split or cut up
spezzeria spice shop, grocery store *(épicerie)*
spezzettare, *p.p.* **spezzettato** to break into pieces
spezzino *(adj.)* of La Spezia
spianare, *p.p.* **spianato** to roll out, flatten
spianatoia work surface, pastry board
spicara see MENOLA
spicchio clove (of garlic), wedge, segment (of lemon)
spiedino, *pl.* **spiedini** skewer, brochette, shish-kebab; *spiedini* can refer to tubes of ridged pasta, slit and twisted
spiedo, *pl.* **spiedi** spit; **allo spiedo**, spit-roasted
spiga, *pl.* **spighe** ear (of grain)
spigola sea bass, striped bass; syn. BRANZINO; **spigola francese**, = LAVARELLO (Lazio)
spigolo = MENOLA OR ZERRO (Toscana); also means corner
spigon = LUCCIO MARINO (Liguria)
spillata, birra beer "on tap"
spina, *pl.* **spine** bone (of a fish)
spina, birra alla draft beer
spina dorsale backbone, spine
spina, uva gooseberry
spinaci *(pl.)* spinach
spinare, *p.p.* **spinato** to bone
spinarolo = PALOMBO (Venezia Giulia)
spinassi = SPINACI (Veneto)
spinola = SPIGOLA (Toscana, Abruzzo, Lazio, Puglia, Campania)
spinula = SPIGOLA (Calabria, Sicilia)
spirito spirit, with the same range of meanings as in English
spollichini white beans or a dish made with them
sporcare, *p.p.* **sporcato** to soil, to get (something) dirty
sporco dirty
sportellacchia = PORTULACA
spratti sprats
spratto syn. PAPALINA

sprecare, *p.p.* **sprecato** to waste
spremere, *p.p.* **spremuto** to squeeze
spremiagrumi hand juicer
spremilimone da tavola (lemon) reamer
spremuta fresh-squeezed fruit juice
spressa hard cheese of Trentino, similar to ASIAGO
spretz tsaori syn. PUZZONE
sproccolati dried figs stuffed with fennel seed
spruzzare, *p.p.* **spruzzato** to spray, to spritz
spugna terrycloth
spugnola morel mushroom *Morchella*
spullecarielli young white beans
spuma foam, froth
spumante full-blown sparkling wine made in Italy with the same techniques as Champagne. Unfortunately, in past decades the popularity of inferior Asti Spumante (which uses another method; see ASTI) gave *spumante* in general a bad name, with the result that the finest Italian specimens do not carry the designation on their labels. Until very recently they were called *Méthode champenoise,* and now are usually labeled METODO CLASSICO or METODO TRADIZIONALE.
spumone a Piedmontese dessert of sweetened, lightened MASCARPONE with rum and candied citron
spuntare, *p.p.* **spuntato** (1) intransitive: to sprout; (2) to cut the points off
spuntature (di costa) *(pl.)* spareribs, usually served with POLENTA, often used to make sauce; the word can also be applied to other regional cuts of meat
spuntino snack
spunto *(adj.)* sour, used when the wine has begun to turn to vinegar
spurgare, *p.p.* **spurgato** to purge (snails, shellfish)—like expurgate
s.q. (secondo quantità) according to quantity; appears on menus in lieu of price for variable-quantity items, such as antipasto from the buffet
squacquerone soft, white cheese from Emilia-Romagna

squadro angel shark, angel fish, monkfish (*Squatina squatina*); syn. *pesce* ANGELO

squagliare, *p.p.* **squagliato** to melt; **lo squaglio**, what has melted

squalena = SQUADRO (Veneto, Venezia Giulia)

squama, *pl.* **squame** (fish) scale, anything in the shape of fish scales

squamapesce fish scaler

squarciarella, alla in a mushroom sauce

squasset GUAZZETTO in Lombardia

squattruncefalo = SQUADRO (Sicilia)

squero, agnello allo skewered lamb seasoned with thyme and other herbs, roasted over a brushwood fire (Puglia)

squisito *(adj.)* exquisite, one of the standard exclamations for something delicious

stabilizzazione stabilization

staccare, *p.p.* **staccato** to detach (think of staccato in music)

stacchiodde = ORECCHIETTE

stadotu = GATTUCCIO (Puglia)

stagionale *(adj.)* seasonal

stagionato *(adj.)* aged, seasoned

stagione *(n.f.)* season

stagnato, rame tin-coated copper

stagnatura solder, tinplating

stagno solder (base metal)

stagnola, carta tin foil, aluminum foil

stambecco, *pl.* **stambecchi** ibex

stampato *(adj.)* stamped out (of a mold)

stampo mold; **stampo a cerniera**, spring-form pan; **stampo a ciambella**, ring mold; **stampo da plum-cake**, pound-cake mold; **stampo rettangolare**, loaf pan

starna gray partidge

steccare to lard

stecchino, *pl.* **stecchini** toothpick, cake tester, anything narrow and sharp that can be stuck into something else

stecco, *pl.* **stecchi** literally, "stick"; (1) softened cracker sheets or a kind of bread pasta with egg, Parmesan, and spices, rolled around skewers of veal brains, SCHIENALI, sweetbreads, and similar items, then fried—a specialty of Chiavari in Liguria; (2) Bolognese recipe for skewered veal, pickled tongue, chicken liver, sweetbreads, truffles, and MORTADELLA, breaded and fried; (3) other mixtures of meats and vegetables on skewers

steglia = TRIGLIA (Veneto)

steit = ALBORELLA (Piemonte)

stella, *pl.* **stelle** star

stelline *(pl.)* small star-shaped pasta for soup

stelo, *pl.* **steli** stem, of a glass

stemperare, *p.p.* **stemperare** to dissolve, to melt, to dilute

stendere, *p.p.* **steso** to stretch out, to hang out (such as the laundry), to spread. The many other meanings of this common verb include "to knock out."

stiacciata flat bread, like FOCACCIA

stiepidire = INTIEPIDIRE

stimpirata, alla (1) varied Sicilian fish preparations in which the fish is floured and fried, and then baked with onions, capers, and olives; (2) a Sicilian dish of marinated rabbit, breaded, fried, and stewed with with celery, raisins, and pine nuts in a sweet-and-sour sauce

stinco veal or pork shank, often roasted, also braised

stipare, *p.p.* **stipato** to press, to cram

stivaletti literally, "little boots"; small, curving pasta tubes

stoccafisso stockfish, air-dried cod; dried (unsalted) cod (cf. BACCALÀ); **stoccafisso accomodato** is flavored with olives, anchovies, potatoes, and pine nuts; **all'anconetana** is slow-cooked with oil, celery, garlic, rosemary, and tomato sauce; **alla giulese** is with peppers, potatoes, olives, and tomatoes; **a burridda** is a stew of the fish and its innards with mushrooms, tomatoes, basil, and wine

stocco = STOCCAFISSO

storione sturgeon (*Acipenser sturio*)

stoviglie *(pl.)* dishes, collectively

stra- prefix meaning "extra," for example, **stravecchio**, extra old

straccare, straccarsi to exhaust, become exhausted; term is used humorously in a number of food names to reflect difficulty of eating or toughness of fabric, e.g., **straccadenti**, very hard cookies

straccetti literally, "rags"; small pieces of beef cooked in oil, often with

RUGHETTA or CARCIOFI, a traditional Roman dish revived a few years ago and going strong in the trattorias of the capital; cf. STRACCIO

stracchino (1) soft, fresh Lombardian cheese, sold in bricks, supposed to be made from the milk of tired cows (see STRACCARE); other types of cheese from the *stracchino* family are usually called by their more characteristic names, i.e., *Stracchino di* GORGONZOLA or *Stracchino* CRESCENZA. *Stracchino* itself refers to milk that is ready for cheese-making. (2) Ice cream sold in bricks like the cheese (southern).

stracciatella an ice cream, sort of like chocolate chip, in which the chocolate supposedly resembles the eggs in the soup called STRACCIATELLA ALLA ROMANA

stracciatella alla romana egg-drop broth in which the egg drops are supposed to resemble rags (STRACCI)

stracciato *(adj.)* (1) of pasta: dried strips of pasta broken into irregular pieces; (2) of eggs: scrambled; (3) potentially any food made to resemble rags (see STRACCIO)

straccio, *pl.* **stracci** (1) rag, dishcloth, cleaning cloth; (2) "rags," foods that in one way or another resemble bits of torn cloth, e.g., handmade Ligurian LASGNETTE, *stracci di Antrodoco* (meat and mozzarella-stuffed egg crêpes of Lazio) or *stracci di Sella di Corno* (veal and SCAMORZA-filled CRESPELLE of Abruzzo). See SCRIPPELLE, STRACCETTI.

stracotto long-cooked beef pot roast, from **stracuocere**, "to cook for a long time"

strangolapreti literally, "priest-chokers." Obviously there is no gastronomic information inherent in the term; rather it is applied to any number of homemade flour-and-water pastas as well as to a kind of green GNOCCHI. In the Padova area, it is often used for the sweetened version called **maneghi**.

strangolaprieve = STRANGOLAPRETI

strangozzi short, hollow, eggless FETTUCCINE

strangugli = STRANGOLAPRETI

strangulaprievete = STRANGOLAPRETI

strapazzate, uova scrambled eggs

strapponi broad noodles

strascenate *(pl.)* shell pasta

strascicato dredged, "dragged" through a sauce; see STRASCINATO

strascinati *(n.)* ridged LASAGNE or pasta shells, ORECCHIETTE; in Umbria, homemade macaroni with sausage, egg, and cheese; in Basilicata, a pasta formed from flour and lard (*minestra strascinata*)

strascinato *(adj.)* in central and southern Italy, describes vegetables that are first boiled or steamed and then sautéed with oil, hot pepper, and garlic; = RIPASSATO

strascnar = STRACENATE

strassi = STRACCI (Liguria)

strato layer; **a strati**, in layers

strattu tomato concentrate

strauben = FRITTELLE

stravecchio very old, aged for a long time

strega (1) a fish; = CAGNETTA; (2) Strega (uppercase) is an herbal liqueur. The word means "witch," and the liqueur is so named because in popular tradition Benevento, where it is made, is also the home of all the witches in Italy, who gather once a year on the feast of St. John, June 24. Meanwhile, in Rome they are eating snails (see LUMACA).

streghe *or* **streghine** kind of crackers or biscuits

stregoli form of STRANGOLAPRETI

strengozzi = STRANGOZZI

stretto *(adj.)* narrow, *p.p.* of STRINGERE

stricchetti pasta in the form of two bow-ties

strigolo, *pl.* **strigoli** wild, spinach-like greens for salads or boiling (*Silene cucubalus*)

stringere, *p.p.* **stretto** to tighten, to grasp

stringhetti egg pasta like TAGLIOLINI

stringozzi = STRANGOZZI

strinù grilled beef and pork sausage

strioli a wild herb that grows only in the Todi area (Umbria)

strofinaccio rag, cleaning cloth, polishing cloth

strofinare, *p.p.* **strofinato** to rub (usually repeatedly to clean or polish)

stronghe long MACCHERONI

stropicciare, *p.p.* **stropicciato** to rub, to scrape

strozzapreti = STRANGOLAPRETI

strucolo pasta STRUDEL (Friuli); thick pasta sheets rolled up with RICOTTA or meat, tied like a sausage and boiled. When cheese-filled, sometimes it is sauced with butter and sugar; **strucolo de spinaze**, with spinach

strudel as a dessert, it means about the same as strudel in English (or German); as a first course, it indicates sheets of pasta layered with RAGÙ, rolled up, sliced into serving portions and then baked

struffoli small balls of fried pasta bound together with honey, decorated with candied fruit; = CHIACCHIERE; see CICERCHIATA

struncatura maccheroni-like egg pasta of Calabria

strutto lard, i.e., rendered and clarified pork fat for use in cooking; cf. LARDO

strutturato *(adj.)* structured (for wine)

struzzo ostrich; ostrich meat is turning up on the menu with increasing frequency

stufare, *p.p.* **stufato** *(q.v.)* to cook covered for a long time over low flame; to braise; to "sweat" (as for onions); to cook without browning. The past participle can also mean "smothered."

stufatino diminutive of STUFATO

sturare, *p.p.* **sturato** to uncork, to unblock (the sink)

sturiòn = STORIONE (Veneto, Venezia Giulia)

sturiun = STORIONE (Lazio, Campania, Sicilia)

stuzzicadente, *pl.* **stuzzicadenti** toothpick

stuzzichino, *pl.* **stuzzichini** what the French call *amuse-gueule* or *-bouche,* the pre-appetizer offered gratis by some restaurants. It comes from the verb **stuzzicare**, which means "to prick," literally or figuratively, as in stimulate or provoke. In other words, a little bite to get the juices flowing while you read the menu. It is now also being called "appetizer" in Italian. In the plural, the term means little tastes, savory snacks, or hors d'oeuvres.

su on

sua (la) its, your

succhia pesce = LAMPREDA (Abruzzo)

succo juice; individual bottles of **succo di frutta**, fruit juice, are a staple of the bar menu; to specify fresh, ask for a SPREMUTA

sucui zucchini

sud south

Sudtirol German name for the bilingual Alto Adige region

sudtirolese *(adj.)* south Tyrolean, referring to the area of Alto Adige on the Austrian border

sugapisci = LAMPREDA (Sardegna)

sugarello = SUGHERELLO; syn. SURO

sugherello = SURO (Toscana)

sughero cork, the natural material; cf. TAPPO

sughi plural of SUGO

sugna = LARDO

sugo sauce, juice; see also *succo*; **sugo d'arrosto**, pan juices from a roast, used as pasta sauce; **sugo d'umido**, the sauce formed during the cooking of a pot roast when used separately, as over pasta; **sugo finto**—literally, "bogus sauce"—describes a kind of almost meatless but hearty sauce for pasta

sugoso *(adj.)* juicy

suino *(n. and adj.)* pork

sul/sulla on, on the

sulfureo sulphurous

sultanina a variety of green grape used for raisins

suo (il) its

suoi (i) their

sûpa = ZUPPA (north)

superalcolico, *pl.* **superalcolici** hard liquor

superficie *(n.f.)* surface

superfino see RISO

superiore wine classification that indicates higher quality and more alcohol than normal due to lower yields and riper grapes

suppa = ZUPPA

supplemento extra charge

supplì rice croquette made and sold in pizzerias. The word, which is Roman, derives from the French, *surprise,* because of what is inside, namely a glob of mozzarella. Mozzarella forms long strings when melted, which gives rise to the full form of the snack's name, **supplì al telefono** (the strings of mozzarella resemble telephone cords).

surecilli literally, "little mice"; small *gnocchi*

surgelare, *p.p.* **surgelato** to preserve by freezing (cf. CONGELARE). Italian freezers and cold-storage comparments are rated and marked with one to four stars, three being a normal home refrigerator freezer (–18°C to –20°C or 0°F to –4°F) and four (less than –30°C or –22°F) a deep freeze.

surgelato *(adj.)* frozen; as substantive, usually in plural, frozen foods

surici herring-like fish (Calabria); = SURUCITTI

suricitti GNOCCHI made from cornmeal with sausage fat fried in lard or oil (Marche)

surmaturo *(adj.)* overmature

suro horse mackerel, jack mackerel (*Trachurus trachurus*); a *pesce* AZZURRO similar to SGOMBRO

surra = VENTRESCA (Sardegna); Calabrian dialect for the fatty part of the swordfish belly

suscìa bean soup with herbs and onions

susciello small asparagus in broth

susina verde greengage

susina, *p.p.* **susine** plums; **susine secche** are prunes

sussapeixe = LAMPREDA (Liguria)

svanito *(adj.)* vanished, pale

sventrare, *p.p.* **sventrato** to gut (also used figuratively, as when urban planning *sventra* an old neighborhood)

svezzare, *p.p.* **svezzato** to wean

sylvaner delicate, dry white wine from northeast Italy

šelinka a minestrone based on potatoes (Friuli)

~ T ~

tabella table, in the sense of a sign giving information, as in a **tabella dei prezzi** (price list), also called LISTINO

taccare, *p.p.* **taccato** to score (as the edges of a steak)

tacchino turkey; **tacchina**, hen turkey; **tacchinella**, small hen turkey

tacchinoto young chicken

taccola, *pl.* **taccole** broad bean; mange-tout; pea pod, snow pea

tacconelle pasta squares

tacconi pasta squares

taccozze puff pastry for noodles

taccozzelle large pasta squares; = TACCOZZELLE (Abruzzo, Molise)

taccunill' = MALTAGLIATI

tacòn pasta from wheat flour and white beans (FAVE)

tagghiarina = TAGLIATELLA

tagghiulini = TAGLIOLINI

tagiadele = TAGLIATELLE

tagio, al RISOTTO with shrimp and eels

tagliacapsule foil cutter

tagliare, *pl.* **tagliato** to cut

tagliata a very thin slice of beefsteak (COSTATA) usually served as several slices and very rare

tagliatelle *(pl.)* flat noodles, often made with egg; **tagliatelle bastarde** are made with equal parts wheat and chestnut flours. In general, the name *tagliatelle* is used in the northern half of the country, FETTUCCINE in the southern half.

tagliere cutting board, breadboard

taglierini flat strands of fresh pasta
taglio (1) cut; (2) blending; *coupage*; mixing of wines; (3) **al taglio**, by the piece, often used in reference to pizza
tagliolini flat strands of pasta
taieddra Pugliese TEGLIA in terra-cotta
tajadele = TAGLIATELLE
tajarille = TAGLIOLINI
tajarin = TAGLIOLINI (Piemonte)
taleggio rich, very slightly sharp cow-milk cheese from Lombardia, closely related to STRACCHINO
talleri thin pasta disks
tanaceto tansy (*Tanacetum vulgare*), an anthelmintic (chases out intestinal worms)
tanfaranu = ZAFFERANO
tannico *(adj.)* tannic
tantatu = DENTICE (Puglia)
tanuta black sea bream (*Spondyliosoma cantharus*)
tapari capers
tappato *(adj.)* stoppered, corked; term also used to describe wine that literally tastes of the cork
tappo cork, stopper; cork the object, not the material, which is SUGHERO
tapulon donkey, mule, horse, and/or beef stewed with wine, herbs, and spices (Piemonte)
taragna buckwheat polenta (Piemonte)
taralli *(pl.)* made and spelled with various dimunitives and superlatives, these are pretzel-textured, ring-shaped breads that may be plain or variously flavored and are nearly always on the Pugliese table
tarallucci diminutive of TARALLI
tarantello cured-tuna salami (Puglia)
tarantiello a type of SALUME of the Salerno area made from tuna belly
tarantina Pugliese fish soup
Taranto important port on the Ionian sea, the name of a province and its capital city in the Puglia region, abbreviated TA

tarassaco dandelion (*Taraxacum officinale*)
tardivo (*adj.*) late, late-season; for wine, late harvest
tardura fresh bread crumbs bound with egg and cheese, and cooked in broth; **riso e tardura** is rice in beef broth mixed with an egg beaten with Parmesan
targone = DRAGONCELLO
tarocco, *pl.* **tarocchi** prized oranges from southern Italy; the best, from Sicilia, are red. Tarot cards are also called *tarocchi.*
tartara tartare; raw, chopped meat
tartaruga turtle
tartina canapé, little bread hors d'oeuvres with varied toppings, French *tartine*
tartrà type of non-sweet pudding of egg, milk, cheese, onion, and spices
tartufato (*adj.*) with a truffle flavor of unstated origin—possibly, but not necessarily, the laboratory
tartufo, *pl.* **tartufi** truffle, with the same range of meanings as in English: (1) truffle, the tuber; (2) chocolate ice cream molded and covered with chocolate supposedly to resemble a real truffle; (3) sea truffle and any other figurative truffle
tartufo d'Alba white Piedmontese truffle
tartufo (di mare) clam, warty venus, baby clam (*Venus verrucosa*)
tartufo nero black truffle
tartufolo = TARTUFO (DI MARE) (Liguria)
tasca literally, "pocket"; often used for stuffed meat slices; **tasca per pasticceria**, pastry bag
tassa bread, wine, and paprika soup
tatto touch, the sense of touch; **al tatto**, to the touch
taverna tavern, pub, OSTERIA; also a basement room (North)
tavola (1) table, in all the senses of the English word; (2) a steam table, shopfront, or part of a bar; a **tavola calda** is an eatery offering (mostly) hot food, (mostly) ready to serve; a **tavola fredda** provides the same service for cold foods; cf. TAVOLO
tavola, da for wine: table wine; for cheese: table cheese, eating cheese
tavolo a table for a specific purpose, e.g., a café table; cf. TAVOLA
tazza cup, teacup; an ESPRESSO cup is a **tazzina**; cf. BICCHIERE

tè tea
tecia earthenware pot or the food cooked in it, generally flavorful stews
tecnica, *pl.* **tecniche** technique
tecnico literally, "technician," but often simply repairman, a frequent visitor to many kitchens
tegamaccio Umbrian fish stew with wine and herbs
tegame pan; frying pan; **in tegame**, fried, baked, braised; pan-roasted
tegamino small frying pan; shallow dish or frying pan
teglia baking pan, baking dish, pie dish, or the food cooked in it, rather like casserole in English
teiera teapot
tellina = CUORE (Toscana); wedge shell, wedge clam (*Donax trunculus*)
tempestina thin-sliced egg pasta for soup
tempia temple (anatomy)
tempo time
tenca de mar = CERNIA (Veneto, Venezia Giulia)
tencozza = TINCA (Campania)
tendere, *p.p.* **teso** to stretch, extend
tenero *(adj.)* tender
tenerume, *pl.* **tenerumi** soft gristle, cartilage, often part of a BOLLITO MISTO
tental = DENTICE (Venezia Giulia)
tenue *(adj.)* thin, subtle
tenuta farm, estate
Teramo the name of a province and its capital city in the Abruzzo region, abbreviated TE
termodiffusore *(adj.)* heat-diffusing
termometro thermometer; **termometro per fritture**, deep-fat frying thermometer
Terni the name of a province and its capital city in the Umbria region, abbreviated TR
Terni, pane tipo bread made without salt
Teroldego grape used to make **Teroldego Rotaliano**, a red DOC wine from Trentino-Alto Adige
terra earth

terraglia earthenware
terreno, *pl.* **terreni** terrain
terrina (1) pieces of meat, fish, and/or vegetables layered in a (usually) ceramic mold and baked; (2) the mold itself; terrine, bowl
terrosità earthy taste
terzo *(n. and adj.)* third, one-third
terzolo cheese (or other products) made in winter, as opposed to MAGGENGO and QUARTIROLO
teso *(adj.)* tight, taut, stretched
tessuto fabric, cloth
testa = *pesce* CAPPONE (Puglia, Venezia Giulia)
testaroli small crêpes, grilled, boiled and usually served with PESTO or other sauces; see PANIGACCI (Liguria, Toscana)
testazza = LATTERINO (Sicilia)
testetti type of TESTAROLI
testicoli testes
testina (di vitello) (calf's) head cut up and dressed to look like an innocent antipasto dish
testo earthenware lid, clay oven; terra-cotta, cast-iron, or sandstone baking tile
testoni young ANGUILLA (Veneto)
testuggine tortoise, turtle
tetto roof
thé tea
tiagallo = GRONGO (Liguria)
tiella, *pl.* **tielle** a shallow baking pan or the food cooked in it; various central or southern dishes of layered ingredients (mostly vegetables)
tiepido *(adj.)* tepid, lukewarm, room-temperature
tigelle fried rounds of dough topped with with oil and rosemary or cheese
tiglio lime tree; linden
timballo timbale; traditionally, a pie or varied ingredients molded and baked; sometimes, = BOMBA; sometimes a filled pastry. Today, even lasagna is sometimes classed as a kind of *timballo.* A *timballetto* or *timballino* is an individual, unmolded serving.
timo (1) thyme (*Thymus vulgaris*); (2) thymus gland

timo serpillo *or* **pepolino** wild or continental thyme (*Thymus serpyllum*)

timoello = TIMO SERPILLO

timpano = TIMBALLO

tinca tench (*Tinca tinca*) is a freshwater fish, not entirely unlike trout, often prepared *in* CARPIONE

tipico *(adj.)* typical, characteristic

tipo type

tiramisù literally, "pick me up"; ubiquitous, rich, layered dessert of spongecake with brandy, espresso, and MASCARPONE with egg and chocolate

tirare, *p.p.* **tirato** to stretch; to roll out (pasta dough)

tirolese Tyrolean

tirreno, mare the Tyrrhenian Sea

tirtl large RAVIOLI stuffed with kraut or spinach and fried

tisana tisane, herb tea

toast *un toast* is a grilled cheese and ham sandwich, available at nearly any bar in Italy; toasted bread is *pane tostato,* but see BRUSCHETTA

toc Friulian stew of pork, liver, white wine, cloves, and cinnamon; pasta sauce of mixed meats, wine, and herbs; = POLENTA in some parts of Lombardia

tocchetto, *pl.* **tocchetti** chunk, piece; in plural, = STOCCAFISSO A BURIDDA

töcco sauce; = *sugo*; a rich pasta sauce with varied regional versions. A traditional Ligurian **töcco di carne** includes minced beef, marrow, white wine, dried mushrooms, and herbs. **Töcco di funghi** is made with PORCINI mushrooms, onions, tomato, garlic, and spices.

tocco, *pl.* **tocchi** chunk, bite-sized piece

tocio = TOC

tofeja (1) a special cylindrical terra-cotta pot with a narrow mouth from the area of CANAVESE; (2) a soup of bean and pork parts made in the pot of the same name

togliere, *p.p.* **tolto** to remove, to take away

toglitorsoli corer

toma fresh or aged cheese of Piemonte, from cow milk or mixture of cow and goat milk; there are a great many local variations

tomata tomato (Sardegna)

tomaxelle *(pl.)* veal rolls stuffed with meat, cheese, pine nuts, and egg stewed with meat sauce, white wine, and tomatoes (Liguria)

tomino small, fresh cheese of Piemonte, usually of cow milk, often flavored with herbs, served with oil and herbs or stuffed with various ingredients and heated or grilled

ton = TONNO (Veneto)

tonco de pontesel slow-cooked stew of mixed meats, broth and, often, a spoonful of coffee (Trentino)

tondo *(adj.)* round

tonica, acqua tonic water

tonnarelli squared strands of pasta

tonnato *(adj.)* in tuna sauce

tonnetto bonito (*Sarda sarda*)

tonno comune tuna (*Thunnus thynnus*)

topinambur, topinambolo Jerusalem artichoke

topini type of GNOCCHI

torba peat—not a food term, but with the popularity of single malt whiskies, it does come up from time to time

torcere, *p.p.* **torto** to wring, to twist

torcetto ring-shaped cookie (Piemonte)

torchio a press, as for grapes, duck, or olives; a special instrument for making certain pastas (e.g., BIGOLI). The name comes from the verb to twist (TORCERE).

torciglioni FUSILLI-like pasta

torcinelli kid or lamb innards roasted or stewed with white wine or tomato sauce

Torcolato a dessert wine from Breganze (Vincenza), in the Veneto

tordelli = TORTELLI; Tuscan half-moon-shaped pasta with a filling of veal brains and meat, eggs, and herbs, dressed with a veal *ragù*

tordo, *pl.* **tordi** thrush

torello young bull

torinese *(adj.)* of Turin

Torino Turin is the fourth largest city in Italy and the regional capital of Piemonte as well as the name of a province and its capital city, abbreviated TO

torlo = TUORLO

torrefazione the roasting of coffee or seeds, or the place where the freshly roasted product is sold

torresani pigeons

torresano = PICCIONE (Veneto)

torricella dog periwinkle (a mollusk) (*Ceritum vulgatum*)

torroncino either a small TORRONE or TORRONE GELATO

torrone nougat candy made of honey, nuts, and egg whites. Among dozens of locally famous versions, there is that of Benevento, the Chieti variant (dried figs and chocolate), or the famous chocolate *torrone* of L'Aquila. **Torrone gelato** is not ice cream, but a mix of candied fruits with almond paste covered by chocolate (though an ice cream shop might also make *torrone*-flavor GELATO).

torsolo core, as of an apple

torta cake, tart, pastry, pie; **torta fritta** is a type of CRESCENTE

torta di/della nonna literally, "Grandma's cake"; a plain, dry cake, some version of which (usually with custard and pine nuts) is offered by nearly every trattoria in Italy

torta rustica a savory pie; version of PIZZA RUSTICA with a dough made from flour, olive oil, and white wine (Puglia, Basilicata)

tortano ring-shaped FOCACCIA of Napoli

tortei mantovani pumpkin-filled pasta of Mantova

tortelli small pie or omelet, sometimes sweetened; large **tortellini**; filled pasta rectangles, often twisted at the ends, thus resembling pieces of candy in wrappers; various filled pastas, such as triangular or bow-tie shaped **tortelli all cremasca**, stuffed with AMARETTI, raisins, candied citron, eggs, and Parmesan (Lombardia) or **tortelli di zucca**, filled with pumpkin squash, and AMARETTI, a specialty of Mantova, Ferrara, and parts of Emilia

tortellini small filled pasta with meat, properly served in BRODO, but sometimes found with a sauce; the classic Bolognese version is stuffed with a mixture of PROSCIUTTO, MORTADELLA, pork loin, turkey breast, Parmesan, egg, and nutmeg. The filling is placed on small pasta squares which are folded along the diagonal and then formed into a ring shape.

tortiera cake pan; **tortiera a molla**, springform pan

tortiglione large pasta tubes with spiral grooves

tortino a small flan; various preparations of eggs fried or baked with other ingredients

tortora turtledove

torzelle *(pl.)* = CIME DI RAPA or fried chicory

Toscana the large north-central Tuscany region has a long Tyrrhenian coast and rolling hills. The region is known for its huge production of high-quality red wines based on the Sangiovese grape, including Chianti, Carmignano, Brunello di Montalcino, and Vino Nobile di Montepulciano.

toscanello sharp sheep-milk cheese, aged at least six months (Toscana)

tosella slices of fresh cheese sautéed in butter

tostapane toaster

tostare, *p.p.* **tostato** to toast (bread), to roast (coffee, nuts)

tostatura roast, roasting (of coffee)

totanassa, totanessa = TOTANO

totano = CALAMARO (Toscana, Liguria, Sardegna)

totariello little squid (*Alloteuthis media*)

tovaglia tablecloth

tovaglietta americana place mat

tovagliolo table napkin

tozzetti hazelnut BISCOTTI, Lazio's answer to Toscana's **cantucci**, dry, hard cookies to dip in dessert wine

tracina weever, stingfish, Trachinidae family

tradizionale *(adj.)* traditional

tramezzino sandwich; crustless creations characterized by a triangular shape, industrial bread (PANCARRÈ) and varied fillings, often with a great deal of mayonnaise. They are typical bar food, sometimes delicious, sometimes tired and stale.

trancia, *pl.* **trancie** slice

tranciante a filo wire cutter for cheese
trancio, *pl.* **tranci** slice, as of a large fish
tranne except
Trapani the name of a province and its capital city in the Sicilia region, abbreviated TP, and an important port on the west coast of the island
trascina TRACINA (Toscana, Lazio)
traslucido *(adj.)* translucent
trattare, *p.p.* **trattato** to treat. If a recipe asks for a *limone non trattato,* it means a lemon (or orange or other fruit) which has not been treated by pesticides, meaning that the rind is suitable for human consumption. Those with leaves still attached are considered untreated.
trattoria, *pl.* **trattorie** see RISTORANTE
travasare, *p.p.* **travasato** to decant, to pour a liquid from one container into another. *La goccia che fa travasare il vaso* means, literally "the drop that makes the vase overflow," and is equivalent to the straw that broke the camel's back.
trazione traction
tre three
Trebbiano ubiquitous white grape of central Italy
treccia braid, hence also anything braided, which for food can be bread, mozzarella, and sometimes fish
treccina diminutive of TRECCIA
tregghia = TRIGLIA (Veneto)
treglia verace = TRIGLIA DI SCOGLIO (Campania)
trenette long pasta, like LINGUINE; most famously served with PESTO AL GENOVESE (Liguria)
Trentino–Alto Adige a bilingual region in northeast Italy that borders on Austria and Switzerland, also known as Sud Tirol
Trento regional capital of Trentino–Alto Adige and the name of a province and its capital city, abbreviated TN
trevigiano *(adj.)* of Treviso
trevisano *(adj.)* = TREVIGIANO
Treviso the name of a province and its capital city in the Veneto region, abbreviated TV, famous, among other things, for its RADICCHIO

tria homemade durum wheat TAGLIATELLE (Puglia, Sicilia)
tricolore tricolor. Unless otherwise specified, it refers to the Italian flag (red, white, and green).
tridd = MANATE
Trieste this historic political football and important Adriatic city is the capital of the Friuli-Venezia Giulia region and the name of a province and its capital city, abbreviated TS, in Venezia Giulia.
triestina, alla Trieste-style; crabmeat sautéed with garlic and parsley
trifola white truffle (Piemonte, Lombard)
trifolato *(adj.)* some other food (usually vegetables or ROGNONI) prepared like a truffle (TRIFOLA in dialect), hence sliced very thin and sautéed with garlic and parsley, and sometimes white wine or anchovies
trigghia i morsu = TRIGLIA DI SCOGLIO (Calabria)
trigghia sapunara = TRIGLIA DI FANGO (Calabria)
triglia, *pl.* **triglie** red mullet; there are several important species of this fish: one is the **triglia di scoglio** (*Mullus surmuletus*), another is the **triglia di fango** (*Mullus barbatus*). Both are eaten, but the former is especially prized for its uniformly fine flesh; the latter sometimes takes on a less agreeable character owing to its diet.
triglia rossa fish of the genus Upeneus, in the Mullidae family, a relative of the TRIGLIA
trigoli water chestnuts
Trimalcione Trimalchio, nouveau super-rich host of the fabulous dinner party described in Petronius' *Satyricon* (first century A.D.); he is invoked on occasions of great ostentation or excess
trinciapollo poultry shears
trinciare = TAGLIARE
triplicare, *p.p.* **triplicato** to triple
tripolini small egg-pasta bow-ties for soup
trippa tripe, in Italy from beef, veal, lamb, goat, and small water buffalo (*bufalino*). There are four varieties: RETICOLO, RUMINE, OMASO, and RICCIOLINO; **alla napoletana** is boiled, sautéed in lard with onions and then mixed with egg and grated cheese; **alla Genovese** is with chopped vegetables and mushrooms;

all'olivitana is with fried eggplant, boiled eggs, and cheese; **alla romana** is a classic preparation in which the tripe is layered with grated PECORINO and MENTA ROMANA, to which sauce from braised beef or plain tomato sauce is added

trippate, uova literally, "triped eggs," i.e., cut in little strips the way tripe is usually handled

trippette STOCCAFISSO innards

trippino pork tripe

tris three-pasta sampler plate. One restaurant association has declared the *tris* to be a corruption of the Italian table and a plague upon the land, but that has stopped few from serving or ordering it.

tritacarne meat grinder

tritare, *p.p.* **tritato** to chop, to mince, to grind (meat)

trito *(adj.)* finely chopped, minced, pounded. Italian speakers and writers may tend toward the verbose, but their language is capable of synthesis practically impossible to render in English. Recipes will instruct to chop a bunch of ingredients, then put *il trito*—that which has been chopped—into a bowl.

trittico literally, "triptych"; = TRIS

troccoli rustic Pugliese TAGLIATELLE of SEMOLA and egg cut with a special grooved rolling pin called a *troccolo*

trofie, troffie GNOCCHI-like pasta from Genoa, usually handmade (though a machine to make industrial quantities of TROFIE was announced in 1989) and sauced with PESTO

trofiette not the Ligurian, but broken spaghetti-like pasta of Puglia

trofiette small pasta twists, sometimes made with chestnut flour

trombette type of ZUCCHINE

tronco *(adj.)* broken (truncated)

Tropea, Rossa di a prized variety of sweet red onion found in the warmer months. It comes from around the town of Tropea, in Calabria, but is sold and used all over Italy.

trota trout, Salmonidae family; **trota di fiume**, = TROTA FARIO; **trota di lago**, lake trout (*Salmo trutta lacustris*); **trota di mare**, sea trout (*Salmo trutta trutta*); **trota fario**, river trout, mountain trout (*Salmo trutta fario*); **trota iridea**, rainbow trout (*Salmo gairdneri*); **trota marmorata**, "marbled trout" (*Salmo trutta marmoratus*)

trota padana = TROTA MARMORATA

trota salmonata any trout that has taken on a salmon-pink tone as a result of feeding on shrimp

trotella small TROTA

truta = TROTA

truteddu = TROTA FARIO

tùccaru sugar

tuffolone large pasta tubes, usually stuffed and finished in the oven

tullore boiled chestnuts served in the cooking broth

tuma extremely fresh, saltless sheep cheese, a type of CAGLIATA

tumbada milk pudding with lemon and AMARETTI (Sardegna)

tummacella fried intestine

tummàla elaborate, layered casserole of rice and meats

tunnariello = TONNO COMUNE (Campania, Puglia)

tunninola = TELLINA (Campania)

tuorlo yolk

turcenelle = TORCINELLI

turchino a shade of blue; bluefish, when used to describe fish

turcinelli = TORCINELLI

turciniateddi = FUSILLI

turdei = TORDELLI

turgido *(adj.)* turgid

turta baked dish of spinach, rice, cheese, and butter; also = TORTA

turtei *tortelli*; **turtei cu la cua** are made by twisting the ends something like candy wrappers

turteln *or* **tirtlen** fried RAVIOLI stuffed with sauerkraut, potato, or spinach; other variations (Trentino-Alto Adige)

turtidduzza lamb intestines and other organs with tomato (Sicilia)

turtlò Christmas RAVIOLI of Bologna, filled with ricotta, egg, cheese, parsley, and nutmeg, and sauced with tomato and Parmesan

tuscia = *pesce* CAPPONE (Liguria)

~ U ~

uardi e fasui bean and barley soup

uberlekke Piedmontese mixed boiled meats with sausage and vegetables

ubriaco *(adj.)* drunken; literally for people and metaphorically for dishes containing a great deal of liquid or alcohol

'u cazini sweet RAVIOLI

uccellaggione hunting birds; fowling

uccelletti small birds

uccelletto, all' literally, "like little birds"; usually indicates cooking with sage or laurel; **fagioli all'uccelletto** are slow-cooked white beans in olive oil, sage, and tomato, not unlike France's *cassoulet*

uccellino, uccelletto small birds, but often refers to small pieces or rolls of meat; **uccelletti scappati**, beef "birds"

uccello, *pl.* **uccelli** bird

Udine the name of a province and its capital city in the Friuli–Venezia Giulia region, abbreviated GO, in Friuli

ugghia = AGUGLIA COMUNE (Sicilia)

uliva = OLIVA

umbra, all' Umbrian; of antipasto, with CROSTINI and mixed sliced meats

Umbria the landlocked region of Umbria is in the center of Italy, just south of Tuscany. Many consider its olive oil the best in Italy, but it is also known for good wines, such as Orvieto.

umbrici fat, handmade spaghetti (Umbria)

umbrina = OMBRINA (Liguria, Puglia, Sicilia)

umido *(adj.)* wet, damp, humid; **in umido**, in liquid (i.e., stewed, moist-cooked); **sugo d'umido** is the stew's sauce which can be served separately over pasta

ungere, *p.p.* **unto** to oil, to grease

ungherese *(adj.)* Hungarian

unità *(sing. and pl.)* (1) unit; (2) unity

uno one

unto *(adj. and n.)* oil, fat

uopa = BOGA (Puglia, Sicilia)

uopilli *(pl.)* young BOGHE (Puglia)

uoppa = BOGA (Sicilia)

uova see UOVO

uova al funghetto =US IN FONGHET

uova in trippa FRITTATA cut in strips and sauced in such a way as to imitate tripe

uovo, *pl.* **uova** egg(s)

urguni *(pl.)* = GHIOZZO (Sicilia)

urtis top of the hops (*cime di luppolo*)

us in fonghet soft-boiled eggs, shelled, halved, and cooked with PORCINI and other FUNGHI TRIFOLATI (Friuli-Venezia Giulia)

uva grape, grapes; **uva passa**, semi-dried grapes (see PASSITO); **uva americana**, Concord grape; **uva fragola**, type of *uva americana* (Isabella) used to make *fragolino*, a wine with a definite strawberry (FRAGOLA) flavor

uva bianca green grape(s)

uva nera grape for red wine

uva secca raisins (singular construed as plural)

uva spina gooseberry (*Ribes grossularia*)

uvaggio grape blend (in wine making)

uvetta raisins; **uva di Corinto**, **uva di Smirne**, **uva di Malaga**, and **sultanina** are the common types

uvoso *(adj.)* grapy, tasting of grapes

V

vacca cow; **zampa di vacca** is a mollusk

vaccaredda = GATTUCCIO (Sicilia)

vaccinara, coda alla tail, "slaughterhouse-style"; oxtail braised slowly with tomato sauce and celery, from the Roman tradition of the QUINTO QUARTO

vaccini the category of cheese made from cow milk

Valdaosta = VALLE D'AOSTA

valdostana, alla Valle d'Aosta-style, frequently indicating the presence of FONTINA cheese; see VALDOSTANA, COSTOLETTA, and CAPRIOLO

valdostana, costoletta alla veal chop stuffed with FONTINA and PROSCIUTTO, breaded and sautéed

valeriana, valerianella lamb's lettuce or corn salad

valigini *(pl.)* literally, "little cases" or "purses"; meat rolls filled with parsley, garlic, egg, cheese, and bread crumbs (Emilia-Romagna); **valigini mantovani** are cabbage rolls stuffed with a similar mixture, plus chicken and potato, braised with tomatoes and onion

Valle d'Aosta small semiautonomous bilingual (French and Italian) region of northwest Italy; capital Aosta

valligiana, alla potentially anything "valley-style," including (1) duck stuffed with bacon, onions, interior parts, and parsley and then boiled; (2) sautéed eel with pepper

vallu = *pesce* SAN PIETRO (Sicilia)

valpellinentze soup of Valpelline made with meat broth, cabbage, and FONTINA cheese

Valpolicella see AMARONE

Valtellina a DOC designation for a number of red wines produced in the province of Sondrio, in Lombardia

valutare, *p.p.* **valutato** to exploit, to take advantage of, to make the most of

vanello = PAVONCELLA

vaniglia vanilla; can also sometimes lend its name to something white, such as the white fat in *cotechino vaniglia*, a sausage from Cremona. However, owing to the scarcity of vanilla ice cream (whose role is filled by CREMA), the figurative meanings of the word are fewer than in English.

vaniglina = VANILLINA

vanillina vanilla-flavored sugar for baking, sold in little envelopes

vapore steam; **(cotto) al vapore**, steamed

varagno = TRACINA (Veneto)

Varese the name of a province and its capital city in Lombardia region, abbreviated VA

variabile *(adj.)* variable

variegato *(adj.)* variegated

varietà *(sing. and pl.)* variety

varietale *(adj.)* varietal

vario *(adj.)* various, different, assorted (usually in the plural, *vari*)

vasca, *pl.* **vasche** tank, pool, vat, tub

vasellame crockery, china, collectively; **vasellame d'argento**, hollow ware

vassoio tray, platter; **vassoio girevole**, lazy susan

vastedda Sicilian roll filled with cheese, spleen, and pork meats

v.d.n. (**vino naturalmente dolce**) literally, "naturally sweet wine," but in fact = MISTELLA; letter order is from the French *vin douce naturale*

VdT Vino da TAVOLA is a wine that does not conform to DOC standards; the labels do not give the origin (except Italy), vintage, or grape varieties; **vino da tavola con indicazione geografica**, or **Indicazione Geografica Tipica** (**IGT**), is a subdesignation of *VdT*, whereby 85 percent of the grapes used must have been grown in the geographic zone indicated on the label

veccia vetch

vedelo = VITELLO
vedere, *p.p.* **visto, veduto** to see
vegetale *(adj.)* vegetable, as opposed to animal or mineral
vegetariano *(n. and adj.)* vegetarian
vellutato *(adj.)* creamy, smooth; **salsa vellutata** is usually flour-thickened broth; **vellutata di** something generally indicates a vegetable purée thickened with egg yolk, though it may also be used to describe a creamy herbal emulsion (e.g., *vellutata di* BASILICO)
velo veil; covering
venatorio *(adj.)* pertaining to the hunt; **stagione venatoria**, hunting season
vendemmia vintage, (grape) harvest; **vendemmia tardiva**, late harvest (to describe dessert wines)
vendemmiare, *p.p.* **vendemmiato** to harvest (grapes)
venerdì Friday
venere chione = FASOLARO
venere tartufo = TARTUFO (DI MARE)
Venessiana = VENEZIANA
Veneto the Veneto region extends from the northern shore of the Adriatic across the flat Po valley to the Dolomites, covering a huge culinary spectrum from the superb seafood of Venice to the famous cheese of ASIAGO and the RADICCHIO of Treviso. Its wines range from the light, sparkling Prosecco and white Soave to the light red Bardolino to the potent Amarone della Valpolicella.
Venexiana = VENEZIANA
Venezia Venice, fabled city of canals on the northern Adriatic coast, capital of the Veneto region and the name of a province and its capital city
veneziana, alla Venetian-style (e.g., liver with onions or boiled crab with oil, parsley, and garlic)
ventaglio (1) (hand-held) fan; (2) = CAPASANTA
ventilatore electric fan, but not the fan above the stove or any fan that sucks air, which is ASPIRATORE
ventosa suction cup, sucker. The same word is used for what is on the octopus's tentacles and what you stick on the wall.

ventresca (1) the preserved belly of the tuna; (2) potentially anything involving belly meat, e.g., a Tuscan dish based on pork belly
ventriglio poultry gizzard
verace *(adj.)* "true"; "real"; most often applied to a type of small clam (VONGOLE VERACI)
Verbano–Cusio–Ossola one of the eight provinces of the Piemonte region, abbreviated VB
verbena vervain (*Verbena officinalis*)
Vercelli the name of a province and its capital city in the Piemonte region, abbreviated VC
verde *(adj.)* green, young, unripe
verdolino *(adj.)* pale green
verdura greens, the category of vegetables (including those of other colors)
verduraio *(m.)*, **verduraia** *(f.)* vegetable vendor
verduriera vegetable crisper (in the fridge)
vermicelli literally, "little worms"; thin spaghetti
vermut vermouth
Verona known for its opera festival and as the home of Romeo and Juliet, as well as for Soave wine, it is the name of a province and its capital city in the Veneto region, abbreviated VR
veronese, alla Verona-style
versare, *p.p.* **versato** to pour, to spill
versin = VERZA
verza Savoy cabbage, cabbage; see also CAVOLO, ROSA
verzada = VERZATA
verzata (di riso) (rice-) cabbage casserole
verze imbracate = VERZE STUFATE COL VINO
verze sofegae = VERZE STUFATE
verzotto, cavolo = VERZA
vescica bladder
veste verde, in wrapped in vine leaves
vestito *(adj.)* dressed, also figuratively
vetro glass, bottle; **di vetro**, (made) of glass
vezzena GRANA-type of cow-milk cheese of Trentino and northern Veneto, used, when aged, for grating, somewhat similar to Asiago
Vialone nano, riso see RISO

vianda dried, homemade pasta of Genova
Vibo Valentia the name of a province and its capital city in the Calabria region, abbreviated VV
viccillo ring-shaped pasta filled with salami, mozzarella, and hard-boiled egg
vicentina, alla Vicenza-style; see BACCALÀ
vicentino *(adj.)* of VICENZA
Vicenza the name of a province and its capital city in the Veneto region, abbreviated VI
vigna, *pl.* **vigne** vineyard
vignaiola grape juice or must
vignarola springtime Roman dish of braised fresh peas, fava beans, and artichokes, with the possible addition of GUANCIALE
vigneto, *pl.* **vigneti** vineyard
vin santo Tuscan aromatic dessert wine traditionally served with CANTUCCI
vinaccia still wash, what remains after grapes are pressed (*vinasse*)
vinaccio plonk, poor-quality wine
vinaggio wine blend
vincisgrassi LASAGNE with chicken RAGÙ, typical of the Marche region
vinello a light, unimportant wine, the kind of bottle you might take on a picnic
vinicola, casa winery
vinificare, *p.p.* **vinificato** to make wine
vinificazione vinification
vino wine; sweet **vino cotto** is made in various forms and ways from boiled grape must or sometimes from figs; **vino della casa**, house wine; **vino da arrosto**, wine for roasts (i.e., big reds); **vino da pasto**, table wine, not a legal designation; **vino da taglio**, blending wine; **vino novello**, see NOVELLO
vinoso *(adj.)* winey, not "vinous"
viola violet, the color and the flower
violini goat prosciutto, hand-sliced using a long blade (as if playing the violin)
virtù, le springtime soup of greens, beans, meats, pastas, and

cheese. The most traditional version contains seven legumes and seven vegetables.

viscidu curdled goat milk, dried and pickled in brine (Sardegna)

visciola, *pl.* **visciole** a type of AMARENA; CROSTATA *di visciole* is a traditional Roman dessert

visner liqueur of red wine, sour cherries, and spices (Lazio)

vitacchioni traveler's joy

vitalba clematis, a wild herb

vite, *pl.* **viti** grape vines; **foglie di vite** are grape leaves

vitel tonné see VITELLO TONNATO

vitella, vitello veal

vitello tonnato often called *vitel tonné,* it is a cold main dish of sliced pot-roasted veal masked in a sauce of mayonnaise, tuna, and capers

vitellone a red meat not yet beef; young ox. Fellini's masterpiece *I Vitelloni* is about a group of young men caught between youth and adulthood.

Viterbo the name of a province and its capital city in the Lazio region, north of Rome, abbreviated VT

vitigno variety of vine or grape

Vittoria a cheese similar to BEL PAESE

vivaio, di farm- or tank-raised

vivanda, *pl.* **vivande** dish (prepared)

vivo *(adj.)* alive; **acqua viva** is spring water

volatili *(pl.)* poultry, fowl

volpina large MUGGINE (Veneto)

volta, *pl.* **volte** time (as in *una volta,* once; *due volte,* twice; *tre volte,* three times)

voltare, *p.p.* **voltato** to turn

volume volume

vongola any of the various clams in the Veneridae family

vongola verace, *pl.* **vongole veraci** small clams (*Tapes decussatus*), easily identifiable by a pair of tiny red "horns" on the meat; the orthodox choice for *spaghetti alle vongole,* but their presence is usually specified

vopa = BOGA (Liguria, Lazio, Campania, Puglia, Sicilia, Toscana)

VQPRD **Vini di qualità prodotti in una Regione Delimitata**, quality wine produced in a specified region (QWPSR), a European Union designation for which DOC and DOCG wines qualify

vruccoli = CAVOLO BROCCOLO (Naples)

VSQPRD same as VQPRD but for SPUMANTE

vucca d'infernu, pisci = GATTUCCIO (Sicilia)

vuopa = BOGA (Abruzzo, Puglia, Sardegna)

vuotazucchine long corer for making a cylindrical space in zucchini for stuffing

vupa = BOGA (Sicilia)

vurpo = POLPO (Puglia)

~ W-X-Y-Z ~

wurstel frankfurter, Vienna sausage

zabaglione a dessert of egg yolk, sugar, and MARSALA; an ice cream of the same flavor. Though this is nearly always a dessert, there exists a recipe from Piemonte that calls for putting *zabaglione* over roasted partridge. Often spelled *zabaione,* especially in Piemonte.

zabaione = ZABAGLIONE; Sabayon

zafarana = ZAFFERANO

zafferano saffron (see also CURCUMA). Note that Italian saffron, which grows in Abruzzo, is usually sold powdered in little envelopes.

zafferano bastardo = CARTAMO; also any designation that suggests bogus saffron

zafferano falso = CARTAMO

zafferano indiano = CURCUMA

zafferanone = CARTAMO
zafran = ZAFFERANO
zagara orange-blossom
zaletti crisp cornmeal cookies
zamarugolo = MURICE SPINOSO (Veneto)
zampa leg (as in **zampa di vitello**, leg of veal); trotter (as in **zampa di maiale**, pig's foot); **zampa di vacca** is a mollusk
zampetto veal, lamb, or pork trotter
zampone boned pork trotter stuffed with chopped pork meat, rind, ears, snout, and sinew, a prized element in a classic BOLLITO MISTO. From its origin in Modena, in EMILIA-ROMAGNA, it has spread nationwide.
zappatora, alla literally, "digger's-style" (*zappa* means hoe); probably indicates a robust sauce with spicy peppers and/or sharp cheese
zarzegna duck, teal
zavagion = ZABAGLIONE
zebra = *pesce* PERSICO
zefaru = MUGGINE (Sardegna)
zembi d'arzillo fish-filled Ligurian RAVIOLI with sauce of clams. The name comes from *zembil*, an Arabic word meaning basket, and *arzillo*, a dialect name for ALGHE DEI FONDALI (see ALGA).
zemin, a = IN ZIMINO
zemino, in IN ZIMINO
zentilot = ALBORELLA (Veneto)
zenzero (1) ginger (see also CURCUMA); (2) in parts of Tuscany, this name is given to PEPERONCINO ROSSO
zenzero giallo = CURCUMA
zeppole *(pl.)* doughnuts; fritters; **zeppole di San Giuseppe**, see BIGNÈ
zero = LATTERINO (Venezia Giulia)
zerola name applied in Lazio to CERNIA, MENOLA, and SCIARRANO
zerro picarel (*Centracanthus cirrus*) and smare (*Spicara smaris*); related to MENOLA
zesti zest
Zibello, culatello di see CULATELLO
zibetto civet

Zibibbo grape and sweet wine, a specialty of Pantelleria (Sicilia); currants or raisins used in Sicilian dishes

ziga = TELLINA (Toscana)

zigar type of RICOTTA made from buttermilk; **zigar asc** is the fermented version

zimino braising mix of tomatoes, olive oil, and parsley, and spinach or chard and hot pepper; fish stew; **zimino di ceci** is a soup of chickpeas and other vegetables

zingorra = ANGUILLA (Sardegna)

zite *(pl.)* long, hollow pasta

ziti = ZITE

zlikrofi a stuffed pasta (like RAVIOLI) from Friuli near Slovenia

zoccoli literally, "clogs"; FRITTATA with PANCETTA and pork liver

zolletta, *pl.* **zollette** (sugar) cube

zona, *pl.* **zone** zone, area; term used especially for designated production area of a legally protected food

zucapesce = LAMPREDA (Campania)

zucca pumpkin, squash; winter squash. See also FIORE; Ferrara and Mantova are famous for RAVIOLI stuffed with *zucca*, using the variety *marina di Chioggia*, similar to American pumpkin.

zuccheraggio chaptalization

zuccherare, *p.p.* **zuccherato** to add sugar; sugared. If you suspect your coffee has been delivered with the sugar already in, you ask, "É già zuccherato?"

zucchero sugar; **zucchero a vela**, confectioner's sugar, powdered sugar, icing sugar; **zucchero di canna**, cane sugar; **zucchero semolato**, granulated sugar; **zucchero turbinado**, Turbinado sugar

zucchetta small squash, zucchini

zucchine *(n.f., pl.)* summer squash, zucchini, courgettes (*Cucurbita pepo*); the Italian dictionary lists both masculine and feminine forms of the word as synonyms, but the feminine is somewhat more common.

zucchini see ZUCCHINE

zuccotto a type of SEMIFREDDO made in a hemispherical mold; the name, used for both the dessert and the mold, probably derives from the slang meaning of ZUCCA, which is "head"

zuf gruel of mixed corn and white flours with milk, topped with cheese and butter (Friuli)

zuncurrunu = ANGUILLA (Sardegna)

zuppa (1) soup, properly one served with or containing bread; cf. MINESTRA; (2) various items of different degrees of soupiness, e.g., ZUPPA LUCCHESE and ZUPPA INGLESE

zuppa inglese not a soup but a rich dessert, literally, "English soup," because it supposedly resembles English trifle. It is subject to wide interpretation and variation, but the usual ingredients include PAN DI SPAGNA layered with CREMA PASTICCIERA and soaked in ALCHERMES or ROSOLIO. **Zuppa angelica** is a similar creation with sponge cake and chocolate cream sauce.

zuppiera soup tureen

Weight, Measure, and Temperature Conversion

ITALIANS do not enjoy wearing seatbelts, and you will not find many Italian cooks carefully leveling off a calibrated measuring spoon with the flat blade of a knife. The dessert spoon *(cucchiaio)*, more or less heaping, the wine glass *(bicchiere)*, and the demitasse *(tazzina)* are the basic tools of volume measurement, and there is little point in imposing more precision than the author of the recipe intended.

Faced with Italian recipe measurements, we strongly advise that you use the metric quantities given, rather than trying to convert anything. This is really not so difficult; most packaged goods these days also list their metric equivalents and even most inexpensive plastic, glass, or metal measuring spoons and cups give both U.S. and metric quantities. For volume measurements, this is pretty straightforward.

On the other hand, measuring flour and other dry ingredients can be a stumbling block, as Italian recipes will specify weight rather than volume. U.S. practice is clearly inferior, since any given weight of flour can vary as much as 100 percent in volume. The very simple solution is that any inexpensive scale is better than using volume equivalents—even if that scale has to be begged or borrowed from a friend. One collateral advantage of weighing dry ingredients is that you don't need to sift and level in order to measure. But if a scale really is out of the question, refer to the table below.*

---

* Karen Hess, who prepared the American edition of Elizabeth David's *English Bread & Yeast Cookery* (New York: Penguin, 1982), after baking her way

There are approximately 454 grams to the pound. For practical on-the-fly cooking purposes, round that up to 460, making every 115 grams an easy quarter pound. Given the variance of most home scales, this is well within the limits of precision required by nearly any recipe.

Measurement and temperature equivalents for baking, as opposed to those for scientific laboratories, can and should be approximated. A workable guesstimate of oven temperature can be obtained by simply doubling the centigrade figure: a 175°C oven, for example, works out to 350°F in the real world. We caution only that this trick works best for mid-range temperatures—greater than that of boiling water (which is 100°C or 212°F) and below the highest spots on the oven dial. For higher temperatures (over 200°C), the rough-and-ready chef will double and then subtract just a little: 250°C works out to 475°F.

If you want to double-check, forget the fractions of your high-school science class and get out your handy, decimal-based calculator. The formula is to multiply degrees centigrade by 1.8 and add 32 to the result. So, $175 \times 1.8 = 315$ and $315 + 32 = 347$. As we said 350°F. In fact, much of this calculating will be moot, as Italian recipes very often fail to specify any particular oven temperature at all. In which case, do what you would do with any similar recipe you are familiar with (and keep a close eye on the cookies).

For volume cooking measurements, treat liquid grams and milliliters as numerically equivalent. So 30 g will be 30 ml and vice versa. It remains just to know that 100 grams is a deciliter (dl) and that the kilogram (kg) and the liter (l) are each 1000 grams. Having got that far (and sticking to our system of approximations):

30 g/ml	1 oz
100 g/ml	4 oz

---

through 500 pounds of flour, reports that the best general volume equivalent for flour is 3 level cups per pound, obtained by dipping into normally settled flour. We bow to her experience in this regard.

225 g/ml	1 cup (for liquids or denser ingredients, such as granulated sugar)
5 g/ml	1 teaspoon
15 g/ml	1 tablespoon
1 liter	1 quart (scant)
a stick of butter	115 grams
a tablespoon of butter	15 grams
1 kilogram (kg)	2.2 pounds (lb) or 36 ounces (oz)

For lengths, the U.S. inch is 2.5 centimeters. Conversely, just divide any measurement in centimeters by 2.5 to find the result in inches.

Selected Bibliography

IN addition to the works listed, information in this book comes from menus, interviews with Italian food professionals, producers' promotional material, and our own notes on our travels in Italy.

Alberini, Massimo, and Giorgio Mistretta. *Guida all'Italia gastronomica.* Milano: Touring Club Italiano, 1984.

Alberto, Carlo, and Anna Lucia Bauer. *La cucina trentina.* Trento: Reverdito Edizioni, 1996.

Alessandri, Paolo Emilio. *Droghe e piante medicinali.* 1915. Reprint. Milano: Istituto Editoriale Cisalpino–Goliardica, 1988.

Anderson, Burton. *Guide to the Wines of Italy.* London: Mitchell Beazley, 1992.

Ashley, Maureen. Rome, 1998. Unpublished course materials.

Ashley, Maureen. *Italian Wines.* London: J. Sainsbury, 1990.

Attore, Antonio, and Valerio Chiarini. *Ricette di osterie e di porti marchigiani.* Bra: Arcigola Slow Food Editore, 1994.

Barendson, Marino. *Addio Cicerchia: piccola storia della cucina caprese.* Capri: Edizioni La Conchiglia, 1991.

Beard, James, et al., eds. *The Cooks' Catalogue.* New York: Harper & Row, 1975.

Bianchi, Anne. *Solo Verdura: The Complete Guide to Cooking Tuscan Vegetables.* Hopewell, N.J.: The Ecco Press, 1997.

Braccili, Luigi. *La Cucina Abruzzese.* Cerchio (AQ): Adelmo Polla Editore, 1992.

Bremness, Lesley. *Erbe e Aromi.* Trans. G. Signori. Milano: Tecniche nuove, 1997.

Bruni, Luigino. *Ricette di sua maestà il raviolo.* Bra: Arcigola Slow Food Editore, 1993.

Bugialli, Guiliano. *The Fine Art of Italian Cooking.* New York: Times Books, 1989.

Castello, Antonio. *Sapori e piaceri d'Italia.* Roma: Editrice Sallustiana, 1996.

Codacci, Leo. *Itinerari dell'antica cucina toscana.* Milano: Idealibri, 1995.

Colacchi, Marina, and Pino Simone. *Firenze e la Toscana.* La Cucina Regionale Italiana. La Spezia: Fratelli Melita Editori, 1990.

Colacchi, Marina, and Pino Simone. *Milano e la Lombardia.* La Cucina Regionale Italiana. La Spezia: Fratelli Melita Editori, 1990.

Colacchi, Marina, and Pino Simone. *Roma e il Lazio.* La Cucina Regionale Italiana. La Spezia: Fratelli Melita Editori, 1990.

del Conte, Anna. *Gastronomy of Italy.* London: Bantam Press, 1987.

Fabbri, Alberto Adolfo. *Ricette di osterie dell'Emilia.* Bra: Arcigola Slow Food Editore, 1997.

Food and Agriculture Organization. *Plants and Plant Products.* Terminology Bulletin 25. Rome: Food and Agriculture Organization of the United Nations, 1983.

Gosetti della Salda, Anna. *Le Ricette Regionali Italiane.* 9th ed. Milano: Solares, 1988.

Gosetti, Fernanda. *I pesci della cucina regionale italiana.* Milano: Fabbri Editori, 1990.

Guarnaschelli Gotti, Marco, ed. *Grande Enciclopedia Illustrata della Gastronomia.* Milano: Selezione dal Reader's Digest, 1990.

Hazan, Marcella. *Marcella's Kitchen.* London: Macmillan, 1987.

Hazan, Marcella. *The Classic Italian Cook Book.* New York: Alfred A. Knopf, 1977.

Hazan, Marcella. *More Classic Italian Cooking.* New York: Alfred A. Knopf, 1978.

Herbst, Sharon Tyler. *Food Lover's Companion.* Hauppage, NY: Barron's Educational Series, 1990.

Johnson, Hugh. *Pocket Wine Book 1997.* London: Mitchell Beazley, 1997.

Kasper, Lynne Rossetto. *The Splendid Table.* New York: William Morrow and Company, 1992.

Krane, Willibald. *Five-language Dictionary of Fish, Crustaceans and Molluscs.* New York: AVI [Van Nostrand], 1986.

Lanterno, Alberta. *Piemonte in bocca.* Palermo: Edizioni e Ristampe Siciliane, 1986.

Maffioli, Giuseppe. *La cucina veneziana.* Padova: Franco Muzzio & c., 1995.

Manzoni, Paolo. *Riconoscere e cucinare i pesci di mare e d'acqua dolce.* Novara: De Agostini, 1993.

Mayr, Christoph. *Erbe aromatiche.* Bolzano: Casa Editrice Athesia, 1995.

Monja y Parellada, Enrique. *Diccionario de Plantas Agrícolas.* Madrid: Ministerio de Agricultura, 1980.

Pacini Fazzi, Maria. *Traditional Recipes of Lucchesian Farmers.* Lucca: Maria Pacini Fazzi Editore, 1988.

Padulosi, Stefano, ed. *Rocket Genetic Resources Network. Report of the first meeting ...* Rome: International Plant Genetics Resources Institute, 1995.

Palombi, Fra' Domenico. *La medicina dei semplici.* Pavia: Edizioni Torchi de' Ricci, n.d.

Parenti, Marco. *Alla ricerca del formaggio perduto.* Cuneo: Edizioni L'Arciere, 1997.

Pellaprat, Henri-Paul. *L'Arte della cucina moderna.* Trans. Natale Rusconi. Milano: Sansoni, 1992.

Pescosta, Rosemarie. *Piatti e dolci delle valli ladine.* Trento: Casa Editrice Publilux, 1996.

Pettiti, Silvia, and Cinzia Scaffidi. *Le ricette di osterie d'Italia: 50 piatti da salvare della cucina di territorio.* Bra: Slow Food Editore, 1994.

Piccinardi, Antonio. *Dizionario dei vini Italiani.* Milano: Rizzoli, 1991.

Piccinardi, Antonio. *Dizionario di gastronomia.* Milano: Rizzoli, 1993.

Piras, Pierangela Pelizza. *L'isola d'Elba in cucina.* 4th ed. Lecco: Editrice Stefanoni, 1991.

Ragazzini, Giusepee. *Dizionario inglese-italiano, italiano-inglese.* Milano: Zanichelli, 1986.

Regione Emilia Romagna, Assessorato Agricoltura Bologna. *Ricette in soffitta.* Forlì: Regione Emilia Romagna, 1993.

Ricette delle osterie di Langa. Bra: Arcigola Slow Food Editore, 1992.

Sartoni, Monica Cesari. *Dizionario del Ghiottone Viaggiatore, Italia.* Bologna: Fuori Thema/Tempi Stretti, 1994.

Sassi, Maria. *Trento in bocca.* Palermo: Il Vespro, 1979.

Serra, Piro, and Ferretti, Lya. *Il grande libro della pasticceria napoletana.* Napoli: Edizioni Coop "Il Libro in Piazza," 1994.

Simeti, Mary Taylor. *Pomp and Sustenance.* New York: Henry Holt and Company, 1991.

Soracco, Diego. *Ricette di osterie e genti di Liguria.* Bra: Arcigola Slow Food Editore, 1995.

Testi, Antonio. *Il Libro dei funghi d'Italia.* Colognola ai Colli (VR): Demetra, 1995.

Ubaldi, Jack, and Elizabeth Grossman. *Jack Ubaldi's Meat Book.* New York: Macmillan, 1987.

United States Department of Agriculture. *Cheeses of the World.* New York: Dover Publications, 1972.

Vialardi, Giovanni. *A tavola con il re.* Torino: Piemonte in Bancarella, 1994.

Willinger, Faith Heller. *Eating in Italy.* New York: Hearst Books, 1989.

Zanini De Vita, Oretta. *Il Lazio a tavola: Guida gastronomica tra storia e tradizioni.* Roma: Alphabyte, 1994.

Zanini De Vita, Oretta. *The Food of Rome and Lazio: History, Folklore, and Recipes.* Translated by Maureen B. Fant. Rome: Alphabyte, 1994.

Zingarelli, Nicola. *Vocabolario della lingua italiana.* 12th ed. Milano: Zanichelli, 1995.

English–Italian Index

This index of terms is meant only to steer the reader to selected entries in the body of this dictionary, not necessarily to offer a straightforward translation of the English term.

abalone aliotide
absinthe assenzio
acid acido
acidulate acidulare
acorn ghianda
add aggiungere
addition aggiunta
additive additivo
adjust aggiustare
adulteration adulterazione, sofisticazione
advance anticipo
aesthetically esteticamente
aflame infiammato
after dopo
aftertaste retrogusto
agaric mushroom agarico
age età
age (*v.*) invecchiare
aged (for a long time) stravecchio
aging invecchiamento
agrarian agrario
alcohol alcol, alcool
alcoholic alcolico
alga alga
alive vivo
alkekengi erba canina
allspice pimento della Giamaica
almond amandola, mandorla
almond paste marzapane
almonds, Jordan confetti
almost quasi
already già
aluminum alluminio, carta argentata
aluminum foil carta argentata
Amanita caesarea ovolo
amino acid aminoacido
ammonia ammoniaca, ammonio
anchovy acciuga, alice
animal animale
anise anice
anisette anisetta
antioxidant antiossidante
apart parte, a
aperitif aperitivo
appearance apparenza, aspetto
appetizer antipasto
apple mela
appliance elettrodomestico
apricot albicocca, meliaca

blackbird merlo
bladder vescica
blade lama
blade (mushroom) lamella
blanch imbianchire, sbianchire
blancmange biancomangiare
blend (e.g., of coffee) miscela
blend (*v.*) miscelare
blender frullatore
blending (of wine) assemblaggio
blood sangue
blood orange sanguinello
blood pudding sanguinaccio, boudin
blue azzurro, blu
bluefish pesce turchino
boar cinghiale, marcassin
body corpo
boil bollire, lessare
boil, to bring to a portare ad ebollizione
boiled lesso
boiler caldaia
boiling bollente
boletus porcino
bologna mortadella
bone (animal) osso
bone (fish) lisca, spina
bone (*v.*) diliscare, disossare, sfilettare, spinare
bone marrow midollo
borage borragine
botrytis botrite
bottle boccetta, bottiglia
bottle opener levacapsule
bowl bacinella, ciotola, insalatiera, scodella
box scatola
braid treccia
brains cervella
braise brasare
bran crusca, cruschello
brand marca, marchio
brandy acquavite
brazier braciere
bread pane, pan
bread (*v.*) impanare
bread crumbs mollica
bread-making panificazione
breaded *panato*
breadsticks grissini
bream sarago
bream (gilt-head) orata
breast petto
breast (veal) cima
brine salamoia
broccoli broccoli siciliani, cavolbroccoli
broccoli raab broccoletti, friarielli
broiled ai ferri
broth brodo
brown bruno
brown (*v.*) dorare, rosolare
brown lightly imbiondire
brush spazzola, pennello
Brussels sprouts cavoli, cavolini, cavoletti di Bruxelles
bucket secchio, secchiello
buckwheat grano saraceno
bud gemma, germoglio
bunch fascio, grappolo, mazzetto
bundle fagottino, fascetto
burdock lappola
Burgundy Borgogna
burn (*v.*) bruciare, scottare
burner (range) fornello
burning ardente
butcher macellaio, macellaro
butcher block ceppo
butcher shop macelleria
butler bottigliere
butter burro
butter (*v.*) imburrare
butterfly farfalla

cilantro coriandolo
cinnamon cannella
citron cedro, chinotto
citrus fruit agrume
civet zibetto
clam arsella, cannolicchio, caparossolo, fasolaro, tellina, vongola
claret chiaretto
clean (*v.*) mondare, pulire
clear (the table) sparecchiare (la tavola)
cleaver mannaia, spaccaossa
clematis vitalba
clementine clementina
cloak (*v.*) ammantare
clove (spice) garofano
coarsely grossolanamente
cock gallo, galletto
cocoa cacao
coconut noce di cocco
cod merluzzo
coffee caffè, espresso
cold freddo, fresco
cold-cuts affettati
composed composto
concentrated concentrato, ristretto
conch buccina
cone cono
confectionery dolciume
confetti coriandolo
conger eel grongo
container barattolo, contenitore
cook cuoco
cook (*v.*) cucinare, cuocere
cooked cotto
cookie biscotto
cookie jar biscottiera
copper rame
coriander cilantro, coriandolo, erba cimicina
cork sughero, tappo
corkscrew cavatappi
corn (maize) granoturco, mais
cornflakes fiocchi di mais
cornstarch amido di mais, maizena
course (of a meal) portata
couscous cuscus, cuscusu
cover coprire, incoperchiare, ricoprire
cow mucca, vacca
crab granchio, granciporro, granseola, moleca
crab apple meluggine
cracker galletta
crayfish gambero europeo, gambero di fiume
cream crema, panna
cream of tartar cremore di tartaro
creamy cremoso
crème brûlée crema bruciata
crêpe crespella, frittatina
cress crescione
croissant cornetto
croquette crochetta, supplì
crouton crostone
crumb briciola, pan grattato
crumble sbriciolare sbriciolato
crumbly friabile
crunchy croccante
crush ammostare, frantumare, pestare, pigiare, schiacciare
crust crosta
cube dado
cucumber cetriolo
cultures (as in yogurt) fermenti lattici vivi
cumin cumino
cup tazza
curd, rennet caglio
curdle cagliare, impazzire
curly riccio
currant Zibibbo

currants ribes
cut ritagliare, tagliare, trinciare
cutlet braciola, braciolett, cotoletta, costoletta
cutting board tagliere
cuttlefish seppia, seppioline
dairy latteria
dandelion dente di leone
decaffeinated decaffeinato
decant travasare
decanter caraffa
deep-fat fryer friggitrice
defrost (the freezer) sbrinare, scongelare
deglaze deglassare
dehydrate seccare
delicious delizioso
demijohn damigiana
dense denso
dessert dolce
deviled (spicy) indiavolato
dextrose destrosio
dice cubetti
dill aneto
dinner cena
dip intingolo
dirty sporco
dish drainer scolapiatti
dishes stoviglie
dishpan bacinella
dishwasher lavapiatti, lavastoviglie
dissolve sciogliere, stemperare
donkey asino, asinello, somaro
dormouse ghiro
double boiler bagnomaria
dough impasto, pasta
dove colombo
dozen dozzina
drain (*v.*) scolare
dredge infarinare
dregs feccia, morchia
dress (*v.*) condire
drumstick fuso
drunk ebbro, ubriaco
duck anatra, germano reale, mazaro, moulard, nana, sarzegna
duckling anatroccolo
ear orecchio
ear (corn) pannocchia
ear (grain) spiga
earthenware coccio
eau de vie acquavite
edible commestibile
eel anguilla, bisato, buratelli, capitone, ciriola
effervescent effervescente, frizzante, gassoso
egg uovo
egg (hard-boiled) uovo sodo
egg white albume
eggbeater battiuova
eggplant melanzana
eggs (coddled) uova alla coque
eggs, scrambled uova strapazzate
elderberry sambuco
elecampane enula campana
elk alce
embers brace
emmer farro
endive cicoria, belga, indivia
entrails frattaglie
escarole scarola
eviscerate eviscerare
extract essenza, estratto
extrude estrudere
eye occhio
eye round girello
farm cascina, fattoria, tenuta
fat grasso, unto
fatback lardo
feather penna, piuma
fennel finocchio
ferment fermentare

fermentation fermentazione
festival sagra
fiber fibra
field campo
fig fico
filet mignon filetto
filigree filigrana
film pellicola
filter filtro
filter (*v.*) filtrare
filtration filtrazione
fin pinna
fine fine
finger dito
fire fuoco
fireplace camino, focolare
firm sodo
first primo
fish pesce
fish farming acquicoltura, piscicoltura
fish scaler squamapesce
fish stock fumetto
fisherman pescatore
flake scheggia
flambé infiammare
flame fiamma
flame diffuser diffusore, spargifiamma
flamingo fenicottero
flan sformato, tortino
flank costato
flask borraccia
flask fiasco
flat piano
flatware posate
flavor gusto, sapore
flavor (*v.*) aromatizzare, profumare
flip rivoltare
flour farina
flour (wheat) semola, semolino
flower fiore
foam schiuma, spuma
fondue fonduta
food mill passaverdure
fork forchetta
form forma
fortified (wine) liquoroso
fragrance profumo
freeze congelare, surgelare
freeze-dried liofilizzato
fried fritto
fritter bombolone, frittella
frog rana, ranocchio
frosted glassato
frozen congelato, gelato, ghiacciato, surgelato
fruit frutta
fruit cocktail macedonia
frustino wire whisk
fry frittura
fry (*v.*) friggere
frying pan padella, tegamino
funnel imbuto
furnace caldaia
galantine galantina
game caccia, cacciagione, selvaggina
garbanzo beans ceci
garden orto, ortolano
garlic aglio
garnish guarnizione
geese (pertaining to) anserino
gelatin colla di pesce
germ germoglio
giblets rigaglie
gill (fish) branchia
gill (mushroom) lamella
ginger zenzero
gingerbread panpepato
gland ghiandola
glass vetro
glazed glassato
glutton leccone
goat capra

kettle marmitta
kid capretto
kidney rognone
kitchen cucina
kiwi actinidia
kiwifruit kiwi
knead gramolare, impastare
knife coltello
knuckle nocca
kosher casher, kasher
lactose lattosio
ladle mestolo, ramaiolo
ladyfingers savoiardi
lamb abbacchio, agnello
lamb's lettuce soncino, lattughella, lattughino, valeriana, valerianella
lamprey lampreda
langoustine scampo
lard lardare, lardellare, steccare
lard strutto
lark allodola
laurel alloro, lauro
lavender lavanda
layer strato
layered cipollato
leaf foglia
lean magro
leek porro
leftovers avanzo
legumes legumi
lemon limone
lemon verbena cedrina
Lenten quaresimale
lentil lente, lenticchia
lettuce lattuga, insalata
licorice liquirizia
lid coperchio
light chiaro, leggero, lievo
linden tiglio
liquefy liquefare
liqueur amaro, liquore
liquid liquido
liquor distillato, liquore, superalcolico
liver fegato, fegatini
loaf pagnotta, panetto
lobster aragosta, astice
loin lombata, lombo
lollipop lecca-lecca
lotte bottatrice
lovage levistico
low-calorie ipocalorico
lukewarm tiepido
lunch pranzo
lung corada, polmone
lupin fusaglie, lupino
mace macis
mackerel maccarello, sgombro
mahimahi lampuga
maize granoturco, mais
malt malto
mandarin mandarino
maple acero
margarine margarina
marinate macerare
marjoram maggiorana, persa
market mercato
marmalade marmellata
mashed franto, purè, purea, sfranto
maturation (of wine) affinamento
mayonnaise maionese
meal (grain) farina
meal (to eat a) pasto
measure misurino
measure (*v.*) dosare, misurare
measuring cup caraffa graduata
meat carne
meat sauce ragù
meatball polpetta
meatless magro
meatloaf polpettone
medallion medaglione
medium medio

medlar fruit nespola
melon cantalupo, melone
melt fondere, sciogliere, squagliare, stemperare
menu carta, menù
meringue meringa
milk latte
mill macinino, macinatoio
millefeuille millefoglie
millet miglio
mince macinare, sminuzzare, tritare
mineral minerale
mineral water acqua minerale
mint menta
mix amalgamare, impastare, incorporare, mescolare, mischiare, rimescolare
mixed misto
mixture impasto, pasta
moisten bagnare
molasses melassa
mold (fungi) muffa
mold (shape) forma, stampo
mollusk mollusco
monkfish bordrò, rana pescatrice
moorhen folaga
moray amurena, murena
morel morchella, morello, spugnola
morello cherry amarena, marena, marasca
mortar mortaio
mugwort artemisia
mulberry gelso
mullet (red) triglia
murex murice spinoso
muscat moscato
mush pappa
mushroom fungo
mushroom cap cappella
musk muschio
mussel cozza
must (grape) mosto, vignaiola
mustard senape
mutton castrato, montone
myrrh mirride
myrtle mirto
napkin tovagliolo
neck collo
nectarine nettarina, pesca noce
nettle ortica
noisette nodino
non-stick antiaderente
nonalcoholic analcolico
nougat torrone
nutmeg noce moscato
oats avena
octopus moscardino, polpo
offal interiora
oil olio, unto
oil (*v.*) ungere
okra bamia, bammia
old antico, vecchio
olive oliva
olive-press frantoio
olive tree olivo
omelet frittata, frittatina
onion cipolla
open aperto
open (*v.*) aprire
orange (fruit) arancia, tarocco
orange, blood sanguinello
orange-blossom zagara
orange tree arancio
orchard frutteto
oregano origano
ostrich struzzo
oven forno
overcook scuocere
overcooked scotto, sfatto
oyster ostrica
package confezione
pan tegame
paper towel Scottex
paprika paprica

parboil sbollentare, scottare
paring knife spelucchino
Parmesan parmigiano, Parmigiano Reggiano
parsley prezzemolo
parsnip navone pastinaca
partridge pernice
passion fruit maracuja
pasta (dry) pastasciutta
pasteurize pastorizzare
pastry pasticceria, sfoglia
pastry bag tasca per pasticceria
pastry cook pasticciere
pastry wheel rotella
pea pisello
pea pod taccola
peach pesca
peacock pavone
peanuts arachide, noccioline americane
pear pera
peel buccia
peel (*v.*) pelare, sbucciare, spellare
peeler pelapatate
pennyroyal mentuccia, puleggio
pepper pepe
pepper (hot) peperoncino
pepper (sweet, bell) peperone
pepper mill macinapepe
perch pesce persico
persimmon loto
pestle pestello
pheasant coturnice, fagiano
pickled salmistrato
pickles acetini, cetriolini, sottaceti
pie torta
pig maiale, porco
pig (suckling) maialino da latte, lattonzolo, porcellino
pigeon colombo, piccione
pilaf pilau
pimpernel pimpinella
pine nuts pignoli, pinoli
pineapple ananas
pink rosa
piquant piccante
pistachio pistacchio
pit (*v.*) snocciolare
pizza cook pizzaiolo
pizza peel pala da forno
plain naturale
plastic wrap pellicola
platter vassoio
plover pavoncella, piviere
pluck (innards) coratella
pluck (*v.*) spennare
plum amolo prugna, susina
poach affogare
pod baccello, guscio
pomegranate melagrana
poppy seeds semi di papavero
pork maiale, suino
pot marmitta, pentola, pentolone
pot holder presina
pot roast arrosto morto, brasato
potato patata
potato chip patatina
potato flour fecola
potato, sweet batata
poultry pollame, volatili
poultry shears trinciapollo
pour irrorare, mescere, versare
prawn scampo
precooked precotto
prepare preparare
preservative conservante
preserved sottaceto, sott'olio
press (olive, wine) torchio
pressure pressione
pressure cooker pentola a pressione
prickly pear fico d'India
process (in a blender) frullare
pudding (U.S.) budino
puffed soffiato
pullet pollastro

pulp midolla, polpa
pumpkin zucca
punch ponce
purée passato, purè, purea
puréed purè, purea
purslane portulaca
quail quaglia
quenelles chenelle
quince cotogna, melacotogna, pera cotogna
quinine chinino
rabbit coniglio
radish ravanello
raised (as with yeast) lievitato
raisin uva secca, uvetta, sultanina
rampion raperonzolo
rapeseed oil olio di ravizzone
rare al sangue, crudo
raspberry lampone
ratatouille rattatuia
raw crudo
recipe ricetta
reduce diminuire, ridurre
refrigerator frigo, frigorifero
reheated rigirato
rennet quaglio
rennet apple renetta
rhubarb rabarbaro
rib costa, costola
rib cage costato
rib steak costata
rice riso, risotto
ricer passapatate
rich grasso
rind cotenna, corteccia, crosta, scorza
roast (*v.*) arrostire
roast beef rosbif
roast, roasted arrosto
roast, roasting (of coffee) tostatura
roasting pan rostiera, rosticciera
rocket ruchetta
roll involtino, rollè, rotolo
roll (*v.*) arrotolare
roll out spianare, tirare
rolling pin mattarello
root radice
rose hip rosa canina
rose rosa
rosé (wine) rosato
rosemary arromaniu, rosmarino
rotisserie girarrosto
rotten marcio
round rotondo, tondo
round (meat) controgirello
royal reale
rubbed stropicciato
rubbery gommoso
ruby rubino
rue ruta
rum rhum
rump culatto, fesa
rutabaga navone
rye segale
saccharine saccarina
saddle groppa, sella
safflower cartamo
saffron zafferano
sage salvia
salad insalata
salad burnet erba noce, salvas-trella
salmon salmone
salmon trout salmerino, trota salmonata
salsify scorzobianca, scorzonera
salt sale
salt (*v.*) salare
salt cod baccalà; cf. stoccafisso
salt pork lardone
salt shaker saliera
salted salato
saltwort barba di frate
sandwich panino, tramezzino
sardine sardina comune

satsuma mandarino
sauce intingolo, salsa, sugo
sauceboat salsiera
saucepan casseruola, marmitta
sauerkraut crauti
sausage salsiccia, insaccato
sauté sotè, souté
sauté (*v.*) ripassare, soffriggere
sauté pan saltiere
sautéed al salto
savarin bordura
Savoy cabbage verza
scale (fish) squama
scale (flake) scaglia scaglie
scale (for weighing) bilancia
scallion cipollotto
scallop (seafood) capasanta
scissors forbici
scraper (rubber) leccapentola di gomma
scraps ritagli
sea mare
seared scottato
season stagione
season (*v.*) condire
seasoning (aging) invecchiamento
seaweed alga
seed seme
selene sclupit, sclopit
semisweet abboccato, amabile
serrated seghettato
sesame sesamo
shad agone, alosa, cheppia
shaker agitatore
shallot scalogno
shank muscolo, stinco
sharpening steel acciarino
shears cesoie
sheep pecora
sheep (pertaining to) ovino
shell conchiglia, guscio
shellfish frutti di mare
sherbet sorbetto
shoot germoglio
shortbread cookies frollini
shoulder spalla
shrimp canocchia, gambero, mazzancolla
side dish contorno
sieve passino, setaccio
sieve (*v.*) passare, setacciare
sift (*v.*) setacciare
sifted passato
sifter setaccio
simmer sobbollire
singe scottare
sirloin costa
skate arzilla
skewer spiedino
skillet padella, tegamino
skim schiumare
skimmed (milk) scremato
skimmer schiumarola
skin cotenna, pelle
skin (*v.*) spellare
slaughterhouse macello
slice fetta, scaloppa, trancia
slice (*v.*) affettare
slicing machine affettatrice
smell (*v.*) odorare
smelling (act of) olfazione
smelt argentina, latterino
smother affogare
snack merenda, spuntino
snail babbalucci, bagioi, bovoleto, chiocciola, grigette, lumaca
snipe beccaccino, croccolone
snow pea taccola
soak ammollare
soda water seltz
soften ammollire, ammorbidire
sole sogliola
sorbet sorbetto
sorghum saggina

tangerine mandarino
tannic tannico
tansy tanaceto
tarragon dragoncello, estragone
tart (pastry) torta
tart (taste) aspro
tartare tartara
taste assaggio, sapore
tavern bettola, taverna
tea tè, thè
tea kettle bollitore
teal alzagola, alzavola
teapot teiera
teaspoon cucchiaino
tender tenero
tenderloin filetto
tepid tiepido
testes granelli, testicoli
thaw decongelare
thermometer termometro
thick denso, fitto, spesso
thicken addensare, legare
thigh coscia, coscetta, coscio, cosciotto
thin magro, sottile, tenue
thrush tordo
thyme timo
timbale timballo
tin (can) scatola, latta, lattina
tin foil carta stagnola
tisane tisana
toast abbrustolire, tostare
toaster tostapane
tomato pomodoro
tomato paste concentrato (di pomodoro)
tomato purée passata (di pomodoro)
tongs molle
tongue lingua
tonic water acqua tonica
toothpick stecchino, stuzzicadente
towel asciugamano, canovaccio
tray vassoio
trim (*v.*) mondare, pulire
trimmings ritagli
tripe busecca, trippa, trippino, ricciolino
trotter piedino, zampa
trout salmerino di fontana, trota
truffle tartufo
truss accosciare
tuna alalunga, tonno
turbot rombo
tureen (soup) zuppiera
turkey dindo, tacchino, tacchinella
turmeric curcuma
turn voltare
turn off spegnere
turn over rivoltare
turn upside down capovolgere, rovesciare
turnip rapa
turnip greens cime di rapa
turtle tartaruga
turtle-dove tortora
uncover scoprire
unleavened azzimo
unrefined grezzo
unsweetened amaro
utensil attrezzo
vacuum-packed sottovuoto
vanilla vaniglia, vanillina
vanilla bean siliqua di vaniglia
vat caldaia
veal vitello
vegetable (*adj.*) vegetale
vegetables ortaggi
vegetarian vegetariano
vein vena
velouté vellutato
venison capriolo, cervo
verjuice agresto
vermouth vermut

vervain verbena
vetch veccia
vine ceppo, vite
vinegar aceto, aspretto
vintage annata, millesimo, vendemmia
violet viola
wafer cialda, ostia
waiter cameriere
walnut noce
wash lavare
wastebasket cestino
water acqua
water buffalo bufalo
water chestnut castagna d'acqua, trigoli
watercress cappuccina, nasturzio
watermelon anguria, cocomero
wattle bargiglio
wax cera
web-footed palmipede
weight peso
well done ben cotto
wheat grano, frumento
whelks scungilli
whey siero
whip (*v.*) montare
whisk frullino, frusta
whole integrale, intero
wild di campo, selvaggio, selvatico
wine vino
wine list carta
wine rack cantinetta
wine shop bacaro, bottiglieria, enoteca
winery azienda vinicola, casa vinicola
wing ala, aletta
wishbone forcella
woodcock beccaccia
wormwood genepi
wrap (*v.*) ammantare
wrapper involucro
yam igname
yarrow achillea
yeast lievito
yolk tuorlo
young giovane

MAUREEN B. FANT is a translator, editor, small publisher, and writer with a special interest in Italian food. A New Yorker who lives in Rome, she is a regular reviewer of European restaurants for the *New York Times* travel section. She holds graduate degrees in Classical Studies and Archaeology from the University of Michigan, and is co-author, with Mary R. Lefkowitz, of *Women's Life in Greece and Rome* and author of *Eat Like the Romans: The Visitor's Food Guide.*

HOWARD M. ISAACS is publisher and editor of *The Italian Traveler,* a monthly newsletter of restaurant and hotel reviews, published since 1988. He has reviewed more than 600 restaurants throughout Italy, in addition to working on other translation projects. He holds a master's degree in Political Science from the University of Chicago and lives in Brooklyn, New York.